Perfect
Party Menus

Perfect
Party Menus

When You Don't Have Time to Cook

Nancy Holmes & Karen Richards

Delacorte Press / New York

Published by
Delacorte Press
1 Dag Hammarskjold Plaza
New York, N.Y. 10017

Photographs by Susan Wood

Food Styling by Luke Reichle

CREDITS: Hand-blown crystal glassware from
Simon Pearce Glass, Quechee, Vt.; flatware from Conran's,
New York, N.Y.; baskets, knives, and serving pieces from Dean & DeLuca,
New York, N.Y.; white glazed plates handmade by Stephen Pearce from Simon
Pearce Glass; all other pottery glazed plates and serving pieces handmade by
Claudia Schweide from Lee Bailey at Henri Bendel, New York, N.Y.;
tablecloth "Taos" designed by Jay Yang for Wamsutta; napkins
from Frank McIntosh at Henri Bendel; bench from
Bloomingdale's, New York, N.Y.

Manufactured in the United States of America

First printing

Designed by Richard Oriolo

Library of Congress Cataloging in Publication Data

Holmes, Nancy, 1921–
Perfect party menus when you don't have time to cook.

Includes index.
1. Menus. 2. Entertaining. I. Richards, Karen.
II. Title.
TX728.H62   1982   641.5'52   82-9976
ISBN 0-440-07224-7   AACR2

We dedicate this book to the women who showed us the difference between cooking and creative cooking; who encouraged us to use our imaginations and take risks in the kitchen; who gave us the gift of their wonderful food and inspired us to do the same for our families, friends, and the readers of these pages. They are: Nancy Newlove, Ellen Parker, Susan Fernie, Peg Richards, Barbara Ryalls, and Carolyn Milke.

We also want to acknowledge the help we received in the form of recipe ideas and professional advice from the following people: Alice Holmes, Wendell Holmes, Daphne Hartwig, Judy Freeman, Pauline Ryan, Bonnie Daly, Muriel White, Diane Mason, Terry Wysong, Jean Hall, Judy Keifer, Edna Greene, and Dorothy Graham.

Finally, we want to thank Jim Freeman, Gil Richards, and Krissy and Gilbert Richards who, in addition to giving daily moral support, tasted every recipe in the book many times over and provided thoughtful criticism to the very last bite.

Contents

1

Getting Ready: Tips on Food & Drink, Equipment, & Table Settings

Getting Ready: Tips on Food and Drink, Equipment, and Table Settings

The idea for *Perfect Party Menus When You Don't Have Time to Cook* was born when we became aware that home entertaining had declined in the past decade because women were going to work outside the home. In spite of the unflagging popularity of cookbooks, food machinery, and classes in the art of cooking, candlelight dinner parties in the warmth and intimacy of people's homes seemed to be on the wane. The reason was simple: A woman who has a full-time job, a house to maintain, and children to care for does not have the time or energy—though ironically, she may very well have the money—to follow through on all the details that add up to a successful dinner party. Nevertheless, we believe that potential hosts and hostesses in this predicament would prefer to entertain friends at home—maybe not as often as they used to but, let's say, on an average of once a month. The at-home dinner party is certainly more enjoyable, convivial, and memorable than dining out in restaurants or clubs where you cannot adjourn to the den after dessert, kick off your shoes, and wind down the discussion of movies or a local election with a brandy in your hand.

We decided it was possible for working women—and working men too—to give great little dinner parties if their definition of such parties could be altered. We totally agree that most women do not have the time or inclination to prepare the kind of menu that was touted in the 1960s and 1970s by cooking gurus like Julia Child, magazines like *Gourmet*, and instructors in widely attended cooking schools. Though they may not personally subscribe to it, these sources of inspiration tend to advance the idea that home entertaining should be rather elaborate and novel, or built around a new ethnic or regional cuisine, or both. Women retreated from the complications of this prevailing culinary spirit; they didn't have the time to fix such dinners, yet they didn't want to serve hot dogs and beans either.

So we have written *Perfect Party Menus* for every working person who would sincerely like to give imaginative, tempting, and truly interesting dinner parties without expending a great deal of physical and mental effort. To accomplish this, we have constructed menus that require only moderate preparation before the party and very little time spent in the kitchen after the guests have arrived. Every menu has been planned to be elegant in presentation, appearance, and taste—in other words, to be acceptable to the most discriminating palates while actually being simple to create. There are no special or unusual ingredients to be purchased, so that every menu should be possible anywhere in the country. Though the menus are easy to prepare, there is little reliance on convenience or prepackaged food. We have gone to great lengths to make each menu look so appetizing on the printed page that no reader should want to consider substitutions; she or he will recognize a winner on sight and therefore won't have to spend an evening poring over cookbooks to come up with a decent menu. No one has time for that sort of thing today.

The main division of the book is seasonal—with an equal number of menus suitable for warmer and for cooler weather. Not only does such organization save the reader time when trying to decide on a menu; it allows for fare that capitalizes on the fresh foods of the season. We are living in a time when fresh, natural, relatively unadorned foods are favored, so a seasonal cookbook makes the most sense to cook and guests alike.

The majority of the menus in the book are for dinner parties of six. This is a number that we regard as rather sacrosanct if one is seriously desirous of entertaining with a minimum of fuss and a maximum of flair. In our extensive experience at giving dinner parties, we have learned that to have eight or ten people to dinner involves disproportionately more unavoidable work (having fewer than six is easier but not nearly as lively and sociable). Therefore six is the magic number for us as far as dinner parties go. Stick to this number, and you will find yourself giving more dinner parties than ever before.

The menus for the brunches, cocktail buffets, and a holiday dinner serve more than six people as such special occasions are apt to do. However, we have not added on more guests for these parties than the hurried cook and hostess can handle. By following our tips for how and when to prepare the food, you should be able to entertain a small crowd without having to take a vacation from your job in order to get the party together.

How to Make This Book Work for You

You are who you are—an individual with a great many responsibilities, commitments, people depending on you. And you are going to give a dinner party. Our most important piece of concerned advice is: Be good to yourself.

At the same time you are calling your friends to invite them to dinner, decide on the menu you're going to serve and carefully read through each recipe. This gives you two to three weeks to get such cooking as you can out of the way—perhaps a frozen dessert or an appetizer that keeps in the refrigerator for several days. You can also begin the grocery shopping, picking up all the nonperishable items.

Though we immodestly believe our menus to be perfect orchestrations of color, texture, flavor, and amount of food, we would be remiss if we didn't discuss how you can execute substitutions or additions, if you must. The best place to make changes in these menus is with desserts. Though each dessert has been calculated to be just the right finishing touch, a dessert is never as integral a part of a meal as the other dishes. So you can mix and match our desserts to some extent.

Another way the menus can be adjusted is to add a simple green salad to those meals that don't have a salad. Most of the menus feature a soup course instead of a salad because we think soups are infinitely more exciting. However, for those people who cannot fathom a meal without a leaf of lettuce, by all means tack on a salad. The salad could be our recipe for green salad with tarragon-mustard dressing (page 65) or a green salad with vinaigrette dressing (page 110), both of which go well with practically any menu. And if you do serve a salad, we encourage you to sandwich it in as a separate course between the main course and the dessert; in this way, the salad does not interfere with the drinking of good wine.

About a week before the dinner party, sit down with a cup of tea or a glass of wine and plan the week's agenda. Determine when and how your house is going to get cleaned. Make a final grocery shopping list of the food that remains to be purchased; early in the week, you will need to order special meats from the butcher and buy certain produce items like avocados for home ripening. Figure out when you are going to prepare each recipe. Plan your table setting and the table centerpiece (see later in this chapter for ideas); if you're not going to eat at a dining table, figure out how the food is going to be served and where guests will eat it. Start making ice for the party, or if freezer space is limited, make a note about picking up a bag of ice the day of the party.

It's a good idea to write up your menu and your agenda and post both of these in plain sight on a kitchen or office bulletin board. Check off the items on the agenda as they get done.

We are assuming that most people who work give dinner parties Saturday evening (or possibly Sunday). This gives you twenty-four hours leading up to the party for preparing food, doing some light housecleaning, setting the table, taking care of the children's needs, and last but not least, readying yourself for the party. If you choose to entertain on a week night, use the previous weekend to accomplish as many of these chores as possible.

Try to give yourself time the day of the party to take a luxurious bath, fix your hair, get dressed, and—if you are really well-organized—lie down for thirty minutes. A tip about dressing: Wear comfortable clothes when you're the host or hostess; save the formal attire for visiting in someone else's home.

Food to Have on Hand at All Times

We don't want to be dictatorial about this, but your life as a social entertainer will be less hassled and more pleasant if you try to keep certain foods on hand as a general principle. Whenever the supply of any of these items runs low, you should immediately replenish it regardless of whether you're planning to use it in the near future. This makes the grocery shopping much less arduous during the week of your dinner party and prevents a lot of last-minute trips to the store. Also, a well-stocked larder increases the possibilities of the recipes you can put together at a moment's notice.

We have included in these lists the ingredients that are used with some degree of frequency in the book's recipes and/or ingredients we think you would use often, whether or not you were cooking from this book.

In the pantry

salt	garlic
flour	soy sauce
granulated sugar	steak sauce
light brown sugar	Worcestershire sauce
confectioners' sugar	hot pepper sauce
cornstarch	chicken broth
baking powder	beef broth
baking soda	unflavored gelatin
vegetable oil	canned tomatoes
olive oil	tomato sauce
red wine vinegar	crackers for appetizers
cider vinegar	semisweet chocolate for grating
medium egg noodles	vanilla extract
long-grain white rice	honey
onions	

In every recipe calling for white rice, we specify that the rice be long-grain. Don't buy anything but long-grain—never use instant or Minute rice—and do buy your rice in large quantities.

Always have several cans of chicken and beef broth on hand. These get used up quickly.

As long as you're investing in olive oil, you should get one of good quality. The best olive oil is an extra-virgin oil from Italy, but you'll pay a lot of money for the product. The French make an extra-virgin olive oil which is lighter than the Italian and almost as good, especially in salad dressing. A lesser grade of olive oil is virgin; this can come from Italy, Greece, Portugal, Spain, or France. There are a number of virgin olive oils on the market which are reasonably priced and perfectly acceptable for cooking. Olive oil keeps for a long time if it is well sealed and stored in a cool, dark place.

In the refrigerator

Parmesan cheese or Romano cheese	tomato paste*
sharp Cheddar cheese in stick form	catsup*
	capers*
cream cheese—3-ounce and 8-ounce packages	walnuts and/or almonds*
	lemons
plenty of butter	parsley
mayonnaise*	frozen chives (if you don't grow fresh)
Dijon mustard*	eggs
sour cream	
horseradish	
peanut butter*	

For people who use margarine instead of butter in their everyday cooking, we suggest you keep butter on hand in the freezer so you won't be caught short when you start preparing dishes for the dinner party; allow plenty of time for it to thaw. Please use butter in the book's recipes; there is no comparison between its flavor and that of any butter substitute.

We keep a jar or sealed plastic bag of walnut meats and almonds in the refrigerator because we use a lot of nuts, in cooking and as toppings or garnishes. Since there are several recipes in the book calling for these nuts, you might want to consider keeping a supply on hand. Nuts spoil if left at room temperature for any length of time.

We go through a large bunch of parsley every week under nor-

* should be refrigerated after opening

mal circumstances, more if we're having company to dinner. It is a good idea to always have a bag in the refrigerator of this most nutritious, flavorful, and useful herb. Keep it sealed to retain crispness.

Most tomato paste is sold in six-ounce cans. Unfortunately, most recipes call for less than six ounces of tomato paste, which means you have to store the leftover paste in the refrigerator, where it sits until mold forms on the surface. Recently, however, gourmet food shops and certain mail-order catalogs specializing in kitchen and food items have offered tubes of imported tomato paste. These work like a toothpaste tube: You simply squeeze out the amount of tomato paste you need, screw on the tube cap and put the tube in the refrigerator where the tomato paste stays absolutely fresh. This is a great innovation, which we hope will be widely available soon.

We believe that no cook should ever be without a supply of Parmesan cheese or Romano cheese. Buy only bulk cheese—never the kind that is sold already grated in jars, plastic bags, or cardboard shakers. Wrap it well and it will keep for many weeks in the refrigerator. Grate the cheese as needed in a food processor fitted with the steel blade or with a hand grater; or you can grate it all at once and store in a tightly-lidded jar. Parmesan cheese grates finer than Romano, and its flavor is not as pronounced.

In the herb and spice rack

black peppercorns	ground cumin
cayenne pepper	sage
white pepper	dry mustard
paprika	ground ginger
curry powder	nutmeg
thyme	cinnamon
basil	whole cloves
oregano	allspice
bay leaf	celery salt
marjoram	garlic powder
rosemary	fennel seeds
tarragon	poppy seeds
dillweed	caraway seeds

We use lots of herbs and spices, as the list above indicates. A well-filled rack of things to perk up or enhance the taste of food is a great comfort, especially in winter, when you can't grow the herbs. Although we advocate the planting of a kitchen herb garden in summer, we realize that not everyone has the space or the desire to grow fresh herbs and thus must rely on the dried product all year long.

Most herbs and spices lose their pungency after long storage (about one year). You might want to write the date of purchase on the label and throw out a herb or a spice when it is past its prime. Buy reputable brands of herbs and spices to insure the best flavor, color, and longest shelf life.

Throughout the book we call for freshly ground black pepper to be added to food—meaning you grind your own with a pepper mill or grinder. Freshly ground pepper is superior to buying pepper already ground because the flavor of the pepper is released into the food at that moment; ground pepper that has been standing around is lackluster by comparison. The best peppercorns are called tellicherry; you probably won't find them in supermarkets, but you can often locate them in specialty food shops and mail-order catalogs. Occasionally a recipe calls for white pepper; this is used primarily in white sauces instead of black pepper to achieve a better visual appearance.

In the liquor cabinet

dry white wine
dry red wine
dry sherry
dry vermouth
brandy

We use a great deal of wine in our cooking, and after that, we probably use more sherry than anything else. You can purchase a reasonably priced California or New York state dry sherry; sometimes it is labeled "dry" and sometimes "cocktail." Such sherry is good for drinking too.

One rule of thumb for wine in cooking is to use the same wine that you're going to drink with the meal, but obviously this could be rather expensive. The white wine we keep on hand for cooking is usually a Chablis, a Blanc de Blancs, or a white table wine; for red wine, we favor a table wine, a Burgundy (not too heavy, though), a Chianti, or a Zinfandel.

Kitchen Equipment

The purchase of top-flight cooking equipment and other food preparation gadgetry is one of the best investments you will ever make. Not that its value will increase so that you'll be able to sell it at a profit. No, we are talking about the connection between excellent equipment, trouble-free and foolproof preparation, and a splendid dinner on the table. Not only should you have the best equipment at your disposal, but you should also have the right equipment.

It is amazing how many amateur chefs spend their whole lives working with skillets that don't conduct heat, tinny and battered saucepans, a single mixing spoon or bowl, the first electric blender ever marketed which boasts one speed only, and other motley equipment which they wouldn't part with or replace for the world. Our guess is that cooking is something of a chore for these people, or perhaps it is a challenge. The truth is they're working unnecessarily hard and taking too many chances on failure.

You will pay a lot of money for some of the equipment we recommend, but most of it should last a lifetime without breaking down or wearing out. Spread the purchase of the more expensive pieces over a period of time as we have done. Eventually you will have a kitchen that is a joy to run because everything in it works smoothly and efficiently, and you never lack the right piece of equipment when you need it the most.

Knives and other utensils

To start with, you should have a set of trustworthy knives made of high-carbon stainless steel with handles of extremely hard wood or plastic. A less expensive knife is one made simply with carbon steel, but this will rust and be a problem to care for. Plain stainless steel knives are difficult to keep sharpened, and are not recommended at all. An adequate set of knives consists of the chef's knife, a paring knife, a six-inch utility knife, and a fruit and bread knife. To this collection you can add a boning knife (and save money by boning your own chicken), a carving knife, and a meat cleaver.

Keep your knives sharp by stroking them against a sharpening steel every time you use them, and by sharpening them on a whetstone whenever the edge seems dull; this will be necessary every few months. Never put your knives in the dishwasher, and wipe them dry the minute you wash them.

A companion to a set of knives is a good pair of kitchen scissors. High on the list of its myriad uses is the cutting of chicken breasts and large fish fillets. For these jobs, scissors are much better than a knife because the latter shreds the meat. Scissors are also preferred for cutting away chicken fat.

Other utensils which are of great help to the cook are:

an assortment of wooden spoons
wooden or plastic spatulas and forks

2-pronged stainless steel fork
slotted spoons and slotted spatulas
wire whisks in several sizes
carrot/potato peeler
kitchen tongs
a pie and cake server

Because we use our knives so frequently in the preparation of food, we keep them on the counter in a handsome butcher block holder; there's a place for the sharpening steel in the holder too. Our wooden spoons are used almost as often as the knives, so we have them standing at the ready in a large earthenware pitcher on the counter.

Pots and pans

Another expensive category of equipment that is worth every penny is a set of stainless steel skillets and saucepans. Copper is the best heat-conducting metal there is, but since a large copper skillet costs over $150 and requires a lot of maintenance, we are enthusiastic endorsers of the second-best skillet you can buy: a stainless steel skillet with either a copper plate or a thick aluminum plate bonded to the base. These plates improve the ability of stainless steel to conduct and distribute heat quickly and evenly; the food never gets discolored and the cleanup is a breeze. The stainless steel with the copper plate is our number one choice for both skillets and saucepans. Make certain the plate is a well-defined plate and not the copper wash you see on the base of some cheaper cooking equipment.

Here is the battery of skillets and saucepans you shouldn't be without; each one of these should be accompanied by a really tight-fitting lid:

12-inch skillet (2 of these are desirable)
10-inch skillet
small skillets, including a 7- to 8-inch skillet with a no-stick sur-
face and sloping sides
3-quart saucepan
1½-quart saucepan
3-cup saucepan
omelet pan

Besides skillets and saucepans, you need dependable baking dishes of varying dimensions and depths. There are many on the market that not only do a commendable job of aiding the cooking process, but they look quite attractive when brought to the table. So keep in mind the advantage of owning eye-appealing baking dishes when making new purchases. Some of these dishes are made with brightly colored enamel coatings; others are imaginatively crafted ceramics which have been treated to withstand high oven temperatures; still others are the old tried and true glass dishes now dressed up with a companion wicker basket into which the dish is slipped before it is brought to the table. Here are the baking dishes we find indispensable:

shallow, rectangular dishes (9 x 13 x 2 inches, 8 x 11 x 2 inches,
   12 x 20 x 2 inches)
deeper casserole dishes (2–2½ quart, 4–5 quart)
8-inch square cake pan
5 x 9 x 3-inch bread loaf pan
9-inch pie plate
10-inch quiche pan, 1¼-inch deep
9-inch round springform cake pan
roasting pan

Other items rounding out the pots-and-pans category are:

a nest of mixing bowls
6-cup ring mold, preferably with a no-stick surface
muffin tin
2 or 3 cookie sheets, about 12 x 15 inches
12-quart stock pot

The food processor and other electrical equipment

If you own this book, you should own a food processor. Along with good knives, skillets, and saucepans, the food processor enables you to feel pleasantly relaxed while being the epitome of speed and professionalism every time you are cooking in the kitchen. By now we imagine most people know what the food processor is capable of doing. Briefly, it purées, chops, grates, crumbles, slices, shreds, and mixes foods in the twinkling of an eye and without any effort on the user's part. This is accomplished with three main attachments that come with every brand of food processor: the steel blade, the slicing disk, and the shredding disk. There are other attachments, but these are the crucial ones. We have recently invested in a new slicing disk that produces ⅛-inch-thick slices, slices that are thinner than those produced by the standard slicing disk. This is quite nice for zucchini and mushrooms.

We cannot indulge in a comparison of food processor brands, but there are considerable differences in quality as well as in price among the many on the market. We suggest you consult *Consumer Reports* and talk to friends who already own a food processor.

A food processor needs to be kept out on the counter to be of maximum use.

The electric blender has almost been put out to pasture by the advent of the food processor, but we still use ours for certain modest jobs. If you don't own a food processor and don't plan to invest in one for a while, the blender will process most of the recipes in the book, though it will take longer and the result may not be as successful.

Another appliance that is extremely useful is an electric hand mixer or beater—mostly for whipping cream and beating egg whites. And two different sizes of hot trays (or two of the same size) come in handy for keeping food warm, especially at cocktail buffets.

Miscellaneous equipment

The following items are pretty self-explanatory, and all will add to your cooking expertise and enjoyment:

2 colanders—medium and large
nest of sieves
measuring cups (a set of ¼-, ⅓-, ½-, and 1 cup measures for dry ingredients; for liquids, two 1-cup, a 2-cup, and a 4-cup measures)
measuring spoons—2 or 3 sets
stainless steel hand grater with 4 sides
cutting board, about 15 x 18 inches
salad spinner
food mill (especially if you don't own a food processor)
pepper mill
kitchen scales
kitchen string
large salad bowl and salad tossing equipment
assortment of serving platters and bowls
corkscrew

Buying, Storing, and Serving Wine

We recommend pretty well-known, easily obtained wines to drink with the meals in this book. When you go to the liquor store armed with our suggestions and are faced either with too many choices of wine or slim pickings, don't hesitate to discuss your wine needs with the liquor store proprietor. If he seems knowledgeable (and not all of them are), tell him exactly what dishes you are serving and let him be a guide.

Wine can run into a lot of money, especially the imported variety. If you are in a cost-conscious mood, buy jug wine instead of the smaller, 25.4-fluid-ounce bottles (a size that used to be referred to as a fifth). There is a lot of excellent wine sold in 1.5-, 3-, or 4-liter bottles. Jug wine can be poured into attractive glass or ceramic decanters for serving at the table.

The amount of wine to buy for a party of six will vary according to your drinking habits and those of your guests. Light drinkers will be satisfied with two of the 25.4-ounce bottles or a 1.5-liter jug (the latter gives you the same amount as the two smaller bottles). More serious drinkers will consume three of the 25.4-ounce bottles of wine and proportionately more jug wine.

We usually delay the pouring of wine at dinner until after the soup course. While one person clears away the soup bowls, another diner can make the rounds with the wine. However, this is a matter of personal preference. Others will want to pour the wine before anyone sits down at the table; or they will ceremoniously pour the wine as soon as everyone is seated and the dinner is about to commence.

All wine should be stored in a cool, dark place such as a basement or closet. Wine that is bottled with a cork should be stored lying on its side to keep the cork from drying out. Wine bottled with a screw cap can be stored upright.

Table Settings and Service

There are so many details rattling around in your head prior to giving a dinner party that the last thing you want to worry about is an attractively set table. This is easily avoided by having on hand table linen that is appropriate to the season of the year and which complements your dining room design; and by thinking through the various possibilities for a table centerpiece and deciding on something that works well for you.

Because formal table linen is so expensive, we own no more than three to four sets. If you have a tablecloth or set of placemats that looks summery, and another that warms you up to look at it in the winter, you really don't need anything more. However, if you do a lot of entertaining, you may want a third tablecloth or set of mats that is all-seasonal in appearance; this could be a solid neutral color against which you could place a variety of patterned napkins, including some of the beautifully designed paper napkins.

There was a time when paper napkins would have been verboten except at family breakfast; and the napkins were always white. Today's paper napkins are generously sized, soft and thick, colored in shades ranging from delicate to brilliant, and very imaginatively patterned. Therefore we say: Use paper napkins when you find designs that complement your table linen. Placemats too used to be considered totally lacking in style or elegance, but no more. This is an era of casualness and informality, and placemats fit right in. One reason for using placemats is a dining table that is a show-off piece of furniture, such as a glass-top or slate-top table or a table with several grains of wood. Another reason to use placemats is the ease with which they can be laundered and stored away.

The use of linen napkins enables you to enhance the table decoration in several simple ways. A linen napkin inside a napkin ring has the look of luxury. It's fun to collect napkin rings to go with different linen; they are generally inexpensive and come in a variety of colors and materials, including wood, pewter, silver, gold, Lucite, straw, and enamel. We like to display linen napkins inside the wineglasses, though this takes a bit of fussing to get the right shapes. Napkins can be folded in a number of fetching ways. There are books and articles on the subject of napkin folding; check in your local library for ideas that appeal to you.

To some extent, your table centerpiece will be determined by the type, color, and design of your table linen and your china. We can only make suggestions here for you to fit into your personal decor. Fresh flowers, of course, are the all-time favorite centerpiece, and we agree there's nothing more soothing to the eyes than a bowl of artfully arranged flowers. But unless it is summertime and your garden is in full bloom, flowers can be expensive and a problem to procure when you have a hundred other items on your agenda.

There are other ways of putting nature on your table besides the fresh garden bouquet or florist's arrangement. Many plant stores, garden centers, and nurseries carry a wide selection of dried plant materials, and these can be assembled into a handsome centerpiece that will last a long time. Some of these places have people on staff who are trained to do the arranging for you in a favorite bowl, basket, or vase that you bring in. If you live in an area where autumn leaves turn to glorious shades of red, yellow, and orange, you can gather a few branches of these for a seasonal centerpiece. A little collection of small, compact flowering plants can look charming on the table either in a basket or on a tray.

We have in mind the African violet, geranium, impatiens, bego-nia, kalanchoe and, at Christmas, poinsettia. A pinecone wreath around a fat candle is another idea for the holidays; or ever-greens and holly with velvet ribbons tucked into a base of Oasis.

Vegetables or fruits in season can be piled into an interesting basket for an easy, natural centerpiece; the corners of a matching napkin or two could be peeking out from this. The brightly col-ored gourds and Indian corn available in autumn can be put in a bowl or basket for a centerpiece that should last from September through Thanksgiving.

Another approach to the table centerpiece is to put art on the table instead of nature. For example, during most of the year our table has a piece of sculpture on it. Other ideas are a collection of decorative bottles or pottery in varying sizes, a collection of miniatures such as animals or a dollhouse room, a beautiful an-tique, a grouping of lacquered boxes.

A bunch of differently sized candles can be an effective, almost mesmerizing centerpiece. Of course, you will probably have can-dles on the table even with another type of centerpiece. Just be sure that the candles and centerpiece harmonize in terms of color, proportion, and placement.

Lighting is very important in establishing the ideal ambiance for your dinner party. Candlelight alone does not usually provide sufficient light; you want guests to be able to see each others' facial expressions clearly and to see the fabulous food you've pre-pared. On the other hand, the light that augments the candlelight should be subtle and indirect. Down lights or track lights around the room's periphery can be quite striking, especially if you have paintings on the walls. A lamp turned low can create another pool of light in the room. Small portable lights called spots or up lights can add to the atmosphere if they are directed at something of interest—a large plant, for instance, or a statue, a painting, a patterned drapery—or are placed inside a lattice-work basket. If the only source of electric light in your dining room is an over-head fixture, add a rheostat control to the light switch so that the lights can be dimmed.

When setting the table, put down at least one pair of salt and pepper shakers, a serving utensil for each dish, an attractive hot pad for each hot dish to sit on, and a small ash tray for a guest who smokes (although you are completely in the right to request such a guest to refrain from smoking while dinner is in progress). To keep the table from being too crowded, we keep the wine on a sideboard or in the kitchen. When coffee is served, bring in a pitcher of milk, the sugar bowl, and small spoons for stirring the coffee.

Many people who own a large set of china do not possess adequate soup bowls; instead they use cereal bowls or dessert dishes. We like a white china soup bowl that holds about one cup of liquid, is rather broad and flat, and has a broad rim. This type of bowl shows off the soup to best advantage, and the soup is handily spooned out of it.

For reasons we have never understood, salad is usually served in bowls of china, glass, or wood. We much prefer to serve all our salads on a plate that measures about eight inches in diameter. The salad has more visual presence on a plate, is easier to eat, and the plates take up less room in the dishwasher.

A divided platter is a nice serving piece to have. The entrée can be in one compartment and the side dish that is most closely related to the entrée (such as noodles or rice) can be in the other. This helps to keep the number of serving dishes on the table to a minimum, a real boon with some of the smaller contemporary dining tables designed for apartments and condominiums.

2

Dinner Party Menus for Spring & Summer

Parsley—Lettuce Soup
Lemon—Lime Chicken Breasts
with Artichoke Hearts
                    Apricot—Cashew Pilaf
                          Peppermint Parfait

The mood of this dinner menu is one of stimulating refreshment, like a glass of iced tea after a volleyball game or a bicycle ride on a cool sunny morning. The flavors of the food are sharp, and the colors evoke either the placidity of long summer days or the perkiness of spring, depending on the season you choose for the menu. In fact, this is a menu that works equally well for spring or summer not only because the ingredients should be available throughout both seasons, but the soup course can be served hot or cold as needed.

Every dish on the menu can be prepared well in advance of the dinner party, but only the parsley-lettuce soup can actually be finished the day before. The soup, with its thickening agent of potato, has a faint flavor of vichyssoise, but we think it's infinitely more interesting, rich, and pretty to look at than that old standby of trains, hotels, and country clubs. In addition, the soup gives you versatility, since it can be served hot or cold.

The parsley in the soup has to be fresh; you simply cannot make the soup with the insipid dried version. We've checked around the country, and have concluded that fresh parsley is available in supermarkets the year around—often in large bunches which are sometimes used as decoration for produce counters. To obtain the required cup of parsley, break off the leaf ends of part of a large bunch (a rough estimate is half a large bunch, or enough parsley to fill the container of a food processor two-thirds full), and chop in a food processor or electric blender; then measure out into the cup, packing down a little as you do. There is no need to clean out the food processor or electric blender containers before puréeing the soup in them.

The Romaine lettuce has been chosen for its deep green color; no other lettuce will work as well. The half a head you'll want to use is the tip end, where the color is most intense. Cut it off, chop coarsely, and then clean in a sieve by running cold water over it; drain thoroughly before adding to the soup.

The lemon-lime chicken on a dinner plate alongside the pilaf with its flecks of apricot is reminiscent of a bouquet of jonquils. These two dishes are like a marriage, with the piquancy of the chicken being the perfect complement to the rich savoriness of sweet apricots and cashew nuts. Both dishes can be prepared in the morning for late evening dining. It is essential to keep the chicken very well covered or the meat will dry out. Our trick of cutting the breast into quarters and pounding it flat like veal enables you to cook the chicken quickly so as not to lose too much moisture before the meat is done. Choose a baking dish you can bring to the table for this pretty entrée.

For our taste, the pilaf is just right with the addition of one-half cup of apricots, but some people might prefer an even sweeter dish, in which case another tablespoon or two of apricots can be added. We recommend unsalted cashew nuts for the pilaf, but we realize that these nuts can be hard to find in small quantities unless you have a health food store in your community. Therefore we tested the pilaf with the salted cashews sold everywhere in small cellophane bags and found the dish just as good; however, you must carefully watch the salting of the rice when you use salted nuts.

The dessert course for this dinner is one of the easiest and most colorful concoctions in the whole book. A teen-age child can make the peppermint parfait while you arrange flowers for the table. The contrasting layers of bright green cream and dark chocolate in the long tall glasses will provoke admiring comments. And so will the deliciously intoxicating taste! Whenever you are whipping cream, especially in the summer or when the cream pretty much stands alone as a basic ingredient, be sure to chill your bowl and the beating attachments in the refrigerator for about 20 or 30 minutes prior to the operation. Chocolate wafers are available at cookie counters in supermarkets in single-layer packages; if you have no other use for the leftover wafers, freeze them to use again in this recipe.

You need a white wine with a lot of authority to hold its own against the lemon in the chicken. We recommend one of our favorite whites, the spicy Gewürztraminer. Traditionally, this wine comes from the Alsatian region of France, but in recent years certain California wineries have been producing good Gewürztraminer wines.

Parsley–Lettuce Soup

Wash and peel the potatoes and cut into quarters or eighths, depending on the size. In a medium saucepan, place the potatoes, onion, garlic, tarragon, salt, pepper, chicken broth, and wine. Bring to a boil, then lower the heat and simmer, covered, until the potatoes are tender, about 15 to 20 minutes. Halfway through the cooking, add 1 cup of parsley and the lettuce, and finish cooking.

In an electric blender or food processor fitted with the steel blade, purée the contents of the saucepan with the cream cheese until quite smooth; this will have to be done in 2 or 3 batches. Taste to correct the seasoning.

If you are serving the soup cold, add the cream, and when the soup has completely cooled, refrigerate until chilled. *At this point, the soup can be stored in the refrigerator, covered, for 1 to 2 days.*

If you are serving the soup hot, refrigerate without adding the cream (again, the soup can be stored for 1 to 2 days). Shortly before serving, reheat the soup over low-medium heat, then add the cream and reheat again without letting the soup boil.

Serve both the cold and hot versions of the soup with the remaining 2 tablespoons of parsley sprinkled over each portion as a garnish.

1 *pound potatoes*

1 *medium onion, coarsely chopped*

1 *clove garlic, finely chopped*

2 *teaspoons fresh tarragon* OR ½ *teaspoon dried tarragon*

Salt and freshly ground black pepper to taste

3 *cups chicken broth* OR *chicken stock*

½ *cup dry white wine*

1 *cup plus 2 tablespoons fresh parsley, finely chopped*

½ *head Romaine lettuce, finely chopped*

4 *ounces cream cheese, softened to room temperature*

1 *cup heavy cream*

Lemon–Lime Chicken Breasts with Artichoke Hearts

6 servings

2½ *pounds whole, bone-less, skinless chicken breasts*

½ *to ¾ cup flour*

Salt and freshly ground black pepper to taste

8 *tablespoons (1 stick) butter*

2 *tablespoons vegetable oil*

1 *large lemon*

1 *large lime*

1 *medium onion, thinly sliced*

2 *cloves garlic, finely chopped*

½ *cup dry sherry*

⅔ *to ¾ cup chicken broth* OR *chicken stock*

1 *teaspoon dried rose-mary, crumbled*

1 *bay leaf*

1 *16-ounce can arti-choke hearts, drained* OR *1 10-ounce pack-age frozen artichoke hearts, thawed*

Cut each connected chicken breast in half and then in half again so that each breast yields 4 pieces of meat; trim away any fat and membrane and dry with paper towels. Place the pieces of chicken on a cutting board and pound flat with a meat pounder or with the heel of your hand. Season the flour with plenty of salt and some pepper and dredge the chicken in the flour, shaking off any excess. Let the chicken stand for 5 minutes, then repeat the dredging process.

In a large skillet, melt 2 tablespoons of the butter and 1 tablespoon of the oil over medium heat; sauté as much chicken as will fit in the skillet without crowding until it is golden brown on all sides and cooked through, about 10 minutes. You will want to lower the heat during the cooking to avoid burning the butter. Remove the chicken with a slotted spoon to a greased, shallow baking dish large enough to hold all the chicken pieces in a single layer, about 9 x 13 x 2 inches. Melt 2 tablespoons of the butter and the remaining oil in the skillet and sauté more of the chicken pieces, removing them to the baking dish when cooked. Depending on the size of your skillet, you may need to cook the chicken in 3 batches, in which case you will have to add extra butter and oil to your skillet.

Cut the lemon and lime in half, squeeze the juice from one half of each fruit and reserve; you should have 2 tablespoons of juice. Thinly slice the other lemon and lime halves and reserve.

In the same skillet in which you cooked the chicken, add 2 more tablespoons of the butter and sauté the onion and garlic briefly, then add the sherry and boil briefly, scraping away the particles from the bottom of the skillet. Lower the heat and add the chicken broth, rosemary, bay leaf, and reserved lemon and lime juice; simmer briefly to blend flavors, then pour the sauce over the chicken pieces. *At this point, the chicken can be held, covered with aluminum foil, for several hours, or it can be refrigerated overnight.* Before cooking, let the chicken come to room temperature for 45 to 60 minutes.

When ready to cook, preheat the oven to 350 degrees.

Cut the artichokes in half if they are canned—the frozen ones can be left whole—and tuck the artichokes around the chicken, spooning some of the sauce over the artichokes and the chicken to moisten. Reheat the chicken, covered, for 20 to 30 minutes. Add the remaining 2 tablespoons of butter to the sauce and garnish the dish with the slices of lemon and lime. Spoon some sauce over each portion of chicken when serving.

Apricot–Cashew Pilaf

6 servings

In a large saucepan, melt 4 tablespoons of the butter over low-medium heat and sauté the onion and garlic until tender. Add the rice, salt, and pepper, and continue to sauté for about 3 minutes, making sure the rice is thoroughly coated with the butter. Pour in the chicken broth and remove from the heat. *At this point, the rice can be held for several hours.*

About 1 hour before serving, bring the chicken broth to a boil, then lower the heat and simmer, covered, until the rice is cooked and the liquid is absorbed, about 50 to 60

6	*tablespoons butter*
1	*large onion, finely chopped*
1	*clove garlic, finely chopped*
1½	*cups brown rice*
	Salt and freshly ground black pepper to taste

3 to 3½ cups chicken broth OR chicken stock

½ cup dried apricots, finely chopped

⅓ cup unsalted cashew nuts, finely chopped

minutes. Off the heat, stir in the apricots, the cashews, and the remaining 2 tablespoons butter. Taste to correct seasoning, spoon into a warm dish, and serve immediately.

Peppermint Parfait

6 servings

20 chocolate wafers

2 cups heavy cream

⅔ cup green crème de menthe

3 tablespoons confectioners' sugar

In an electric blender or food processor fitted with the steel blade, crush the chocolate wafers until very fine; you should have 1 cup.

In a large mixing bowl, whip the cream until it forms stiff peaks, then stir in the crème de menthe and sugar until thoroughly blended.

Have ready 6 parfait or tall wineglasses. Spoon into the bottom of each glass one-third of the whipped cream mixture, smooth over and top with an even ½-inch layer of the crushed chocolate wafers. Repeat the procedure with another third of the whipped cream mixture and ½-inch layer of crushed wafers. Add the remaining whipped cream mixture and top each serving with a sprinkling of crushed wafers. Refrigerate the parfaits immediately until ready to serve. *At this point, the peppermint parfaits can be stored in the refrigerator for 4 to 6 hours.*

Chicken Teriyaki with Pineapple, Peppers, and Onion
Curried Corn Pudding
Tomato–Parsley Salad
Chocolate–Mint Cheesecake

Summertime and the living is easy . . . at least you want it that way if you are contemplating having company. Food should be light, seasonal, and as colorful as a bevy of girls in their summer dresses. Decks and patios are natural places for people to congregate, which is why the cook might as well join the party by preparing the main course outdoors over charcoal (the chicken can also be cooked in the oven; see recipe instructions). The menu is easily multiplied to serve eight or ten with the addition of two more food-laden skewers for the chicken teriyaki.

Thick chicken breasts work best for the teriyaki because they can be cut into more uniform chunks. If you are stuck with thin chicken breasts, you will have to fold over some of the pieces to achieve chunks suitable for spearing on the skewer. We use canned pineapple in the recipe in order to have juice for the marinade, but also to omit the step of preparing a fresh pineapple. However, fresh pineapple really is a whole lot better than canned— especially for cooking over a fire—so if you want to buy the fresh fruit, do it! Then either buy some canned pineapple juice for the marinade or just increase the sherry by a small amount. We are assuming few people grow their own onions, but the smaller garden onions are perfect for this dish; and they're so sweet, you might want to use four per skewer instead of two.

Whether you cook the chicken over a charcoal or gas grill or in the oven, it is important to baste the vegetables and pineapple as well as the chicken with the marinade—otherwise the food will tend to char or dry out. Be sure to clean the grill before lighting the fire so as to prevent the food from sticking to it; you can even *lightly* oil the grill. When the teriyaki is done, push the food onto a warm serving platter; if you have a platter with divided compartments, you can separate the meat and vegetables. Another serving possibility is to place the skewers intact on individual plates at the table; just make sure your plates are big enough for this.

Our corn pudding captures as much of the essence of corn as eating it off the cob does—yet how much easier and neater the preparation and cleanup. The key to the success of the dish lies in selecting the freshest, youngest corn you can locate. Avoid big, thick ears and husks that are dark green all over; the best corn has a husk that is pale green at the base and shades into an even lighter green near the top. Richness is imparted to the corn by cream instead of butter, and the hint of curry gives the dish an interest that will be identified only by curry freaks like ourselves (we have known children who couldn't be dragged to an Indian restaurant to wolf down this corn). We recommend that you try to orchestrate your predinner time so that the corn pudding goes into the oven just as the guests arrive. That way you won't have to hold it very long or reheat it before serving; and it's true that the fresher the corn the better—even when cooked.

The tomato-parsley salad not only adds brilliant color contrast to the menu, it shares with the corn pudding an authentic summer flavor by being its unadorned self. We do not spoil the tomatoes with a complicated dressing; instead, at the last minute, we pour the simplest dressing imaginable—one made with lemon juice and oil—over them. We recommend that you serve the tomatoes on a platter to reinforce the color contribution they make; overlap the slices, then sprinkle on the onion and parsley, and refrigerate until ready to use.

This is a good menu to serve buffet-style because you have two good-sized platters to contend with, plus the dish of corn. Grouped on a sideboard or kitchen island, these dishes are symbolic of summer at its finest.

We have chosen an unusually rich dessert for this menu because the rest of the food is relatively light; therefore this seemed the perfect menu in which to include America's favorite sweet flavor—chocolate. Actually, our chocolate-mint cheesecake is not as fattening as it sounds. There is no crust and very little sugar, and the amount of chocolate is not overwhelming. We might also point out that the cake does serve eight to ten people. If you are still calorie-conscious after reading our arguments, consider omitting the whipped cream topping; the cake is delicious when served plain. This is our only dessert for the spring and summer seasons which does not feature fruit. Thus it's a good recipe to have on hand for those unpredictable times when fruit is suddenly scarce or whatever fruit is available looks weeks away from ripening.

As for wine, we think a slightly fruity white wine from Germany or one of the California Rieslings would go well with the main-course dishes.

Chicken Teriyaki with Pineapple, Peppers, and Onion

6 servings

Drain the juice from the can of pineapple and reserve ¼ cup; reserve the pineapple. In a medium mixing bowl, put the pineapple juice, soy sauce, sherry, garlic, ginger, and honey; whisk in the oil until thoroughly blended.

Trim away any fat and membrane from the chicken and cut into 2-inch cubes. Place the chicken in a shallow dish and pour over the marinade, turning the cubes until thoroughly coated; marinate at least 2 hours, turning occasionally. *At this point, the chicken can be stored in the refrigerator for several hours.* Let it stand at room temperature for 20 to 30 minutes before cooking.

Wash and seed the peppers and cut each one into approximately 2-inch squares, for a total of 12 squares. Cut the large onion into 6 pieces, or the 2 smaller onions into 3 pieces each. Cut 3 of the pineapple slices into 4 sections. *At this point, the pepper, onion, and pineapple can be stored in the refrigerator, covered, for several hours.*

About 30 minutes before cooking, light the coals in a charcoal grill and let them burn down until they have a light coat of gray ash; with a gas grill, you need no such advance preparation for the fire. Spear the chicken, pepper, onion, and pineapple onto 6 18-inch metal skewers, alternating the cubes of poultry with the other ingredients. Brush the vegetables with the marinade. Place the skewers over the charcoal or gas grill fire and grill the food, turning occasionally and basting everything constantly; the total cooking time will be about 20 minutes. Serve immediately.

(Instructions for oven broiling: Preheat the oven to BROIL, place the chicken teriyaki on

1	*8-ounce can sliced pineapple in unsweetened juice*
½	*cup soy sauce*
¼	*cup dry sherry*
1	*teasoon garlic, finely chopped*
¼	*teaspoon ground ginger*
1	*teaspoon honey*
¼	*cup vegetable oil*
2½	*pounds boneless, skinless chicken breasts*
2	*green peppers*
1	*large onion* OR *2 small onions*

the broiler pan and cook 6 inches from the broiler heat for 15 to 20 minutes; turn and baste as you would on an outdoor grill.)

Curried Corn Pudding

6 to 8 servings

8	ears fresh corn
3	eggs
1	pint whipping cream
2	to 3 teaspoons curry powder
1½	teaspoons salt
	Several dashes hot pepper sauce

Preheat the oven to 350 degrees.

Scrape the corn kernels from the cobs and put in a large mixing bowl. In a medium mixing bowl, lightly beat the eggs and whip in the cream, curry powder, salt, and hot pepper sauce. Pour the cream mixture into the corn and stir vigorously until well blended; pour the corn into a greased, deep 2½-quart baking dish. Bake for 60 to 70 minutes, or until a straw or knife inserted into the center comes out clean. *At this point, the corn pudding can be held, uncovered, for 2 to 3 hours.*

Shortly before serving, cover the corn pudding and reheat in a 325-degree oven for 20 to 30 minutes while grilling the chicken.

Tomato–Parsley Salad

6 servings

5	medium, ripe tomatoes
¼	cup scallions (white part only), finely chopped
½	cup fresh parsley, finely chopped

Peel the tomatoes and slice into ½-inch slices (you should have about 3 slices per person). Arrange the tomato slices on a serving platter and sprinkle them with the scallions and then the parsley. *At this point, the tomatoes can be stored in the refrigerator, covered, for several hours.*

In a small mixing bowl, prepare the dressing by combining the garlic, salt, pepper, and lemon juice; then whisk in the olive oil until the ingredients are blended. Let the dressing stand several hours until ready to use.

When ready to serve, discard the garlic clove halves from the dressing and whisk it again until everything is thoroughly blended. Pour the dressing evenly over the tomatoes.

Dressing

1   *clove garlic, halved*

   Salt and freshly ground black pepper to taste

2   *tablespoons fresh lemon juice*

6   to 7 *tablespoons olive oil* OR *a combination of olive and vegetable oil*

Chocolate–Mint Cheesecake

8 to 10 servings

Preheat the oven to 350 degrees.

In the bottom of a double boiler, heat some water to a simmer. Break up the chocolate into chunks and place in the top of a double boiler. Melt the chocolate over the simmering water, stirring occasionally. Off the heat, stir in the hot water and the crème de menthe.

In a food processor fitted with the steel blade, place the cream cheese and the chocolate and process until blended; add the flour and the egg yolks and continue processing until completely blended and smooth. Spoon into a large mixing bowl.

In a large mixing bowl, beat the egg whites until they form stiff peaks. Fold the egg whites into the chocolate mixture until everything is thoroughly blended; this will take a few minutes.

Grease a 9-inch round springform pan and dust the bottom and sides with about 1 tablespoon of the confectioners' sugar. Pour the chocolate batter into the pan and bake for 35 to 40 minutes, or until a toothpick inserted into the center comes out clean. Cool the cake

2   *4-ounce packages sweet chocolate*

2   *tablespoons hot water*

3   *tablespoons green* OR *white crème de menthe*

1   *8-ounce package cream cheese, softened to room temperature*

2   *tablespoons flour*

6   *eggs, separated*

   About 5 tablespoons confectioners' sugar

1   *cup heavy cream (for 6 people, ¾ cup)*

on a rack. Remove the outer rim of the spring-form pan and refrigerate the cake for 3 to 4 hours. *At this point, the cake can be stored in the refrigerator, covered with plastic wrap, for 2 to 3 days.*

Shortly before serving, whip the cream to stiff peaks (you will need a whole cup of cream if you are serving 8 to 10 people, only ¾ cup for 6 people) and sweeten to taste with the remaining sugar. Cut the cake into wedges and serve on dessert plates with a generous dollop of whipped cream on top of each serving.

Chilled Cucumber Soup
Chicken in Wine–Herb Sauce
Zucchini Stuffed with Sausage and Walnuts
Limeade Mousse

Into every summer a heat wave will surely fall. If you have invited people to dinner and, as the date approaches, the temperature keeps climbing toward 100 degrees, you may want to consider this menu. Three of the dishes can be made as much in advance as the day before, and only one dish—the zucchini—is served hot.

Actually, the menu is delicious for any kind of summer weather and for the spring too, because a variation on the chicken entrée is to serve it hot. Thus a lot of versatility is built into a menu that is not only a snap to prepare but is also inexpensive. Because it requires no cooking, the cucumber soup recipe can be put together in the time it takes to set a table—maybe less. Most cucumber soups are made by simmering cucumbers in chicken broth, but we think that dulls the vegetable's very special yet delicate flavor; and we guarantee you've never tasted such essence of cucumber as you will in this light but authoritative soup. If any of your guests are weight watchers, you might want to use low-calorie mayonnaise in the recipe instead of the regular kind.

The chicken dish has evolved from a Greek treatment for fish. Certainly bay leaf and rosemary are herbs that transport us immediately to whitewashed cottages perched amid olive groves on hillsides above the blue Aegean; in the recipe, these two herbs achieve a prominence in the wine sauce that gives it an unusual pungency. Chilling a dish often decreases the flavor impact, but that doesn't happen when this chicken sits on ice. You should end up with enough sauce to cover the chicken breasts; if not, turn the chicken occasionally in the sauce while refrigerating it.

Because most vegetable dishes would fade in a competition with the chicken in wine-herb sauce, we pair our zucchini with a little sausage. What we end up with is a recipe for an absolutely first-rate stuffed zucchini which could stand by itself as a luncheon or supper entrée; yet as a complement to the chicken, it can't be rivaled for taste, color, and a balance of hot with cold. We know some people are going to have trouble obtaining Italian sausage, but we want to emphasize that if you have a choice between regular pork sausage and Italian, buy the latter because it really has a lot more zip.

Now about our limeade mousse. We admit that mousses have been a headache throughout the writing of this book. Having failed on several occasions, we think we finally have a success on our hands. We wish we had numerous "never-fail" tips to pass on to our readers, but we have followed several such tips either read about or gleaned from friends, and we've still failed. One thing we do know for sure is to mix *cold* water with the gelatin and let this stand for a few minutes because if the gelatin doesn't soften—which is what this step accomplishes—forget it. Another word to the wise about mousses or any other dish requiring whipped cream: If the weather is hot, chill all your utensils before you whip the cream, including the bowl. This helps to get the cream really whipped up so that the folding is easier and the end product is more mousselike. The mousse, by the way, makes a delicious filling for a pie with a coconut or regular crust, but you need to reduce the cream by one-half cup.

The red wine sauce dictates that a light red wine be drunk with the meal—a Beaujolais, for instance; however, if you're a red wine buff, the dish could actually take a heavier red, perhaps a Chianti or a Burgundy. Cool the wine for an hour in the refrigerator for drinking on a hot summer night.

Chilled Cucumber Soup

Wash, peel, and seed the cucumbers; cut the cucumbers into 1-inch chunks. In the container of a food processor fitted with the steel blade or in an electric blender, place the cucumber, mayonnaise, yogurt, parsley, and fresh dillweed (if using dried dillweed, do not add at this stage) and purée until smooth; this will have to be done in 2 to 3 batches. Scrape into a large mixing bowl and stir in the lemon juice, cream, and the dried dillweed if that is used. Chill in the refrigerator for at least 3 to 4 hours. *At this point, the soup can be stored in the refrigerator, covered, for 2 to 3 days.*

When ready to serve, stir the soup well before ladling into soup bowls or cups. Garnish each serving with slices of radish and, if you wish, a light sprinkling of dill.

4	to 5 *cucumbers*
½	*cup mayonnaise*
2	*8-ounce containers plain yogurt*
¼	*cup fresh parsley, finely chopped*
1½	*tablespoons fresh dillweed, finely chopped* OR 2 *teaspoons dried dillweed*
2	*tablespoons lemon juice*
1	*cup half-and-half cream*
4	to 6 *radishes, thinly sliced*

Chicken in Wine–Herb Sauce

In a small mixing bowl, combine the first five ingredients and set aside.

Cut each connected chicken breast in half, trim away any fat and membrane, and flatten slightly with the heel of your hand; dry with paper towels. Season the flour with plenty of salt and some pepper, and dredge the chicken in the flour, shaking off any excess. Let the chicken stand 5 minutes, then repeat the dredging process.

In a large skillet, melt 3 tablespoons of the

2½	*tablespoons tomato paste*
2	*tablespoons red wine vinegar*
2	*bay leaves*
1	*teaspoon dried rosemary, crumbled* OR 2 *teaspoons fresh rosemary, finely chopped*

1½ cups dry red wine

2½ pounds whole, boneless, skinless chicken breasts

½   to ¾ cup flour

Salt and freshly ground black pepper to taste

8   tablespoons (1 stick) butter

¼   cup vegetable oil

1   large clove garlic, finely chopped

¼   cup fresh parsley, finely chopped

butter and 2 tablespoons of the oil over medium heat and sauté half the chicken until it is golden brown on all sides and cooked through, about 15 to 20 minutes. Lower the heat during the cooking to avoid burning the butter. Remove the chicken with a slotted spoon to a shallow baking dish large enough to hold the chicken in a single layer, about 9 x 13 x 2 inches. Melt 3 tablespoons of the butter and the remaining oil in the skillet and sauté the rest of the chicken, removing the pieces to the baking dish when cooked.

In the same skillet, sauté the garlic over low-medium heat until golden; do not let it burn. Add the wine-herb mixture and bring to a gentle boil, scraping away the particles from the bottom of the skillet. Continue cooking the wine-herb mixture until it is reduced and slightly thickened, stirring frequently. Off the heat, stir in the remaining 2 tablespoons of butter and pour the sauce over the chicken, turning each piece until well coated. Cool the chicken and then refrigerate for at least 2 hours, or until it is chilled. *At this point, the chicken can be stored in the refrigerator, covered, for 1 to 2 days.*

When ready to serve, spoon the sauce over the chicken and garnish the dish with the parsley.

(Note: If you choose to serve the chicken hot, bring the dish to room temperature for 1 hour, then reheat it in a 350-degree oven for 20 to 30 minutes.)

Zucchini Stuffed with Sausage and Walnuts

6 servings

Wash the zucchini and trim away the ends (but do not peel the skin). Cut each zucchini in half lengthwise. Using a melon baller, hollow out the zucchini to within ¼ to ⅓ inch of each zucchini rim. Chop up the zucchini meat into very small pieces and reserve.

Remove the casing from the Italian sausage and crumble, or if using pork sausage, simply crumble. In a medium skillet, place the sausage and cook over medium heat, breaking up the sausage into small pieces, until it is completely cooked through and done, about 10 minutes. Remove the sausage with a slotted spoon to a dish, pour out the sausage grease, and wipe the skillet clean with a paper towel.

Using the same skillet, melt 3 tablespoons of the butter over low-medium heat and add the onion, walnuts, and the chopped zucchini meat; sauté over low heat until the onion and zucchini are tender and the walnuts are beginning to brown, about 7 minutes. Off the heat, stir in the sausage, bread crumbs, basil, oregano, parsley, salt, and pepper. When the mixture has cooled, stir in the egg and blend thoroughly.

Spread the remaining 2 tablespoons of butter in the zucchini cavities and sprinkle each with salt and pepper. Pack the sausage filling into the hollowed-out zucchini, mounding the filling until you have used it up; sprinkle the tops of the zucchini with the Parmesan cheese. Lightly grease a shallow baking dish big enough to hold the zucchini in a single layer and place the vegetable in it. *At this point, the zucchini can be stored in the refrigerator for 3 to 4 hours.* Let the zucchini come to room temperature for 30 to 45 minutes before cooking.

3   *medium to large zucchini*

½   *pound sweet Italian sausage OR bulk pork sausage*

5   *tablespoons butter, softened to room temperature*

1   *small to medium onion, finely chopped*

⅓   *cup walnuts, finely chopped*

1   *cup fresh bread crumbs*

2   *teaspoons fresh basil, finely chopped OR ½ teaspoon dried basil*

½   *teaspoon dried oregano*

2   *tablespoons fresh parsley, finely chopped*

  Salt and freshly ground black pepper to taste

1   *egg, well beaten*

6   *tablespoons Parmesan cheese OR Romano cheese, grated*

Preheat the oven to 350 degrees.

Bake the zucchini, uncovered, for 30 to 40 minutes, or until the tops are golden brown and bubbly. Serve immediately from the baking dish or a warm platter.

Limeade Mousse

6 servings

4	*eggs*
	Scant ⅔ cup sugar
½	*cup cold water*
1	*package unflavored gelatin*
1	*6-ounce can frozen limeade, slightly thawed*
1	*cup coconut, loosely packed*
½	*teaspoon lime rind, grated*
1¼	*cups heavy cream*

In the top of a double boiler, break the eggs and beat them well; add the sugar and continue beating until satiny smooth. Add the cold water and gelatin and stir to blend; let this mixture stand for a few minutes to soften the gelatin. Bring a little water to a boil in the bottom half of the double boiler, then reduce the heat to simmer. Set the egg mixture over the water and cook, stirring constantly, until the gelatin is completely dissolved. Pour the egg mixture into a large mixing bowl and stir in the limeade concentrate, then place in the refrigerator until partly set (this will take about 1 hour).

While the limeade mixture is jelling, toast the coconut in the oven broiler, about 3 inches from the heat, watching very carefully so it doesn't burn; this takes only 2 or 3 minutes. In a small mixing bowl, combine the toasted coconut and the grated lime rind.

In a large mixing bowl, whip the cream until stiff peaks form, then fold the whipped cream into the limeade mixture until thoroughly blended. (Note: If the limeade mixture has jelled so much that it isn't going to mix with the cream without remaining clumpy, stir it up with an electric beater on the "stir" or "mix" setting until it is smooth, then proceed to fold in the whipped cream.) Pour the mousse into a 1½-quart container such as a soufflé dish, and sprinkle the coconut-lime rind combination over the top. Chill in the refrigerator until set, about 4 to 6 hours. *At this point, the mousse can be stored in the refrigerator, covered, for 1 to 2 days.*

Tomato–Orange Soup
Fillets of Sole with Cheese and Herbed Butter
Zucchini–Mushroom Custard
Peach–Cassis Ice

The harvests of red, ripe tomatoes and delectable peaches tend to coincide in many parts of the country around the middle of July, which makes mid- to late summer the ideal time to plan a dinner party around these special fruits. Neither the soup nor the dessert calls for any cooking—a blessing if your party comes during a heat wave.

The dessert of peach-cassis ice is your first responsibility because it can be frozen well ahead of time (in fact, we have enjoyed this dessert from the freezer as much as seven months after it was made—to dine on it in February assures us that summer will indeed come around again). A blend of peaches at their sweetest, the popular liqueur cassis (a distillation of black currants), yogurt, and a little honey add up to an exotic conclusion to a memorable meal. The interesting thing about the combination of these particular ingredients is that they retain their identity, possibly because each is so forceful in its own right. The flavor of the peach-cassis ice is powerful and dense, which is why we offer the option of tempering it with a little vanilla ice cream.

The tomato-orange soup is one of the most unusual recipes in this book. We hope you get a chance to serve it on a fiercely hot day because it is almost as effective a thirst quencher as ice-cold water. But whatever the weather, the soup looks absolutely beautiful in the soup bowl (especially if your bowls are clear glass or white china)—a small pool of sharp red and mellow orange. One might question whether the merging of two such distinctive flavors as tomato and orange can succeed, but they seem as made for each other as ham and eggs or peanut butter and jelly. This is the sort of recipe your company will remember you for, so don't give it away.

Since the soup and dessert are prepared at least a day in advance, the only dishes you have to worry about on the day of the dinner are the fish and the vegetable. The zucchini-mushroom custard involves several steps, and we suggest that you assemble the whole thing in the morning and refrigerate it until ready to bake. Unlike the soup, this dish features two vegetables with delicate flavors which create an extremely subtle taste experience when they are blended. In fact, the zucchini-mushroom custard serves to play up the authoritative flavors of the fresh herbs and aged cheese in the entrée.

We invented the fish dish for people who have a modest kitchen herb garden. So few recipes in magazines and books call for fresh herbs, yet the fresh ones are vastly superior in taste to the dried. When you buy dried herbs, you can't be sure how long they've been sitting on the shelf—yet a dried herb loses its flavor after nine or ten months. A herb garden specializing in herbs for cooking brings great pleasure to the gardener/chef. We encourage our readers to consider planting one by the kitchen door. Herb gardens are easy to establish, require minimal maintenance, and just keep coming up green year after year.

The fillets of sole with cheese and herbed butter are very easy to make, and you can assemble them entirely before guests arrive. Of course, if you don't have the fresh herbs called for in the list of ingredients (though you should have the parsley and, we hope, the chives), dried herbs can be substituted. The fish cooks while you are dining on the soup. You can serve the platter of fish at the table and be sure to spoon the lovely, herb-flecked drippings of butter, wine, and cheese over each portion; use it all up.

Serve a light, dry, very cold white wine with the sole, say a Chablis or Soave or Blanc de Blancs.

Tomato–Orange Soup

6 servings

Peel, seed, and chop the tomatoes into small cubes and place in a large mixing bowl.

Wash one of the oranges and peel away the zest in approximately 1 x 2-inch strips (zest is the outermost, orange surface of the fruit's skin; it should not include the white part of the skin). Cut each strip of zest into 1-inch lengths and cut lengthwise into very thin strips (thinner than a matchstick). Add the zest to the tomatoes. Cut each orange in half and, using a serrated grapefruit knife, cut all the sections out of the oranges and add to the tomatoes along with the juice of both oranges.

Add the onion, vinegar, wine, tomato juice, chicken broth, salt, pepper, and hot pepper sauce to the tomatoes. Stir everything together and refrigerate for at least 4 to 6 hours. *At this point, the soup can be stored in the refrigerator, covered, for 2 to 3 days.*

When ready to serve, stir in the parsley.

2	*pounds very ripe tomatoes*
2	*oranges*
1	*medium onion, finely chopped*
1	*tablespoon red wine vinegar*
½	*cup dry white wine*
1	*12-ounce can tomato juice, chilled*
1½	*cups chicken broth OR chicken stock*
	Salt and freshly ground black pepper to taste
	Dash hot pepper sauce
¼	*cup fresh parsley, finely chopped*

Fillets of Sole with Cheese and Herbed Butter

6 servings

In a small mixing bowl, cream together the butter with the herbs and spread just enough of this mixture to cover the bottom of a 9 x 13 x 2-inch shallow baking dish which can be brought to the table.

Pat the fish dry and arrange half of the fil-

12	*tablespoons (1½ sticks) butter, softened to room temperature*
3	*tablespoons fresh parsley, finely chopped*

1 tablespoon fresh chives, finely chopped

1 teaspoon fresh thyme, finely chopped OR ½ teaspoon dried thyme

2¼ pounds fresh fillets of sole OR flounder

1½ cups Gruyère cheese OR Monterey Jack cheese, grated

⅓ cup dry white wine

Dash paprika

lets in a single layer in the baking dish. Spread the fish with half of the remaining butter mixture and sprinkle with half of the cheese. Arrange the rest of the fish on top of the cheese, spread the rest of the butter over the fish, and sprinkle the rest of the cheese over all. Pour the wine around the fish and dust the top of the cheese with a little paprika. *At this point, the fish can be stored in the refrigerator for 2 to 3 hours.* Let the fish come to room temperature for 30 to 45 minutes before cooking it.

Preheat the oven to 400 degrees.

Bake the fish for about 15 minutes, until the cheese is bubbling and golden. Spoon the drippings over the fish as you serve.

Zucchini–Mushroom Custard

6 servings

½ cup long-grain white rice

1 cup chicken broth OR chicken stock

6 tablespoons butter

¾ pound fresh mushrooms, chopped

2½ pounds zucchini

Salt to taste

2 tablespoons olive oil

1 small to medium onion, finely chopped

2 cloves garlic, finely chopped

Freshly ground black pepper to taste

4 eggs

In a medium saucepan, place the rice, chicken broth, and about ¼ cup of water. Cover tightly and bring quickly to a boil, then lower the heat to a simmer and cook, stirring once, for 10 to 12 minutes, until the rice is done but still firm. Drain the rice into a large sieve and rinse with cool water; reserve.

In a large skillet, melt 2 tablespoons of the butter over low-medium heat and sauté the mushrooms until they have released their juice; remove to a dish and reserve.

Wash the zucchini and trim away the ends (but do not peel the skin). In a food processor fitted with the shredding disk, or with a hand grater, grate the zucchini and place in a colander or sieve set over a bowl; sprinkle generously with salt and let stand for 20 to 30 minutes. Squeeze the excess juice from the zucchini with your hands, then dry on paper towels to get rid of even more moisture (it is important to get the zucchini quite dry to avoid a runny custard).

In the same skillet in which you sautéed the mushrooms, melt the remaining 4 tablespoons of butter and the olive oil over low-medium heat and sauté the onion and garlic until tender; add the zucchini and continue cooking for about 7 minutes, tossing constantly. Off the heat, add the mushrooms, rice, salt, and pepper to the skillet, mixing everything very gently but thoroughly. Taste to correct the seasoning; you will probably need to add more salt.

Spoon the zucchini-mushroom mixture into a greased, shallow baking dish measuring approximately 8 x 12 x 2 inches. *At this point, the dish can be stored in the refrigerator for several hours.* Let it come to room temperature for 30 to 45 minutes before cooking.

Preheat the oven to 375 degrees.

In a medium mixing bowl, beat the eggs lightly, then beat in the cream and the mustard until completely blended. Pour the egg mixture evenly over the zucchini and, using a fork, let the liquid seep down into the dish so the liquid is evenly distributed. Bake for 35 to 45 minutes, or until the center is firm like a custard and a toothpick inserted into the middle comes out clean. Cut into squares and serve immediately.

1   *cup light cream*
2   *tablespoons Dijon mustard*

Peach–Cassis Ice

6 servings

Cut the peaches into chunks and place in a food processor fitted with the steel blade or in an electric blender. Add the yogurt, crème de cassis, and honey and process until smooth; you will have to do this in 2 or 3 batches. Pour into a fairly shallow, plastic container and freeze until firm around the edges, about 2 to 3 hours. Spoon the ice into a chilled mixing

5   *peaches, peeled*
1½   *cups plain yogurt*
½   *cup crème de cassis*
⅓   *cup honey*
      Vanilla ice cream (optional)

bowl and beat with an electric beater until smooth and fluffy. Return the ice to the plastic container and freeze until firm, about 12 hours. *At this point, the ice can be stored, covered, for 1 to 2 months.*

Shortly before serving, remove the peach-cassis ice from the freezer and let it stand at room temperature for 15 to 20 minutes, until it has softened slightly. Serve plain or with a small scoop of vanilla ice cream.

Shrimp in Wine–Butter Sauce
Mushroom–Celery Pilaf
Green Beans Marinara
Blueberries in Maple Cream

Considering how much we love shrimp, it may seem surprising that we have included only one menu in the book featuring fresh shrimp. The reason is simple: Good, fresh shrimp are not readily available in certain parts of the country, and wherever they *can* be found, the price is inevitably sky-high. So, fond as we are of shrimp, we decided it would be unfair to many of our readers to make demands on their pocketbooks or to use an ingredient hard to obtain for one reason or another. Consequently, our one-and-only shrimp menu contains a classically prepared dish that presents the full flavor of shrimp without any interference from other ingredients like vegetables, other seafoods, or complicated sauces.

First, we marinate the shrimp in a simple mixture of oil, lemon juice, garlic, and a dab of mustard. Then, instead of discarding the marinade and broiling or sautéing the shrimp—a common treatment erroneously labeled *shrimp scampi* on many restaurant menus—we quickly cook the shrimp in the marinade, to which we add butter and wine. This prevents the shrimp from turning tough or dry—a frequent problem for amateur chefs—and produces a wonderfully succulent dish. Furthermore, after the marinade gets cooked down, it becomes a delicious sauce for the mushroom-celery pilaf.

Where fresh seafood is marketed, shrimp will usually be available in three sizes—medium, large, and jumbo (the last is often called "stuffing" shrimp). If you have a choice, we recommend getting the large size because you won't have as many shrimp to peel, and the larger the shrimp, the more dramatic the appearance on the plate. However, some people will prefer the medium shrimp just because there will be more shrimp per person. Medium or large shrimp—it's an individual's decision. Actually, many seafood markets, and supermarkets too, handle only the medium shrimp; this is true whether the shrimp are fresh or frozen. When buying frozen shrimp, be sure the shrimp are in the shell; otherwise, you're buying precooked shrimp. Finally, avoid any shrimp labeled "cocktail"; these are smaller than medium and not suitable for an entrée such as this.

If you have already read the individual recipes, you know that the shrimp have to be served the minute the cooking is finished. Therefore, your rice and the green bean dish must be ready before guests sit down to eat. The mushroom-celery pilaf is our first choice as an accompaniment because the vegetables in it enrich the shrimp without fighting a flavor battle with the shellfish or marinade. It is a more complex and interesting rice treatment than plain boiled rice or even our parslied rice in the beef shish kebab menu; however, either one of these simpler rice dishes could be considered as a substitute, as could a plain pilaf without the addition of mushrooms and celery.

The green beans marinara is a superlative summer vegetable dish. Nothing beats it for gorgeous color, advance preparation, and ease of cooking. We can guarantee that once you have made the recipe, it will become a standby in your summer culinary repertoire; in fact, we bet you'll find yourself sneaking it in as the vegetable in several other menus in this book.

The presentation of the dinner can be handled in one of two ways. We think that nicer looking individual plates can be assembled in the kitchen for carrying to the table. In this case, the shrimp can be arranged with some artistry over or around the mushroom-celery pilaf. On the other hand, a dramatic presentation at the table before serving would be to pile the rice in the center of a large platter, with rows of shrimp marching across in some pattern. The latter approach means that when you dish up the rice and shrimp, you're not going to achieve as neat a look on individual plates as you would if serving in the kitchen.

The blueberries in maple cream is one of our pet desserts. It is easy, delicious, and with blueberries enjoying a long season, the dessert can be relied on from spring into late autumn. We encourage people to use authentic maple syrup for the recipe and not the insipid, maple-flavored kind sold in supermarkets. Pure maple syrup is sold in gourmet sections of grocery stores, in gourmet food shops, cheese shops, and health food stores; many gift catalogs offer pure maple syrup too.

The elegant ingredients and special tastes of this dinner call for a fuller-bodied white wine, like a Chardonnay or Orvieto. However, a light, dry white works well too, with Chablis and Muscadet leading our list of favorites.

Shrimp in Wine–Butter Sauce

6 servings

Shell and devein the shrimp, rinse in cold water, and dry on paper towels. Place the shrimp in a shallow dish large enough to hold them in a single layer.

In a small mixing bowl, combine the mustard, garlic, and lemon juice, then whisk in the oil until well blended. Pour the marinade over the shrimp and turn the shrimp so they are coated. Marinate at least 6 hours, and preferably overnight; turn occasionally. *At this point, the shrimp can be stored in the refrigerator, covered, for 1 day.* Let the shrimp come to room temperature for 30 minutes before cooking.

Remove the shrimp from the marinade with a slotted spoon and reserve both shrimp and marinade. In a large skillet, melt the butter over medium heat, add the wine and the marinade, and cook over medium-high heat until reduced by half. Lower the heat to medium, add the shrimp, and cook until done, stirring constantly; this will take about 3 minutes. Serve the shrimp immediately, arranging them over individual portions of the mushroom-celery pilaf; spoon some of the sauce over each portion, and garnish with the parsley.

2¼	*pounds medium to large shrimp, fresh or frozen*
1	*teaspoon Dijon mustard*
4	*cloves garlic, finely chopped*
¼	*cup lemon juice*
½	*cup vegetable oil* OR *a combination of vegetable and olive oil*
4	*tablespoons butter*
1	*cup dry white wine*
¼	*cup fresh parsley, finely chopped*

Mushroom–Celery Pilaf

6 servings

In a medium skillet, melt 2 tablespoons of the butter over low-medium heat and sauté the mushrooms and celery until the mushrooms have released their juice and are cooked

6	*tablespoons butter*
½	*pound mushrooms, thinly sliced*

3	celery stalks, finely chopped
1½	cups long-grain white rice
	Salt and freshly ground black pepper to taste
3	to 3½ cups chicken broth OR chicken stock

through; remove from the heat and reserve.

In a large saucepan, melt 3 tablespoons of the butter over low-medium heat. Add the rice, salt, and pepper, and sauté the rice for about 3 to 5 minutes, making sure it gets thoroughly coated with butter. Pour in the chicken broth, bring to a boil, then lower the heat and simmer the rice, covered, until it is cooked and the liquid is absorbed, about 20 to 25 minutes. Remove from the heat and keep covered. *At this point, the rice as well as the mushroom-celery mixture can be held for 2 to 3 hours.*

About 30 minutes before serving, preheat the oven to 350 degrees.

Melt the remaining 1 tablespoon of butter with 1 tablespoon water until hot and pour over the rice. Gently stir in the mushrooms and celery, along with their pan juices. Turn the pilaf into a greased, deep 2½- or 3-quart casserole dish and reheat the pilaf, covered, for 15 to 20 minutes. Serve immediately.

Green Beans Marinara

6 servings

2	pounds fresh green beans
¼	cup vegetable oil OR a combination of vegetable and olive oil
2	cloves garlic
3	medium to large tomatoes, peeled, seeded, and coarsely chopped
2	teaspoons fresh basil OR oregano, finely chopped; OR ½ tea-

Break off the stem end of the beans and snap them into approximately 2-inch lengths. In a large kettle, bring to a boil 4 to 6 quarts of salted water and plunge in the beans; cover until the water returns to the boil, uncover and boil for no more than 3 to 5 minutes, until barely tender. Drain the beans in a colander and run cold water over them until they are cool. Dry the beans on paper towels. *At this point, the beans can be stored in the refrigerator, covered, for 1 day.* Let the beans come to room temperature for 45 to 60 minutes before reheating.

In a large skillet, heat the oil over medium

heat and sauté the garlic cloves until golden on all sides; discard the garlic. Lower the heat and add the tomatoes, herb, salt, and pepper, and simmer about 15 minutes, until you have a thick sauce; remove from the heat and reserve. *At this point, the sauce can be held for several hours.*

Just before serving, add the beans to the marinara sauce in the skillet and reheat until the dish is hot (but don't really cook it). Place in a warm serving bowl and sprinkle with the parsley; serve immediately.

spoon dried basil OR oregano

Salt and freshly ground black pepper to taste

¼ *cup fresh parsley, finely chopped*

Blueberries in Maple Cream

6 servings

Pick over the blueberries to remove stems and discard any crushed berries; rinse thoroughly in cold water and dry on paper towels. Place in a large bowl, reserving 18 berries for a garnish.

In a medium mixing bowl, blend the sour cream and maple syrup until smooth. Pour over the blueberries and stir gently with a wooden spoon until the berries are coated. *At this point, the blueberries can be stored in the refrigerator, covered, for 1 to 2 days.*

Stir the berries and spoon into individual dessert dishes, garnishing each serving with 3 of the reserved berries.

1½ *pints fresh blueberries, about 4½ cups*

1   *8-ounce container sour cream*

4   *tablespoons pure maple syrup*

Charcoal–Broiled Swordfish in Mustard Marinade
Pasta Primavera
Garlic–Buttered Bread
Strawberries in Raspberry Sauce

This is definitely a menu to consider for a soft spring evening when you've hauled the charcoal grill out of winter storage and the view from deck or patio is colored by rhododendrons and azaleas in full bloom. Furthermore, strawberries are back in season, fresh swordfish has returned to the market, and our pasta dish can be varied so you can use just about any fresh vegetable that happens to be around. We hasten to add that the swordfish can be grilled in an oven if you don't have access to an outdoor cooker.

We know from experience what a busy season spring and early summer can be. The lawn has to be fertilized, vegetables and flowers are scheduled for prompt planting, the windows need to be washed and screens put on; the list of weekend chores is overwhelming. But take our word for it: You will have plenty of time to prepare this impressive menu for friends *and* clean out the garage or prune the forsythia.

The main chore on the day of the party will be to assemble the pasta primavera ("primavera," by the way, means spring). This takes about an hour, and the closer to the time of your guests' arrival you can do this, the prettier the dish will be. For people whose idea of pasta is spaghetti and meatballs, this dish will be a revelation; for others more knowledgeable about Italian cuisine, it will be a delight. Essentially, we marry spaghetti with a medley of vegetables and bind the two with a creamy cheese sauce. As is true of many stews, the pasta primavera can be varied according to what's available in garden or grocery store. For example, you can substitute yellow squash, broccoli flowerettes, green peas—you can even use green beans if you break them into one-inch pieces. The important thing is to have some green, red, and yellow flashes among the strands of spaghetti. Fresh basil won't be ready for picking in the spring, of course; but if you serve this dish later in the season and you grow basil in your garden, you'll need about 16 basil leaves for ¼ cup.

Unfortunately, swordfish is not available to everyone in this country, and we debated at length about including an entrée which can be scarce at times or nonexistent in some places. However, we believe the demand for all kinds of fish is going to increase as people grow more concerned about healthy diets; and since swordfish is one of the most freezable seafood products, we think it will soon be more widely distributed to frozen food counters everywhere. We are also featuring swordfish in a menu because of its immense popularity even with people who ordinarily shun fish like a fever. On the West Coast, a suitable substitute is albacore; and another very acceptable choice in lieu of swordfish is mako shark. When you buy the swordfish, try to get pieces that are no more than 1½ inches thick (we prefer 1 inch); anything thicker will take proportionately longer to cook, which tends to dry out the exterior meat. You will undoubtedly have to buy two or three pieces of swordfish to get a total of 3 pounds.

The garlic-buttered bread should be a loaf of a reliable Italian, French, or Portuguese bread baked on the premises of a local supermarket or trucked in from a local bakery. Carefully flavor a stick of softened butter with a little garlic powder or a small clove of mashed garlic, and butter the bread slices either on one or both sides. Wrap in aluminum foil and warm up the whole loaf in a 350-degree oven for 15 to 20 minutes.

The strawberry dessert with its rich, red coating of raspberry sauce is surely one of the most visually inviting sweet treats in the book. This is definitely the dessert to tack onto your meal when the strawberry season is at its peak—when the berries are a uniform shape, perfectly textured, and at their most flavorful. While the whipped cream is not essential, it does serve to intensify the red colors of the two berries.

The wine choice for this menu depends on whether you favor white or red wine in the general eating scheme of things. Our own choice would be an Italian Soave or Ischia, if you can get it. But food and wine purists would no doubt insist on a light but commanding red—especially a Chianti or a Valpolicella.

Charcoal–Broiled Swordfish in Mustard Marinade

6 servings

2 tablespoons Dijon mustard

2 tablespoons onion, finely chopped

1 large clove garlic, finely chopped

¼ cup fresh parsley, finely chopped

½ teaspoon oregano

2 tablespoons lemon juice

¼ cup dry white wine

½ cup vegetable oil

3 pounds swordfish, fresh or frozen, approximately 1 inch thick

2 tablespoons butter, softened to room temperature

In a small mixing bowl, combine the mustard, onion, garlic, 2 tablespoons of the parsley, oregano, lemon juice, and wine; gradually pour in the oil, whisking vigorously to blend.

Place the swordfish in a shallow dish big enough to hold it in a single layer, pour over the marinade, and turn to coat. Marinate for at least 4 to 6 hours in the refrigerator, turning occasionally. *At this point, the swordfish can be stored in the refrigerator, covered, for 1 day.* Let the fish come to room temperature for 1 hour before cooking.

About 30 minutes before cooking, light the coals in a charcoal grill, and let them burn down until they have a light coat of gray ash; with a gas grill, you need no such advance preparation for the fire. (See below for instructions on oven broiling the swordfish.) Place the fish over the charcoal or gas grill fire and cover the grill (the vents usually remain open unless the fire is too hot, in which case you may want to partly close the bottom vent). Cook the fish approximately 4 to 5 minutes on one side; then turn the fish, baste with the marinade, and cook 5 to 6 minutes, covered, on the other side. Test for doneness in the center of the fish by cutting with a sharp knife. (Note: If you have a thicker piece of fish, you will need to increase the cooking time accordingly.)

Remove the fish to a warm serving platter, spread with the butter, and sprinkle with the remaining parsley. Serve immediately.

(Instructions for oven broiling: If you choose to cook your swordfish indoors, you will lose the hint of charcoal flavor but you will end up with a very moist, succulent piece of fish. Preheat the oven to BROIL and place the fish on the broiler pan. Cook the fish 3 inches from the heat for 1 to 2 minutes to sear, then lower the oven rack to 6 inches from the heat and cook 5 minutes. Turn the fish and baste with the remaining marinade. Raise the oven rack to 3 inches again, sear for 1 minute, then lower the rack to 6 inches from the heat and cook for another 5 to 6 minutes. Omit the soft butter but garnish with the parsley and serve.)

Pasta Primavera

6 to 8 servings

Trim the ends of the carrots and radishes, scrape them and cut into a ½-inch dice. Wash the zucchini, trim the ends (but do not peel the skin) and cut into a ½-inch dice. Wash the optional leeks thoroughly to remove all traces of sand, then finely chop the white part.

In a large skillet, melt 3 tablespoons of the butter and the oil over low-medium heat and sauté the onion, garlic, carrots, radishes, and leeks until almost tender, about 10 minutes. Add the zucchini, parsley, basil, chicken broth, salt, and pepper (be generous with the salt—you may use as much as 2 or 3 teaspoons); cover, and simmer over low heat, stirring occasionally, until the vegetables are tender, about 10 minutes. Remove the vegetables from the skillet with a slotted spoon and reserve both the vegetables and the juice in the skillet.

In a large kettle, bring to a boil 6 to 8 quarts salted water to which you have added a little vegetable oil. Break the spaghetti into thirds and add to the water; cook over high heat until barely tender, about 7 minutes. Drain the spaghetti in a colander and run cool water over it; drain well again and place in a greased 7 x 11 x 2-inch baking dish. Spoon the vegetables over the spaghetti and poke them down into the pasta a little bit.

2	*medium carrots*
6	*to 8 radishes*
2	*medium zucchini*
2	*leeks (optional)*
8	*tablespoons (1 stick) butter*
3	*tablespoons vegetable oil*
1	*medium red onion, finely chopped*
1	*large clove garlic, finely chopped*
½	*cup fresh parsley, finely chopped*
¼	*cup fresh basil, finely chopped OR 1 tablespoon dried basil*
1	*cup chicken broth OR chicken stock*
	Salt and freshly ground black pepper to taste
12	*ounces thin spaghetti*

1   cup Parmesan cheese
     OR Romano cheese,
     grated

¾   cup heavy cream

In the same skillet in which you cooked the vegetables, melt 4 tablespoons of the butter over low heat in the remaining juice. Stir in the cream until it is warmed through; then add ¾ cup of the cheese, and continue cooking and stirring over very low heat until the cheese is melted and the sauce is thickened and smooth (the cheese does not have to be entirely melted). Pour the sauce evenly over the pasta and vegetables. *At this point, the dish can be held, covered, for 2 to 3 hours.*

About 45 minutes before serving, preheat the oven to 350 degrees.

Dot the dish with the remaining 1 tablespoon of butter and reheat in the oven, covered, for 20 to 30 minutes. Serve the dish immediately, sprinkling a little of the remaining ¼ cup of cheese over each portion as you serve.

Strawberries in Raspberry Sauce

6 servings

1   *quart fresh strawberries*

¼   *cup orange liqueur (Grand Marnier, Cointreau, Curaçao)*

1   *10-ounce package frozen red raspberries, thawed*

½   *cup heavy cream*

2   *to 3 tablespoons confectioners' sugar*

Wash and hull the strawberries; do not slice. In a large mixing bowl, place the strawberries and pour the orange liqueur over them.

In a food processor fitted with the steel blade or in an electric blender, purée the raspberries and their juice. Place a medium sieve over a bowl and strain the raspberry purée through the sieve in order to separate the seeds from the purée. Pour the seedless raspberry sauce over the strawberries and gently stir to coat each berry. Refrigerate the strawberries for 6 hours, stirring occasionally. *At this point, the strawberries can be stored in the refrigerator, covered, for 1 day.* Let the strawberries stand at room temperature for 30 to 45 minutes before serving.

Just before serving, whip the cream to stiff peaks and stir in the sugar. Place a dollop of whipped cream on top of each individual serving.

Steak and Vegetable Sauté
Curried Rice with
Artichokes and Olives
Tomato Aspic Salad
Pineapple Slush

When we and suburbia were growing up in the fifties, the favorite form of summertime entertaining was the backyard or patio cookout, which usually meant a steak grilled over charcoal, accompanied by a green salad and garlic-buttered bread. Plain. Easy. Satisfying. But that was before Julia Child, the food processor, and group charters to Europe—cultural changes that have grown into a determination to make a dinner party a memorable experience. However, most cooks still want to keep the menu preparation as simple and brief as possible without resorting to throwing a slab of porterhouse or sirloin on the fire. One of the most popular cuisines highlighting both speed and simplicity is Chinese, which we've borrowed from in this menu for our entrée of steak and vegetable sauté.

Probably the outstanding characteristic of Chinese cooking is its nutritional value, which is achieved by a reliance on fresh vegetables and quick cooking over high heat. Whether you use a regular or electric skillet or the more authentic wok, you will be cooking the ingredients in the stir-fry Chinese fashion, which guarantees a crisp and fresh dish, ready for the table as soon as you've executed the last stir. The several seasonal garden vegetables in the recipe can be varied according to what produce is plentiful—for example, Swiss chard or Romaine lettuce can be substituted for the spinach, leeks for the scallions, the zucchini can be replaced by yellow squash, a little celery can be added. The important thing is to strive for a variety of color in the vegetables, because essentially the vegetables are an elaborate garnish for your meat. As for the steak, there's a real advantage to the cheaper cut of top round over its twice-as-expensive relations, yet because of the way we treat it, the tenderness and flavor rival Kansas City's finest.

No special dexterity is needed for the last-minute cooking required in this menu, nor is the cooking complicated by outside distractions. Everything else scheduled for the table is already prepared and ready to serve. The steak has to be sliced and marinated ahead of time and the vegetables are cut up in advance. Thus, the only step to be undertaken while guests are enjoying their drinks is the cooking; and this takes about eight minutes! Naturally, you will have placed the individual aspic salads on the table just before you start cooking; ditto the bowl of rice. Warn guests that dinner isn't far off, turn up the heat, and spring into action. When you finish cooking each batch of steak, remember to place the meat on a previously warmed platter in an oven preheated to WARM; keep the meat there until you serve it. The thin slices of steak cool off very quickly when exposed to room temperature.

A word about the tomato aspic salad. While we think our recipe is absolutely tops in texture and flavor, we concede that there are some good tomato aspics available in grocery stores and specialty food shops. Therefore anyone who is too pressed for time to make the recipe (which is extremely easy), or who doesn't want to bother, can purchase an aspic, chill it, and serve it with our mayonnaise-sour cream dressing. The best lettuce leaf to use under the aspic is Boston or iceberg.

The pineapple slush is one of several summer desserts in the book which have to be taken from the freezer for 20 to 30 minutes before eating, to allow it to thaw to a wonderfully slushy but still spoonable consistency; the necessary time out of the freezer depends on the heat and humidity of the day.

Because the flavors of the dinner are a blend of the subtle and the exotic, we recommend a light red wine such as a Gamay Beaujolais or a Valpolicella. What you want is a wine that won't overpower the fresh vegetables in the steak dish, yet will hold its own with the distinctively tangy curry and olives in the rice. You may be familiar with a good but inexpensive table red which will go down nicely with this particular menu.

Steak and Vegetable Sauté

6 servings

Pat the steak dry with a paper towel and trim away any fat. With a very sharp knife, cut the steak into ⅛-inch-thick strips by cutting across the grain at a 45-degree angle (this is much easier to do if the meat is slightly frozen).

In a large mixing bowl, make the marinade by combining the cornstarch, sugar, and baking soda, then stir in the soy sauce and water. Place the steak in the marinade and toss the strips with your fingers until they are thoroughly coated. Marinate the steak for at least 30 minutes. *At this point, the steak can be stored in the refrigerator, covered, for several hours.* Let it come to room temperature for 20 to 30 minutes before cooking.

Wash the vegetables and dry thoroughly, especially the spinach. Trim away the ends of the zucchini and scallions (do not peel the zucchini), and cut into matchstick-size pieces approximately 2 inches long. Seed the peppers and cut into thin strips. Place the zucchini, scallions, and peppers in a bowl. Remove and discard the spinach stems, then cut the spinach into thin strips or chop coarsely; place in another bowl. *At this point, the vegetables can be stored in the refrigerator, covered, for several hours.*

When ready to cook, preheat the oven to WARM.

In a small mixing bowl, make the sauce by combining the cornstarch and salt, then stir in the water, soy sauce, and sherry.

In a large skillet or wok, melt 1 tablespoon of the butter and 1 tablespoon of the oil over medium-high heat. When very hot, add half the steak strips and sauté quickly until done, tossing frequently; this will take about 2 minutes. Remove the steak with a slotted spatula to the middle of a warm serving platter. Melt

2¼	pounds top round steak
2	small zucchini
6	scallions with part of green tops
2	green peppers OR red peppers
1	10-ounce bag fresh spinach OR 1 pound fresh loose spinach
4	tablespoons butter
3	tablespoons vegetable oil
	Juice of ½ lemon

Marinade

2	tablespoons cornstarch
3	teaspoons sugar
1	teaspoon baking soda
¼	cup soy sauce
2	tablespoons water

Sauce

1	teaspoon cornstarch
½	teaspoon salt
3	tablespoons water
2	tablespoons soy sauce
1	tablespoon dry sherry

1 tablespoon of the butter and 1 tablespoon of oil and sauté the rest of the steak in the same way; place the platter of steak in the oven to keep warm while you cook the vegetables.

Add the remaining 2 tablespoons of butter and 1 tablespoon of oil to the skillet and when melted and hot, add the zucchini, peppers, and scallions, and sauté quickly, tossing constantly, about 2 minutes; add the spinach and continue cooking until the spinach is tender but not too limp, about 1 minute. Lower the heat and pour the sauce over the vegetables, tossing until they are completely coated and the sauce begins to thicken and glaze. Remove from the heat.

Pile the vegetables over and around the steak strips and squeeze the lemon juice over all. Serve immediately.

Curried Rice with Artichokes and Olives

6 servings

1½	*cups long-grain white rice*
3	*cups chicken broth* OR *chicken stock*
2	*6-ounce jars marinated artichoke hearts*
16	to 18 *pimiento-stuffed green olives, sliced*
6	*scallions with part of green tops, finely chopped*
2	*teaspoons curry powder*
⅔	*cup mayonnaise*

In a large saucepan, place the rice and pour over the chicken broth, cover, and bring to a boil, stirring occasionally; lower the heat and simmer, covered, until the rice is cooked and the liquid is absorbed, about 15 minutes. Spoon into a large mixing bowl and let cool.

Drain the artichoke hearts, reserving the marinade; cut each artichoke into a small dice. Add the artichokes, olives, and scallions to the rice.

In a small mixing bowl, combine 5 to 6 tablespoons of the reserved artichoke marinade with the curry powder, mayonnaise, salt, and pepper (you may have to adjust the amount of marinade; the important thing is to avoid a greasy consistency in the rice). Pour this mixture over the rice and stir gently to blend. Taste to correct the seasoning. Refrigerate the rice for 3 hours to chill. *At this point, the rice can be stored in the refrigerator, covered, for 1 to 2 days.* When ready to serve, sprinkle some paprika over the top.

Salt and freshly ground black pepper to taste

Paprika

Tomato Aspic Salad

6 to 8 servings

Two to 3 hours before making the aspic, chill 1½ cups of the tomato juice until quite cold.

In a large saucepan, combine the remaining 3½ cups tomato juice, the celery, onion, Worcestershire sauce, basil, parsley, sugar, salt, and peppercorns. Bring to a boil, then reduce the heat and simmer for 30 minutes.

Into a small mixing bowl, pour the chilled tomato juice and sprinkle the gelatin over it; stir to remove any lumps. Let the gelatin soften for 10 minutes.

Into a large mixing bowl, strain the hot tomato juice mixture through a sieve and discard all the solid ingredients. Stir the softened gelatin into the hot liquid until completely dissolved. Pour into a 6-cup no-stick or greased mold; a ring mold is best for this, but you can use another kind of mold, if desired. Chill the aspic until firm, about 4 to 6 hours. *At this point, the aspic can be stored in the refrigerator, covered, for 1 week.*

Shortly before serving, stir together the mayonnaise and sour cream in a small mixing bowl until thoroughly blended. Unmold the aspic (you may have to dip the mold quickly in hot water to do this) and cut into 6 or 8 portions. Place the aspic on the lettuce leaves, which are on individual salad plates. Spoon some of the mayonnaise-sour cream dressing over each serving and sprinkle with a few capers. Serve immediately.

5 *cups tomato juice*

2 *celery stalks, cut in 2 or 3 pieces*

2 *medium onions, coarsely chopped*

2 *teaspoons Worcestershire sauce*

4 to 6 *large fresh basil leaves* OR 1 *teaspoon dried basil*

4 *sprigs fresh parsley*

1 *teaspoon sugar*

½ *teaspoon salt*

4 to 6 *black peppercorns*

3 *packages unflavored gelatin*

¼ *cup mayonnaise*

¼ *cup sour cream*

6 to 8 *lettuce leaves*

Capers for garnish

Pineapple Slush

6 servings

1	20-*ounce can un-sweetened, crushed pineapple*
2	*tablespoons lemon juice*
3	*tablespoons sugar*
½	*cup kirsch*
1	*cup fresh blueberries*

Drain the juice from the pineapple into a small mixing bowl, add the lemon juice and 2 tablespoons of the sugar; stir until the sugar is dissolved.

In a food processor fitted with the steel blade or in an electric blender, purée the pineapple and sweetened lemon juice until mushy (this may take 2 batches in an electric blender); don't purée more than a few seconds, as you want the dessert to have some texture. Pour the pineapple purée into a freezer container, stir in the kirsch and freeze for 6 to 8 hours. *At this point, the pineapple slush can be stored in the freezer, covered, for 1 month.*

Several hours before serving, wash the blueberries and sprinkle with the remaining 1 tablespoon of sugar; chill.

Shortly before serving, check to see if the pineapple slush has hardened; if so, allow it to thaw 15 to 20 minutes, or until it has a nice, mushy consistency. Serve in individual dishes garnished with the blueberries.

Green Pea Soup
Veal in Champagne Sauce
Buttered Noodles
Green Salad with
Tarragon–Mustard Dressing
Frozen Strawberry–
Banana Cream

Among the glories of late spring and early summer are peas and strawberries—along with the first tender leaves of lettuce in your garden. This menu capitalizes on all three of these delicacies, yet there are perfectly acceptable substitutions for these key ingredients, so that the menu is a distinct possibility for many more weeks of the year.

If you can find fresh peas for the soup and want to go to the trouble of shelling them, this menu could definitely herald the coming of summer's lazy days. And if there's a nip still in the air, the soup is just as tasty when served hot instead of chilled. It might seem redundant to call the soup a *green* pea soup, but we stress the color because the green is so vivid. We also need to emphasize the importance of using small peas only in the case of frozen peas, buy only those labeled "tiny," "baby," or "petite." The skin on larger peas doesn't purée smoothly in the food processor (and fares even worse in an electric blender). Of course, if you don't own a food processor, you can always press the peas through a sieve or food mill, in which case you can use any size of pea.

The soup should be made at least one day in advance to give yourself plenty of time the day of the party. And the dessert has to be prepared ahead of time so it can be frozen. If this dessert is made when local strawberries are in season, the berries will probably be exquisitely sweet. But if the strawberry season hasn't arrived yet or is on the wane, the berries you buy will be imports, and therefore could be on the tart side. Taste the recipe as you make it to determine if you need to add more sugar; with tart berries, we have had to increase the sugar by as much as a quarter cup. It is for this reason that we recommend you make up several batches of this dessert recipe when strawberries are at their peak where you live.

Veal has become almost as precious as gold in your teeth, yet there is nothing more elegant than this meat when it's cut from the leg. And the nice thing about serving veal is that your guests know they are special company. To get the greatest mileage out of splurging on veal, be sure to buy only veal that is a milky-pink color; avoid any veal tinged with gray or brown, or veal that is vividly pink. Cut away any thick membrane. And finally, avoid overcooking your veal, because this mistake will give you tough pieces of meat.

The best kind of lettuce for your salad is a soft leaf variety, or better yet, try a salad of lettuce thinnings from your garden if you need to weed them out around the time of your party; add some pieces of Romaine for a contrast of textures. The flavor in the dressing of the herb, tarragon, is a favorite of ours; but it can be omitted, or you can use tarragon-flavored vinegar instead of the red wine vinegar.

If you are celebrating a birthday or anniversary, consider serving dry champagne with the dinner; otherwise, any dry but full-bodied white wine will do.

Green Pea Soup

6 servings

In a large saucepan, place the onion and potatoes and add 4 cups of the chicken broth. Bring to a boil, then lower the heat and simmer, covered, for 15 minutes, or until the potatoes are tender. Add the peas to the broth, along with the basil, salt, and pepper, and simmer for another 5 to 7 minutes.

In a food processor fitted with the steel blade, process the contents of the saucepan until you have a smooth purée; this will have to be done in 2 batches. Return the purée to the saucepan and add the remaining chicken broth and the vermouth. Reheat the soup over low heat, stirring occasionally, to let the flavors blend, about 15 minutes. Taste to correct the seasoning.

If you are serving the soup cold, let it cool completely and then refrigerate until chilled. *At this point, the soup can be stored in the refrigerator, covered, for 2 to 3 days.*

If you are serving the soup hot, reheat it after refrigeration over low-medium heat until it is piping hot, stirring occasionally; do not let the soup boil.

Serve both the cold and hot versions of the soup with a tablespoon of sour cream on top of each portion.

1	*small onion, quartered*
2	*medium potatoes, peeled and cut into eighths*
5½	*cups chicken broth* OR *chicken stock*
2	*to 2½ pounds fresh peas, shelled* OR *2 10-ounce packages frozen tiny peas*
½	*teaspoon dried basil, crumbled*
	Salt and freshly ground white pepper to taste
¼	*cup dry vermouth*
6	*tablespoons sour cream*

Veal in Champagne Sauce

6 servings

Dry the veal on paper towels. Place it on a cutting board covered with a piece of waxed paper and pound flat with a meat pounder or with the heel of your hand; cut into bite-size

2¼	*pounds veal scallops, cut thin*
½	*cup flour*

Salt and freshly
ground black pepper
to taste

8 tablespoons butter

2 tablespoons vegetable
oil

2 tablespoons shallots
OR scallions (white
part only), finely
chopped

1 pound fresh mush-
rooms, thinly sliced

½ teaspoon thyme

¼ teaspoon marjoram

1¾ to 2 cups dry cham-
pagne

2 cups light cream

2 teaspoons nutmeg

¼ cup fresh parsley,
finely chopped

pieces approximately 2 inches square. Season the flour with salt and pepper, and dredge the veal in the flour, then toss the pieces with your hands to remove any excess flour.

In a large skillet, melt 2 tablespoons of the butter and 1 tablespoon of the oil over medium heat and quickly sauté as much veal as will fit in the skillet without crowding until it is golden and cooked through, no more than 2 minutes per side; you may have to lower the heat to avoid burning the butter. Remove the veal with a slotted spoon to a warm plate. Melt 2 tablespoons of the butter and the remaining oil in the skillet and sauté more of the veal, removing it to the plate when cooked. Depending on the size of your skillet, you may need to cook the veal in 3 batches, in which case you may have to add some extra butter and oil to the skillet.

In the same skillet, melt 2 more tablespoons butter over low-medium heat and sauté the shallots and mushrooms until the shallots are tender and the mushrooms have released their juice; season with the thyme and marjoram. Add the champagne and cook over high heat until the liquid is reduced by half, stirring and scraping up the particles from the bottom of the skillet. Lower the heat and return the veal to the skillet. Add the cream and nutmeg and simmer for 3 to 4 minutes, until the sauce is somewhat thickened; taste to correct the seasoning and remove from the heat. *At this point, the veal can be held, covered, for 2 to 3 hours.*

Shortly before serving, reheat the veal over low heat until piping hot (do not let the sauce boil), then swirl in the remaining 2 tablespoons butter until melted. Transfer the veal to a warm serving dish and sprinkle with the parsley. Serve immediately.

Buttered Noodles

6 servings

In a large kettle, bring to a boil 6 to 8 quarts salted water to which you have added a little vegetable oil. Add the noodles and cook over high heat until they are barely tender, about 7 to 9 minutes. Drain the noodles in a colander and run cool water over them. Return to the kettle and toss with the butter, poppy seeds, salt, and pepper. Pour the noodles into a greased, deep 4-quart casserole dish. *At this point, the noodles can be held, covered, for 3 to 4 hours.*

About 45 minutes before serving, preheat the oven to 350 degrees.

Pour the warmed milk or cream over the noodles, toss gently, and reheat, covered, for 20 to 30 minutes. Serve immediately.

1 *12-ounce package medium egg noodles*

6 *to 8 tablespoons butter, melted*

1 *tablespoon poppy seeds*

Salt and freshly ground black pepper to taste

¼ *cup milk* OR *light cream, warmed*

Green Salad with Tarragon— Mustard Dressing

6 servings

Wash the lettuce and dry thoroughly; tear into bite-size pieces and refrigerate in a lidded, plastic container lined with paper towels or in a plastic bag twisted to a close.

In a small mixing bowl or a jar with a tight-fitting lid, combine the salt, pepper, and mustard, and stir in the vinegar. (Note: If you are using stronger lettuces such as Romaine, escarole, or chicory, you may increase the mustard to 1 tablespoon.) Add the oil, beating it in thoroughly with a wire whisk if using a bowl, or shaking the ingredients together vig-

2 *to 3 heads soft lettuce (Boston, leaf, salad bowl, Bibb and the like)*

Salt and freshly ground black pepper to taste

About 2 teaspoons Dijon mustard

2 *tablespoons red wine vinegar*

6 tablespoons olive oil OR a combination of olive and vegetable oil

½ to 1 teaspoon dried tarragon, crumbled OR 2 teaspoons fresh tarragon, finely chopped

orously in a jar. *At this point, the lettuce and salad dressing may be held for several hours.*

Shortly before serving, place the lettuce in a salad bowl. Mix the salad dressing again as you did before, pour it over the lettuce and toss until well coated. Sprinkle the tarragon over the lettuce and toss again. Serve on salad plates.

Frozen Strawberry–Banana Cream

6 servings

1 quart fresh strawberries

1 banana, peeled

½ to ¾ cup confectioners' sugar

1 8-ounce container vanilla yogurt

1 cup heavy cream

Wash the strawberries, reserving 6 whole berries for garnish if you're going to be serving the dessert within 2 days. Cut the banana into 1- to 2-inch chunks. In a food processor fitted with the steel blade or in an electric blender, place the strawberries and banana and process until fairly smooth, then add the sugar and yogurt and continue processing until smooth; this may have to be done in 2 batches. Pour the purée into a large mixing bowl and taste to correct the amount of sugar, if necessary; stir in the cream.

Pour the strawberry-banana mixture into a fairly shallow freezer container or 2 ice-cube trays and freeze until partially frozen, about 4 hours. Remove, spoon into the food processor or electric blender, and process until smooth to remove all ice crystals; you can also use an electric beater for this. Return to a freezer container and freeze until hard, about 8 to 10 hours. *At this point, the strawberry-banana cream can be stored in the freezer, covered, for 1 month.*

About 1 to 2 hours before serving, remove the frozen cream from the freezer and let it thaw at room temperature. If the cream seems to be on the verge of thawing completely, put it in the refrigerator. What you want is a semimushy consistency, something between frozen solid and mushy. Just before serving, stir the cream vigorously and then spoon it into individual dessert dishes; garnish with a whole berry, if desired.

Mixed Grill of Lamb, Pork, and Liver
Baked Bourbon Beans
Gazpacho Salad
Peach Upside–Down Cake

This is the perfect menu to serve when you have a reliable outdoor chef and a bunch of people coming to dinner who traditionally have farmhand or boardinghouse table appetites. The fare is gutsy and filling, yet the flavors and colors of the meal elevate it far above what you would expect at a popular truck dining stop. In fact, this is one of our favorite dinners—not only because it contains so much deliciously dressed-up down-home cooking, but also because the food is so *easy* to prepare. There's no excuse for a last-minute rush in the kitchen because the entire dinner, except for grilling the meat, can be ready to go by noon the day of the party.

The gazpacho salad can be made a day in advance because the longer it sits, the more flavorful it gets. Don't worry about the zucchini getting soggy; the dressing works to preserve the crispness of each vegetable. The ingredient in the salad which imparts an unusually rich and complex tang is the spicy hot vegetable cocktail juice. Though this is a fairly new product on the market, it appears to be readily available and widely distributed under at least two well-known brand names. If you can't locate the spicy hot variety, you can substitute regular vegetable cocktail juice; but do *not* use plain tomato juice.

The nice thing about the meat entrée is its flexibility and the pleasing mix of pork, lamb, and liver, each of which retains its own flavor entirely because we marinate each in a different marinade. The only tricks to the meat preparation are the arrangement of meat on the grill and the timing of the cooking. Assuming you have a medium-to-large grill, you should be able to fit the lamb and pork on the grill together, placing the pork in the center, with the lamb chops surrounding it. The liver, of course, goes on last—after the lamb chops have been removed. Be very careful not to overcook the meats; you want tender morsels, not charred or dried-out leather.

We recommend rib lamb chops because they are cheaper and they afford about one generous mouthful of food, which is all a guest needs in addition to a pork chop and slice of liver. However, if you were just given a salary raise and want to buy the slightly larger but more expensive loin lamb chops, do it. Guests will be impressed. That's what we mean by flexibility. For that matter, if you abhor liver and don't want to serve it even to friends who might be liver lovers (and we've never met anyone over twenty-five who isn't), you can skip the liver altogether and increase the size or number of your pieces of pork or lamb chops.

The baked bourbon beans recipe is one of the few instances in this book when we resort to canned goods for a main ingredient. We feel justified in doing this because the baked beans which are widely available in supermarkets are of such superior quality that a person would be crazy to want to make baked beans from scratch. However, you must buy the brick-oven baked beans and no other kind; these are the tiny pea beans which hold their shape through the cooking. Once you have finished doctoring up the beans according to our recipe, you will have a dish that is far removed from what is served with hot dogs in cafeterias. These are sophisticated baked beans; and watch them disappear.

One way to serve the dinner is buffet style, either on a dining room sideboard piece, a kitchen island, or a patio or porch table. The meat can be arranged on a platter garnished with some parsley sprigs, the beans served from the dish in which they bake, and the salad in lettuce cups, with the extra salad for second helpings placed in a bowl. Be sure to serve the salad with a slotted spoon.

Though the dessert is called a cake, there's not much cake to it, which may be why the recipe is so easy and so foolproof. We normally don't like cakes, finding them too dry or bland, or with far too much emphasis on frosting; we also don't like to make them. But this cake, with its upside-down method, is allowed to sit in a lot of yummy peach and brandy juice which eventually soaks into the cake and creates a delectably moist concoction. Moreover, the flavor and texture of the peaches are not significantly disturbed by the baking of the cake. We think you'll find the peach upside-down cake a novel way to serve peaches at the peak of their season.

The heartiness and spiciness of the food in this menu dictates a robust, full-bodied red wine; however, you don't want a red that's too heavy, especially because you might want to cool it slightly before serving if the day is a scorcher. Any recommended red table wine, such as a California Burgundy or a Chianti from either California or Italy, should do. If you feel like spending more money, consider a Saint-Julien or a Volnay from France.

Mixed Grill of Lamb, Pork, and Liver

6 servings

6	*rib lamb chops, about 2 pounds*
1½	*pounds pork from rib or loin, cut into 2-inch cubes* OR *2-inch medallions*
1¼	*pounds calves' liver* OR *beef liver,* sliced ¾-inch thick*
	Parsley sprigs for garnish

Marinade for Lamb

1	*large clove garlic, finely chopped*
2	*teaspoons Dijon mustard*
1	*teaspoon rosemary, crumbled*
	Salt and freshly ground black pepper to taste
¼	*cup lemon juice*
½	*cup vegetable oil*

Marinade for Pork

1	*large clove garlic, finely chopped*

In a small mixing bowl, prepare the lamb marinade by combining the garlic, mustard, rosemary, salt, pepper, and lemon juice; whisk in the oil until thoroughly blended. In a shallow dish big enough to hold the lamb chops in a single layer, place the chops, pour over the marinade, and turn to coat.

In a small mixing bowl, prepare the pork marinade by combining the garlic, oregano, salt, pepper, catsup, honey, Worcestershire sauce, vinegar, and wine; whisk in the oil until thoroughly blended. In a shallow dish or bowl big enough to hold the pork in a single layer, place the pork, pour over the marinade, and turn to coat.

Marinate both the lamb and the pork for at least 2 hours, turning occasionally. *At this point, the lamb and pork can be stored in the refrigerator for 1 day.* Let both meats come to room temperature for 1 hour before cooking.

In a small mixing bowl, prepare the liver marinade by combining the catsup, wine, and butter. In a shallow dish big enough to hold the liver in a single layer, place the liver, pour over the marinade, and turn to coat. Marinate for 1 hour at room temperature.

About 30 minutes before cooking, light the coals in a charcoal grill, and let them burn down until they have a light coat of gray ash; with a gas grill, you need no such advance preparation for the fire. Place the cubes or medallions of pork over the charcoal or gas grill fire in the center of the grill. (The pieces of pork should be big enough to stay on a grill

---

* *If using beef liver, soak the meat in milk to cover for 2 or 3 hours in the refrigerator; then remove, dry on paper towels, and proceed with the marinade.*

without falling through; if you are concerned about this, you can thread the pork on a couple of metal skewers, making sure the pieces of meat aren't touching.) Place the lamb chops around the pork. Cover the grill (vents should be open on top and bottom) and cook for 8 to 10 minutes. Remove the cover, turn the meat, and cook for 8 to 10 more minutes with the cover back on.

Remove the cover and take the lamb chops off the grill, if you like your lamb medium rare (if you like lamb medium to well-done, leave the chops on the grill another 5 minutes); place the lamb on a warm serving platter. Push the pork to the sides of the grill and add the liver to the grill's center. Cover again and cook for 5 minutes. Remove the cover and turn the liver; at this point, you can remove the pork to the warm serving platter, as it should be done (you can cut into it with a sharp knife to be sure). Return the cover and cook the liver for another 5 minutes. Remove the liver, add to the serving platter and cut into 6 pieces; the inside of the liver should be slightly pink. Serve the meat on the platter with sprigs of parsley tucked in among the meat.

½	teaspoon oregano
	Salt and freshly ground black pepper to taste
1	tablespoon catsup
1	tablespoon honey
1	tablespoon Worcestershire sauce
1	tablespoon red wine vinegar
½	cup dry red wine
¼	cup vegetable oil

Marinade for Liver

½	cup catsup
3	tablespoons dry red wine
1	tablespoon butter, melted

Baked Bourbon Beans

6 servings

Preheat the oven to 325 degrees.

In a large mixing bowl, empty the cans of beans and discard the pieces of salt pork. Add the garlic, catsup, thyme, bay leaf, mustard, cloves, and cayenne pepper, and stir thoroughly but gently to blend. Pour the beans into a greased, 8-inch square baking dish and smooth over the top. Cover with aluminum foil and bake for 1 hour.

Remove the beans from the oven and place

3	16-ounce cans brick-oven baked beans
2	cloves garlic, finely chopped
3	tablespoons catsup OR chili sauce
½	teaspoon thyme
1	large bay leaf, crumbled

2   *teaspoons dry mustard*

2   *whole cloves*

     Dash cayenne pepper

4   *slices bacon*

1   *medium red onion, sliced*

½   *cup strong black coffee*

2   *tablespoons bourbon*

the bacon and then the onion over the top. Return to the oven and bake, uncovered, about 30 minutes, or until the bacon appears fairly crisp.

Remove the beans from the oven and pour the coffee and bourbon over them, using a fork to let the liquid seep down. Let the beans sit for at least 1 hour. If you're going to serve them within 1 or 2 hours, you can leave them in the turned-off oven, covered. If you plan to serve later, keep the beans out of the oven, uncovered. *At this point, the beans can be held for several hours.*

About 45 minutes before serving, preheat the oven to 325 degrees. Cover the beans and reheat for 20 to 30 minutes. Serve immediately.

Gazpacho Salad

6 servings

1   *medium green pepper*

1   *cucumber*

2   *small yellow squashes*

1   *small red onion, finely chopped*

2   *cloves garlic, finely chopped*

3   *large, ripe tomatoes, peeled, seeded, and coarsely chopped*

1   *tablespoon fresh basil, finely chopped (optional)*

¼   *cup fresh parsley, finely chopped*

Wash the pepper, cucumber, and squashes, and dry with paper towels. Seed the pepper and cut it into a ½-inch dice. Peel the cucumber, seed it and cut into a ½-inch dice. Trim away the ends of the squashes (but do not peel the skin) and cut into a ½-inch dice.

In a large bowl, combine the pepper, cucumber, and squash with the onion, garlic, tomatoes, basil (optional), and parsley; refrigerate until chilled. *At this point, the vegetables can be stored in the refrigerator, covered, for 1 to 2 days.*

In a medium mixing bowl, prepare the dressing by combining the paprika, salt, pepper, and tomato paste; whisk in the vinegar and vegetable juice until well blended. Whisk in the oil until thoroughly blended and then add the hot pepper sauce a dash at a time, until you can taste it on the roof of your mouth; be careful with the hot pepper sauce at this stage because you can always add more when combining the vegetables with the dressing. *At this point, the dressing can be held for several hours.*

Before the party begins, carefully pour off any juices that have accumulated at the bottom of the bowl holding your vegetables. Beat the dressing again until well blended and pour over the vegetables, stirring gently to coat everything well. Taste and correct the seasoning, adding more hot pepper sauce if desired. Refrigerate until ready to serve. Serve in small bowls or on salad plates with a lettuce leaf underneath.

6 *lettuce leaves (optional)*

Dressing

¼ *teaspoon paprika*

Salt and freshly ground black pepper to taste

1 *tablespoon tomato paste*

3 *tablespoons red wine vinegar*

½ to ¾ *cup spicy hot vegetable juice*

6 *tablespoons vegetable oil* OR *a combination of vegetable and olive oil*

Hot pepper sauce to taste

Peach Upside–Down Cake

6 to 8 servings

In a shallow dish, place the peaches and sprinkle over them the brown sugar, cinnamon, and brandy; stir gently to blend. Refrigerate for 1 to 2 hours, or overnight if you wish.

Preheat the oven to 350 degrees.

In a medium skillet, melt 2 tablespoons of the butter over medium heat. Add the peaches and when they are bubbling, lower the heat and cook 5 to 7 minutes. Pour the peaches into a greased, 8-inch square baking dish and distribute evenly over the bottom.

In a medium mixing bowl, beat the eggs well; add the granulated sugar and continue beating until smooth. Stir in the vanilla extract. Sift together the flour, baking powder,

6 *large peaches, peeled and sliced*

¼ *cup light brown sugar, packed*

¼ *teaspoon cinnamon*

¼ *cup brandy*

4 *tablespoons butter*

2 *eggs*

½ *cup granulated sugar*

1 *teaspoon vanilla extract*

½ *cup flour*

2 teaspoons baking pow-
der

Pinch of salt

¾ cup heavy cream

3 tablespoons confection-
ers' sugar

and salt, and beat into the egg mixture until smooth. Carefully and evenly drizzle the cake batter over the peaches until they are completely covered. Dot the batter with the remaining 2 tablespoons of butter.

Bake the cake for 30 minutes or until the top is brown and crusty and a toothpick inserted into the center comes out clean. Let the cake cool on a rack for a minimum of 2 hours. *At this point, the cake can be held for 8 to 10 hours.*

The cake can be served at room temperature, or you can warm it up in a 250-degree oven for 15 to 20 minutes. When ready to serve, whip the cream to stiff peaks and stir in the confectioners' sugar. Cut the cake into squares, place each square *with the peaches side up* on a dessert plate, and top with a generous dollop of whipped cream. (Note: Do not attempt to turn over the entire cake before cutting it into squares.)

Hamburgers Stuffed
with Blue Cheese and Bacon
New Potato Salad
Italian Garden in a Skillet
Cherry–Nectarine Crisp

This is our all-American, red-white-and-blue bunting, band concerts in the park, Frisbees at the shore, sunburn and sparklers dinner. We decided that even a dinner party cookbook needs one menu with a universal appeal for kissing cousins, sage grandparents, restless teen-agers, and weekend guests who aren't returning to the city until Monday. We are also assuming that our readers aren't going to send out for pizza or fried chicken when the party occasion is strictly informal. Instead, we imagine everyone is going to rely on this menu for many occasions, ranging from a family birthday party to a fancier gathering, such as a dinner for close friends you're not overly concerned about impressing.

The dinner is so easy, too, even though everything except the potato salad gets prepared the day of the party. Actually, if your house is clean and your grocery shopping done, you will have plenty of time to make the potato salad the day of the party, but since it is just as tasty if it sits a day or two in the refrigerator, you might as well get it out of the way as early as possible.

We strongly recommend using new potatoes in the salad, as the flesh is much firmer than other boiling or baking potatoes, thus holding up better in the cooking. We suggest red onions or scallions for their color in the salad, but if you grow your own onions and they're ready for harvest, be sure to use them even though they're white; their sweetness and freshness will be worth the absence of color flecks.

The next thing to prepare is the cherry-nectarine crisp, which goes together like one-two-three because there is no peeling or chopping of fruit, no pie crust, and no separate cooking on the stove. Be sure the granola you purchase is the straightforward variety with no special spices like cinnamon or additions of raisins, dried apples, etc.; the ingredients will usually consist of rolled oats, coconut, brown sugar, and honey, with perhaps some almonds, wheat germ, or sesame seeds. One popular variety found in most supermarkets is called "natural cereal" instead of granola. We should mention that the crisp can be made a day in advance, but the nectarines lose their color.

Once you have assembled the hamburgers, you really don't have much left to do before the party commences, because the cooking of the vegetable dish is strictly a last-minute operation. However, you can—and should—have the garlic cloves peeled, the cheese grated, and the peppers, basil, parsley, and chives chopped up in advance; only the zucchini has to be sliced just before it goes into the skillet. If your skillet is good-looking enough to bring to the table, you might want to serve the vegetables right out of it instead of in a serving bowl as directed.

The blue cheese in the hamburgers can be Roquefort or Gorgonzola cheese, but since these are very expensive and possibly hard to locate in some areas, we recommend you purchase supermarket blue cheese either in wedge form or crumbled up in a plastic container. The recipe calls for slices of cheese, but the crumbled product works just as well. It keeps a long time, too.

A simple red burgundy is the best wine for this meal, served slightly chilled if the weather is sizzling hot or you are eating outdoors.

Hamburgers Stuffed with Blue Cheese and Bacon

6 servings

In a skillet, fry the bacon until crisp; drain on paper towels and when cool enough to handle, crumble into small pieces and reserve.

Divide the ground beef evenly into 12 sections of meat to make 12 patties of equal size. When you have flattened the patties, smear a dab of horseradish on 6 of the patties. On top of the horseradish, place a slice of blue cheese, making sure that each slice comes to no more than an inch of a patty's edge. Place some of the crumbled bacon on top of the blue cheese.

Now take the other 6 patties and place over the patties with cheese and bacon, sealing carefully around the edges with your thumb and fingers. Salt and pepper both sides of the hamburgers. *At this point, the hamburgers can be stored in the refrigerator for several hours.* Let them come to room temperature for 30 to 45 minutes before cooking.

About 30 minutes before cooking, light the coals in a charcoal grill, and let them burn down until they have a light coat of gray ash; with a gas grill, you need no such advance preparation for the fire.

In a small saucepan, combine the chili sauce, red wine, and Worcestershire sauce, and cook over low heat to blend the flavors; keep warm while the hamburgers cook.

When the fire is ready, place the hamburgers on the charcoal grill—or gas grill—and cook for a total of approximately 15 minutes, bearing in mind that these hamburgers are thicker than most and thus will take more time to cook than you are used to. Remove the hamburgers to a warm serving platter, pour over the chili-wine sauce, and serve immediately.

(Instructions for oven broiling: Preheat the

6   *slices bacon*

3   *pounds ground beef*

Horseradish to taste

6   *slices blue cheese, about 2 ounces*

Salt and freshly ground black pepper to taste

¾   *cup chili sauce*

¼   *cup dry red wine*

Dash Worcestershire sauce

oven to BROIL and place the hamburgers on the broiler pan. Cook 6 inches from the heat for 8 to 10 minutes on *each* side.)

New Potato Salad

6 servings

3   pounds medium red
    (*new*) potatoes

1   *medium red onion,*
    finely chopped OR 1
    bunch scallions with
    part of green tops,
    finely chopped

1   *cup celery, finely*
    chopped

1   *tablespoon fresh basil,*
    finely chopped OR 1
    teaspoon dried basil

¼   *cup fresh parsley, finely*
    chopped

3   *hard-boiled eggs, finely*
    chopped (*optional*)

    Paprika

Dressing

½   *teaspoon salt*

¼   *teaspoon freshly*
    ground black pepper

1   *tablespoon Dijon mus-*
    tard

2   *cloves garlic, finely*
    chopped

3   *tablespoons red wine*
    vinegar

Wash the potatoes. In a large saucepan, bring to a boil enough salted water to cover the potatoes; add the potatoes and simmer, covered, until just cooked through, about 10 to 15 minutes. Drain, and when cool enough to handle but still warm, peel away the skins and cut the potatoes into a ½-inch dice; place in a large mixing bowl.

In a medium mixing bowl, make the dressing by combining the salt, pepper, mustard, garlic, and vinegar; stir in the mayonnaise and then whisk in the oil until thoroughly blended. Pour the dressing over the potatoes and toss gently to coat everything. Let the potatoes stand until cool, then add the onion, celery, basil, and parsley, and stir gently to combine. Cover and chill in the refrigerator for 3 to 4 hours. *At this point, the potato salad can be stored in the refrigerator, covered, for 1 to 2 days.*

Shortly before serving, add the optional egg and stir to blend; or you may garnish the top of the salad with slices of egg. Sprinkle some paprika over the salad and serve immediately.

½ cup mayonnaise

½ cup vegetable oil OR a combination of vegetable and olive oil

Italian Garden in a Skillet

6 servings

Wash the zucchini and yellow squash, trim away the ends (but do not peel the skin) and slice into ¼-inch slices. Wash the peppers, seed them, and cut into 1-inch squares.

In a large skillet, heat the oil over low-medium heat and sauté the onion and garlic until slightly tender. Add the zucchini, yellow squash, peppers, parsley, chives, oregano, salt, pepper, and bouillon cube to the skillet and toss to coat everything with the oil. Cover the skillet and let the vegetables steam over very low heat for 5 to 10 minutes, until the vegetables are tender but still crisp; stir once to mix the bouillon in with the vegetables.

Turn the vegetables into a warm serving bowl, sprinkle with the cheese, and serve immediately.

3 small to medium zucchini

3 small to medium yellow squash

3 medium frying peppers

3 tablespoons olive oil OR a combination of olive and vegetable oil

1 medium red onion, thinly sliced

1 clove garlic, finely chopped

2 tablespoons fresh parsley, finely chopped

1 tablespoon fresh chives, finely chopped

1 teaspoon dried oregano, marjoram OR savory

Salt and freshly ground black pepper to taste

1 chicken bouillon cube, crumbled

6 tablespoons Parmesan cheese OR Romano cheese, grated

Cherry–Nectarine Crisp

6 servings

2   to 3 *nectarines*

12 to 16 *seedless green grapes*

1   *21-ounce can cherry pie filling*

1   *cup regular granola*

⅓   *cup light brown sugar, packed*

½   *teaspoon allspice*

½   *teaspoon fresh lemon peel, grated*

5   *tablespoons butter, melted*

10 to 12 *tablespoons sour cream*

Preheat the oven to 350 degrees.

Wash the nectarines and cut into thin slices; do not peel. Wash the grapes and slice in half. In a medium mixing bowl, combine the nectarines, grapes, and cherry pie filling and stir gently to blend. Pour the fruit into a greased 9-inch pie plate.

In a small mixing bowl, combine the granola, brown sugar, allspice, lemon peel, and melted butter; stir to blend. Carefully spoon this mixture over the top of the fruit, patting it down as you go, until the fruit is completely covered.

Bake the crisp for 30 minutes, until the top is a dark golden brown. Cool the crisp on a rack. *At this point, the crisp can be held for 6 to 8 hours.* Spoon the crisp into dessert dishes and top each portion with a generous dollop of sour cream.

Cold Loin of Pork
in Ham–Mustard Crust
Corn and Zucchini au Gratin
Broiled Tomatoes
Stuffed with Herbed Crumbs
Cantaloupe Frappé

This is a menu that requires a bit of work but not enough to generate a decent sweat, especially because the entrée and the dessert are both made at least a day before the dinner party. Summertime weather can really cast a pall over kitchen activity. No one likes to stand over a hot stove, especially a stove that has a pot of boiling water for corn on the cob, or an oven turned on for the long cooking of a pork roast. For those weeks in summer when you are having a heat wave, we have created a menu that allows you to eat heartily but does not leave you feeling flagged or looking like the pioneer woman at the end of the trail.

Much of the pork available in your standard supermarket tends to be tough, dry, and tasteless, an epicurean experience not unlike dining on the telephone book. Therefore we have striven to concoct offerings of pork that are succulent and flavorful, delicious enough to be considered a mainstay selection on an elegant restaurant's menu. In one pork recipe, the meat is marinated, another recipe calls for stuffing the pork, and in the recipe here, the pork receives the most tender loving care of all by being wrapped in a blanket of mustard, brown sugar, and ham. The result of such attention is not only a tasty piece of meat but a visual presentation to serve with pride: the rounds of pork on a platter are accentuated by the crust that forms in the baking and are dotted with scoops or cubes of the jellied pan juices plus the parsley.

The preparation of the pork may appear tricky, but it really isn't. The main thing you have to be careful about is the browning of the pork before you put it in the oven. If your heat is too high, the sugar in the brown sugar-mustard coating will burn and blacken the bottom of your casserole pot, possibly imparting a charred taste to the pan juices. However, if you watch the heat so that it browns the sugar but doesn't burn it, you'll be okay. After this step, the pork is cooked like any other pork roast. We should add here that the pork is just as good served hot as it is cold, though we prefer it cold with this particular menu, since the side dishes must be served hot.

A blend of two of summer's most popular vegetables, the corn and zucchini *au gratin* complement each other nicely in taste, texture, and color. Again, there is some advance preparation which takes time, but is not at all complicated. We recommend that you cook the corn, scrape the kernels off the cobs, and refrigerate the kernels in advance. We treat the corn this way for the same reason we carefully extract as much juice as we can from the zucchini: Fresh corn usually exudes some juice while standing, and we want to get rid of it before adding the corn to the *au gratin* dish, otherwise the mixture will be runny or there'll be vegetable liquid on the bottom. As we indicate in the recipe, you can prepare both the corn and the zucchini early on and refrigerate them together, then pour off both juices before proceeding to assemble the dish.

They say you can't have too many recipes for the prolific zucchini, and we think the same is true for summer's most bountiful fruit, the tomato. For example, as we researched and experimented with recipes just for *stuffed* tomatoes, we found dozens of them and still wished for more. At any rate, we have put together a wonderful treatment for the tomato whereby we clean out the seed cavities, fill them with an aromatic, colorful mixture of fresh herbs and toasted crumbs and cover the top surface with a spread of mayonnaise and Parmesan cheese that puffs up when it cooks. The only important thing to remember about this recipe is to remove the tomatoes from the refrigerator a good hour ahead of cooking so as to really bring them to room temperature; otherwise the broiling process won't warm up the tomatoes sufficiently and you'll end up with tomatoes with cold bottoms (we also have you bake the tomatoes ever so briefly before you broil them; this helps take away the frostbite).

Nothing could be simpler than the cantaloupe frappé, yet many people will consider this a most unusual, even exotic dessert. Though the recipe calls for only a single melon, the flavor of cantaloupe comes through loud and clear and the orange flesh colors the frappé with a pretty but definite blush. Because the frappé is so easy to make (takes about 5 minutes), so refreshing to eat, and so different, consider making several batches to have on hand in the freezer long after the cantaloupe season is over.

Pork would ordinarily call for a red wine, but since this is a hot-weather menu, we recommend serving a chilled rosé as long as it's not overly sweet, or a truly full-bodied white wine that can stand up to the flavors in the meat and the spicy tomatoes. Such a white could be a Pinot Chardonnay or a Sauvignon Blanc from California.

Cold Loin of Pork in Ham–Mustard Crust

6 servings

Preheat the oven to 325 degrees.

Dry the pork roast with a paper towel and remove the string. Rub the outside of the roast's surface with a mixture of the thyme, sage, and pepper. Wrap the roast with the ham slices (try to cover the surface without too much overlap; do not attempt to cover the ends) and retie with kitchen string to hold the ham slices to the roast.

In a small bowl, mix the mustard and brown sugar and spread half of this over the entire top surface of the roast. In a heavy lidded casserole large enough to hold the pork roast, melt the butter and oil over medium heat; add the roast and brown the top surface, taking care not to let the sugar burn (though it will caramelize). Brush the entire bottom surface of the meat (now turned up) with the remaining mustard-sugar mixture, and turn the roast completely over to brown this surface. Make sure each side of the roast gets browned, too; you may have to hold it in place with wooden utensils to accomplish this. At this point, lower the heat and add the onion to sauté until tender. Add the wine and bring to a boil. Cover the casserole and cook the roast in the oven for approximately 2½ hours, or 40 minutes per pound.

Let the pork roast cool before removing it to another container and refrigerating, covered, for at least 4 to 6 hours. Strain the wine sauce into a small container and refrigerate, covered, until thoroughly chilled. *At this point, the pork and the wine sauce can be stored in the refrigerator for 2 to 3 days.*

When ready to serve, place the pork roast on a cutting board, remove the string, and slice the meat into ¾-inch-thick slices. Remove the

3½ to 4 *pounds boneless pork roast, loin end*

1½ *teaspoons thyme*

½ *teaspoon ground sage*

Freshly ground black pepper to taste

4 to 6 *thin slices boiled ham*

⅓ *cup Dijon mustard*

⅓ *cup light brown sugar*

1 *tablespoon butter*

1 *tablespoon vegetable oil*

1 *medium onion, finely chopped*

1 *cup dry white wine*

¼ *cup fresh parsley, finely chopped*

congealed fat from the surface of the wine sauce and discard. Arrange the slices of pork on a serving platter, spoon over the jellied wine sauce that was underneath the congealed fat, and garnish with the chopped parsley.

Corn and Zucchini au Gratin

6 servings

6	ears fresh corn
1½	pounds zucchini
4	tablespoons butter
3	tablespoons flour
1½	cups light cream
2	egg yolks, well beaten
1	cup sharp Cheddar cheese, grated
1	teaspoon Worcestershire sauce
½	teaspoon thyme
¼	teaspoon oregano
	Dash cayenne pepper
	Salt and freshly ground black pepper to taste
⅓	cup Parmesan cheese OR Romano cheese, grated

In a large kettle, bring to a boil 4 to 6 quarts water. Drop in the corn and cover until the water returns to the boil. Remove the kettle from the heat, remove the cover, and let the corn stand 5 minutes. Take the corn out of the water, and when cool enough to handle, scrape off the kernels; reserve.

Wash the zucchini and trim away the ends (but do not peel the skin). In a food processor fitted with the shredding disk, or with a hand grater, grate the zucchini and place in a colander or sieve set over a bowl; sprinkle generously with salt and let stand for 20 to 30 minutes. Squeeze the excess juice from the zucchini with your hands, then dry on paper towels to get rid of even more moisture (it is important to get the zucchini quite dry or the casserole will be runny). *At this point, the corn and zucchini can be stored in the refrigerator in a lidded, plastic container lined with paper towels for several hours.*

In a large saucepan, melt 3 tablespoons of the butter over low heat and stir in the flour until smooth. Stir in the cream and cook, stirring constantly, until thickened and smooth. Lower the heat to warm and stir in the egg yolks and the Cheddar cheese until the cheese is completely melted. Remove the cheese sauce from the heat and stir in the Worcestershire sauce, thyme, oregano, salt, and pepper until completely blended.

Fold the corn and zucchini into the cheese sauce and pour the mixture into a greased, shallow baking dish measuring approximately 7 x 11 x 2 inches. Sprinkle the Parmesan cheese over the casserole and dot the top with the remaining 1 tablespoon of butter. *At this point, the casserole can be stored in the refrigerator for 2 to 3 hours.* Let it come to room temperature for 30 to 45 minutes before baking.

Preheat the oven to 350 degrees.

Bake the casserole for 30 to 45 minutes, until the top is golden brown and bubbly. Serve immediately.

Broiled Tomatoes Stuffed with Herbed Crumbs

6 servings

Wash the tomatoes and cut off the tops to expose the seed cavities. Using your little finger or a small spoon with a pointed end, scoop out the seeds from the cavities and drain the tomatoes on paper towels with the cut sides down for 15 to 20 minutes.

In a small skillet, melt the butter over low heat and stir in the bread crumbs, parsley, chives, basil, and salt; sauté for a few minutes, then remove from the heat and allow to cool slightly.

In a small mixing bowl, combine the mayonnaise and Parmesan cheese. Press the herbed crumbs loosely into the tomato cavities, poking them down into the cavities with your fingers. Spread the mayonnaise and cheese mixture on top of the tomatoes, taking care not to disturb the crumbs. *At this point, the tomatoes can be stored in the refrigerator for*

6	*medium, ripe tomatoes*
6	*tablespoons butter*
1½	*cups fresh bread crumbs*
1	*tablespoon fresh parsley, finely chopped*
1	*tablespoon fresh chives, finely chopped*
1	*tablespoon fresh basil, finely chopped* OR 1 *teaspoon dried basil*
	Salt to taste
6	*tablespoons mayonnaise*

6   tablespoons Parmesan
    cheese OR Romano
    cheese, grated

3 to 4 hours. Let them come to room temperature for 1 hour before cooking.

Preheat the oven to 300 degrees.

Place the tomatoes in a shallow baking dish large enough to hold them, and warm in the oven for 5 to 10 minutes. Remove from the oven and preheat the oven to BROIL. Return the tomatoes to the oven and broil 6 inches from the heat until the tops are brown and bubbly, about 5 minutes. Serve immediately.

Cantaloupe Frappé

6 servings

1   *ripe, medium canta-*
    loupe

1   *quart vanilla ice cream,*
    slightly softened

¼   *cup honey*

6   *fresh mint leaves* OR *6*
    cantaloupe balls for
    garnish (optional)

Cut the cantaloupe into 4 sections and remove the seeds. Cut away the cantaloupe flesh from the rind in 1- to 2-inch chunks and place in a food processor fitted with the steel blade, or in an electric blender; process the cantaloupe until coarsely puréed, then add the ice cream and honey, and continue processing until smooth (this whole procedure will have to be done in 2 or 3 batches). Pour the frappé into a freezer container and freeze until fairly hard, about 6 to 8 hours. *At this point, the cantaloupe frappé can be stored in the freezer, covered, for 1 to 2 months.*

Shortly before serving, remove the frappé from the freezer and let it stand at room temperature for 30 to 45 minutes in order to soften it slightly. If desired, garnish each serving with a sprig of mint or a cantaloupe ball.

3

Dinner Party Menus for Fall & Winter

Mushroom Soup
Chicken Breasts with Ham and Cheese
Sautéed Green Beans and Cucumber
Apricot Whip

This is one of those perfect little dinners we wish we'd had in our repertoire when we were operating out of kitchens the size of a coat closet. Opening with a rich brown mushroom soup and concluding with a creamy whip studded with apricots, the dinner highlights warm colors, fascinating textures, and a feast of wonderful things to taste. Yet the dinner is extremely easy to put together in very little time and space, and with minimal equipment.

One reason the menu can be prepared without trauma is because each dish can be assembled in its own separate time. Thus you're not cluttering your mind with myriad directional details or your countertop with pots, bowls, and pans. As one dish gets made, you are free to move on to the next. First on your schedule is the apricot whip, which is whipped into shape a day or two before the dinner party and stored in the refrigerator.

Early on the morning of the party, fix the chicken breasts with their coat of crumbs and put them in the refrigerator; you can boil the green beans around that time, too. Clean and slice the mushrooms in the afternoon, and sauté them. In the late afternoon, sauté the chicken breasts and cut the cucumbers into their crescent shapes. With these steps out of the way, you shouldn't have to spend more than 20 solid minutes in the kitchen after the party has started to roll; this will be to make the sauce for the chicken, heat up the soup, and warm the beans with the cucumbers and almonds.

A word about chicken breasts to help you select the right size for the chicken with ham and cheese. Boneless chicken breasts are usually sold as whole breasts. You want 3 whole breasts, each one of which weighs about 12 ounces, for a total weight of 2¼ pounds. If the packaged breasts at the meat counter are smaller than this—and they probably will be—simply tell your butcher what you need and have him provide it. If he says he can't, then you will have to cope with smaller breasts and buy more of them.

The mushroom soup has the most concentrated mushroom flavor we have ever enjoyed. Literally afloat with mushrooms, the soup will be savored by your guests over many minutes; its dense goodness does not go down with the swiftness of a broth or consommé. Therefore keep the chicken and the green beans well covered while the soup is being consumed; you could have one or both of these dishes on an electric hot tray or in the oven on WARM.

Most people don't realize that cucumbers are as delicious when served hot as they are when cool and crisp. Actually, even cooked cucumbers don't lose their crispness; the texture just gets rounded off a little. Thus the vegetable dish is a presence of commanding textures from the cucumber to the quickly boiled beans to the crunchy nut of the almond. Don't skimp on the butter, and you'll serve a dish that many guests will attempt to duplicate in the very near future.

One concern that you might have about this menu: Is there enough food, since it does not include pasta, rice, or potato? We have cooked the dinner dozens of times as it appears here and always staggered away from the table. Somehow that mushroom soup and the apricot whip sneak up on you like someone's secret recipe for rum punch.

In keeping with the dinner's simplicity, serve a fine Chablis or a Muscadet.

Mushroom Soup

6 servings

6	to 8 *tablespoons butter*
1½	*pounds fresh mushrooms, thinly sliced* *
½	*cup dry white wine* OR *dry sherry*
1	*cup fresh parsley, finely chopped*

In a large skillet, melt the butter over low-medium heat and add the mushrooms. Sauté gently until the mushrooms have released their juice and are tender. Remove the mushrooms with a slotted spoon to a large saucepan. Add the wine to the skillet and cook over high heat until reduced to ¼ cup; pour over the mushrooms. *At this point, the mushrooms can be held for 3 to 4 hours.*

* The mushrooms can be sliced in a food processor fitted with the slicing disk.

About 1 hour before serving, add the parsley and beef broth to the mushrooms and heat just to boiling, but do not let boil. Remove from the heat.

In a small mixing bowl, blend together the sour cream and cream until smooth. Spoon a tablespoon or two of the hot beef broth into the sour cream mixture, stirring quickly so it doesn't curdle. Then very slowly pour the sour cream mixture into the saucepan, stirring constantly. Season the soup to taste with salt and pepper and reserve. Shortly before serving, reheat the soup over low heat to piping hot, taking care that the cream doesn't curdle. Serve the soup immediately in warm bowls or cups, with a sprinkling of paprika on top.

4½	cups beef broth OR beef stock
¾	cup sour cream
¾	cup light cream
	Salt and freshly ground black pepper to taste
	Paprika for garnish

Chicken Breasts with Ham and Cheese

6 servings

Ask your butcher for chicken breasts that are large, so that when you cut each in half, the single pieces will weigh 6 ounces. After cutting each connected breast in half, trim away any fat and membrane and flatten with a meat pounder or the heel of your hand; dry with paper towels. Season the flour with plenty of salt and some pepper, and dredge the chicken in the flour, shaking off any excess. With the beaten egg on one plate and the bread crumbs on another, dip each breast first in the egg and then in the bread crumbs until completely coated; pat the bread crumbs to make them adhere. Place the chicken on some waxed paper and refrigerate for at least 1 hour.

In a large skillet, melt the butter and oil over medium heat and sauté the chicken until it is golden brown on all sides and cooked through, about 15 minutes. You will want to lower the heat during the cooking to avoid burning the

3	whole, boneless, skinless chicken breasts, each weighing about 12 ounces
½	to ¾ cup flour
	Salt and freshly ground black pepper to taste
2	eggs, lightly beaten
1½	cups fresh bread crumbs
4	tablespoons butter
2	tablespoons vegetable oil
¾	cup chicken broth OR chicken stock

½	cup dry white wine
1	bay leaf
½	teaspoon thyme
2	to 3 sprigs fresh parsley
¼	cup heavy cream
2	egg yolks, beaten
6	thin slices boiled ham
6	thick slices Gruyère cheese OR Swiss cheese

butter. (If you have trouble fitting 6 large breast halves in your skillet, cook the pieces in 2 batches, using a little less butter and oil for the first batch.) Remove the chicken to a greased, shallow baking dish large enough to hold the pieces in a single layer, about 9 x 13 x 2 inches. *At this point, the dish may be held, covered, for 2 to 3 hours.*

When ready to cook, preheat the oven to BROIL.

Into a medium saucepan, put the chicken broth, wine, bay leaf, thyme, and parsley; bring to a boil and cook until reduced to approximately 1 cup. Off the heat, remove the bay leaf and parsley and stir in the cream; season to taste with salt and pepper. Stir in the egg yolks and cook over low heat, stirring constantly, until the sauce is thickened, about 10 minutes.

Cover each chicken breast with a slice of ham and a slice of cheese cut to fit the breast. Pour the sauce over and around the chicken. Place the dish 6 inches from the broiler heat and cook for 6 to 8 minutes, or until the cheese is melted and golden brown. Serve immediately, spooning the sauce over each portion as you do.

Sautéed Green Beans and Cucumber

6 servings

1½	pounds green beans
2	cucumbers
6	to 8 tablespoons butter
¼	cup sliced almonds OR whole almonds, coarsely chopped

Snap off the stem end of the beans and break into approximately 2-inch lengths. In a large kettle, bring 4 to 5 quarts salted water to a boil, plunge in the beans, cover until the water returns to a boil, and then cook, uncovered, for 5 to 7 minutes, until barely tender. Drain in a colander and run cold water over the beans. Pat the beans dry with paper towels.

At this point, the beans can be held for several hours or they can be refrigerated, covered, for 1 day. Let the beans come to room temperature for 45 to 60 minutes before sautéing.

Wash the cucumbers, trim off the ends and peel them. Cut each cucumber in half lengthwise and scoop out the seeds with a sharp-edged spoon. Slice the cucumber halves into ½-inch slices; each slice will resemble a squared-off crescent (see diagram). At this point, the cucumber can be stored in the refrigerator, covered, for several hours. Let it come to room temperature for 30 to 45 minutes before sautéing.

In a large skillet, melt the butter over medium heat until bubbly. Add the beans and sauté for 2 minutes. Lower the heat, add the cucumber and almonds, and continue sautéing for another 2 to 3 minutes, until the vegetables are completely heated through. Season to taste with salt and pepper. Cover the beans to keep them warm while eating the soup course. Serve in a warm serving dish with the butter poured over all. Garnish with the parsley.

Salt and freshly ground black pepper to taste

3 tablespoons fresh parsley, finely chopped

Apricot Whip

6 servings

In a medium saucepan, bring 2 cups of water to a boil. Add the apricots; when the water has returned to a boil, lower the heat and simmer, covered, about 20 minutes until the apricots are tender. Off the heat, stir in the sugar until dissolved. Using a slotted spoon, transfer the apricots to a food processor fitted with the steel blade; reserve the apricot juice.

While the apricot juice is still very hot, prepare the lemon gelatin. In a medium mixing bowl, place the contents of the package and

6 to 8 ounces dried apricots

2 tablespoons sugar

1 3-ounce package lemon-flavored gelatin

2 teaspoons lemon juice

1 cup heavy cream

stir in 1 cup of the hot apricot juice until dissolved. Stir in 1 cup of cold water and the lemon juice. Refrigerate until the gelatin is beginning to set, about 1 hour.

In the meantime, purée the apricots briefly in the food processor until you have a coarse texture; you can also mash by hand with a fork or purée through a food mill. Reserve the apricot purée.

When the gelatin is ready, stir in the apricot purée. In a large mixing bowl, whip the cream to stiff peaks and fold thoroughly into the gelatin mixture. Chill the dessert until firm, about 4 to 6 hours. *At this point, the apricot whip can be stored, covered, for 1 to 2 days.*

Celery Broth
 Chicken Breasts
 Stuffed with Crab Meat
  Tomato Pilaf
   Hot Honey Sundae
   with Macadamia Nuts

This menu opens with a soup which we think is fairly unusual—at least we haven't run into it in any restaurant, and there is no can of it on the supermarket shelf. What we have done is to marry fresh celery with chicken broth, simmer them until the flavor of the celery becomes subtly predominant, then cloud the whole affair with a touch of cream. The results will have guests amazed at your ingenuity.

We accept the fact that homemade chicken stock is preferable to the canned varieties when you're recovering from some terrible illness and all you want is a bowl of chicken soup. However, we think the canned chicken broth is fine under practically any other circumstance; and besides, we don't know any working woman personally who goes to the trouble of keeping on hand a goodly supply of homemade chicken stock.

When buying the chicken broth for this recipe, get either three 11-ounce cans of the type to which you add an equal amount of water, or a 46-ounce can and a 13-ounce can of the type which does not get diluted. These amounts will give you about 7½ cups of broth.

Thin soups like the celery broth don't stay hot for long, so we recommend that you keep the soup hot on the stove until everyone is actually seated for dinner; then bring it to the table in its pot, if presentable, or in a warm tureen. Have one of your more steady-handed guests pass the individual bowls as you fill them (rather than passing hand to hand around the table). Sprinkle the celery leaves over each individual serving so they fleck the surface of the soup.

The celery broth actually whets the appetite instead of dulling it, as thicker soups are apt to do—and this is a good thing because the next act in the dinner is deliciously rich. Once again, your guests may be surprised to discover a crab meat stuffing inside an ordinary chicken breast; and they'll also discover that the combination of fish and fowl is a winner. Our recipe calls for canned crab meat, because frozen crab these days is astronomically expensive and the difference in taste—when using crab meat as a stuffing—isn't all that discernible. However, for those who want to splurge on frozen crab meat or who live where they can buy fresh crab, we give another version of the recipe with the directions.

The colorful tomato pilaf is a perfect complement to the chicken, offsetting the creamy richness of the entrée with the gentle bite of onions and tomatoes. Serve the pilaf and chicken-crab meat dish at the table for best presentation, and spoon over lots of sauce.

Before you clear the table, put the honey for the dessert on the stove over a low heat until it becomes nice and hot. If your ice cream is impenetrably hard, you might want to remove it from the freezer about 15 to 20 minutes before serving to make it more spoonable. Of course, you will have chopped your macadamia nuts much earlier in the day. You may think this is a cop-out dessert because of its simplicity, but reserve judgment until you taste. There is an extraordinary harmony between honey and vanilla ice cream, with the nuts lending just the proper foil. Macadamia nuts are expensive, but one little jar should give you many sundaes over a period of time; just be sure to refrigerate the nuts after opening the jar.

We don't think you can err with a Chablis here, though if you want to live it up, the meal would be beautifully set off by a Pinot Chardonnay from California or a Verdicchio from Italy.

Celery Broth

Wash the celery and break each stalk into 2 or 3 pieces. In a large kettle, place the celery and the chicken broth and bring to a boil. Reduce the heat to low, cover and simmer for 20 to 30 minutes. *At this point, the soup can be held off the heat for 3 to 5 hours, or it can be kept warm on the stove over very low heat for up to an hour.*

Shortly before serving, reheat the soup to piping hot, discard the celery, and stir in the cream; reheat again, but do not let the soup boil after adding the cream. Serve the soup in warm cups or bowls, and garnish each portion with a sprinkling of the celery leaves.

6 *celery stalks with leaves*

7 to 8 *cups chicken broth* OR *chicken stock*

2 to 3 *tablespoons light cream* OR *heavy cream*

2 *tablespoons celery leaves, finely chopped*

Chicken Breasts Stuffed with Crab Meat

6 servings

In a medium skillet, melt 3 tablespoons of the butter over low-medium heat and sauté the mushrooms until tender; remove the mushrooms with a slotted spoon to a dish and reserve. Add the sherry to the skillet and cook down over high heat until almost evaporated. Off the heat, melt the remaining 1 tablespoon of butter in the skillet and stir in the flour. Whisk in the chicken broth until smooth, return the skillet to the heat, and cook over low heat, stirring constantly, until thickened. Add the cream to the sauce, and continue cooking and stirring until thickened; remove from the heat.

In a small mixing bowl, shred the crab meat

4 *tablespoons butter*

½ *pound fresh mushrooms, sliced*

½ *cup dry sherry*

2 *tablespoons flour*

1 *cup chicken stock* OR *chicken broth*

1 *cup heavy cream*

1 *7-ounce can crab meat, drained*

¼ *cup fresh parsley, finely chopped*

3 whole, boneless, skin-
less chicken breasts,
each *weighing about* 12
ounces

*Salt and freshly ground
black pepper to taste*

½ to ¾ *teaspoon mar-
joram, crumbled*

¼ *cup Gruyère cheese* OR
Swiss cheese, grated

Paprika

and add the parsley; spoon in just enough of the sauce from the skillet to cause the ingredients to stick together and form a stuffing.

Ask your butcher for large chicken breasts, so that the single pieces will weigh 6 ounces, when you cut each in half. After halving each connected breast, trim away any fat and membrane, and flatten with a meat pounder or the heel of your hand. Rub the breasts with salt, pepper, and marjoram. Put equal portions of the crab meat stuffing in the middle of each breast and spread out slightly. Fold each breast in three parts over the stuffing as if you were folding a business letter (see diagram of fish recipe on page 108). Tucking in any loose, ragged edges, place the breasts, seam side down, in a greased, shallow baking dish measuring 9 x 13 x 2 inches. Pour the remaining cream sauce over the chicken and sprinkle the mushrooms over the dish. *At this point, the dish can be held, covered loosely with foil, for 1 to 2 hours.*

When ready to cook, preheat the oven to 350 degrees.

Bake the chicken, still covered loosely with foil, for 1 hour. Remove the chicken from the oven, and turn the oven to BROIL. Sprinkle the cheese over the chicken and dust with a little paprika. Place the dish under the broiler 6 inches from the heat, and broil until the cheese is golden and bubbly, about 6 to 8 minutes. Serve immediately, spooning the sauce over each portion as you do.

Instructions for using fresh or frozen crab meat:

Buy approximately ½ pound of lump crab meat—frozen or fresh. Instead of mixing the crab meat and parsley with some of the sauce to form a stuffing, simply place pieces of crab meat in the middle of each chicken breast and fold over once. Proceed with the recipe, sprinkling the parsley over the cream sauce with the mushrooms.

Tomato Pilaf

6 servings

In a large saucepan, melt 3 tablespoons of the butter over low-medium heat and sauté the onion until tender. Add the rice, basil, oregano, salt, and pepper, and continue to sauté for about 3 minutes, making sure the rice is thoroughly coated with butter. Pour in the chicken broth and stir in the tomato paste until dissolved. Bring the broth to a boil, then lower the heat and simmer the rice, covered, until the rice is cooked and the liquid is absorbed, about 20 to 25 minutes. Remove from the heat and keep covered. *At this point, the rice can be held for 2 to 3 hours.*

About 45 minutes before serving, preheat the oven to 350 degrees.

In a small saucepan, melt the remaining 3 tablespoons of butter and stir into the rice, along with the chopped tomato. Spoon the pilaf into a greased, deep 2½- or 3-quart casserole, cover, and reheat in the oven while the chicken is cooking, about 20 to 30 minutes. Serve immediately.

6	*tablespoons butter*
1	*large onion, thinly sliced*
1½	*cups long-grain white rice*
¼	*teaspoon basil*
¼	*teaspoon oregano*
	Salt and freshly ground black pepper to taste
3	*to 3¼ cups chicken broth* OR *chicken stock*
2	*teaspoons tomato paste*
1	*16-ounce can tomato wedges, drained and chopped*

Hot Honey Sundae with Macadamia Nuts

6 servings

In a small saucepan, heat the honey over low heat until quite warm; do not boil. Spoon the ice cream into individual dessert dishes, pour over the honey, and top each portion with a sprinkling of the nuts. Serve immediately.

4	*to 5 tablespoons honey*
1	*quart rich vanilla ice cream*
⅓	*cup (heaping) macadamia nuts, finely chopped*

Broccoli–Cheese Soup
Brandied Chicken with a
Sauté of Apples, Celery, and Nuts
Paprika–Poppy Seed Noodles
Chocolate Pot de Crème

One of the intriguing aspects of this menu is that while the soup and dessert courses are practically staples of good restaurant fare, the treatments given them here put them in the unusual—even novelty—category. This is accomplished by tossing a handful of Cheddar cheese into the broccoli soup, and by injecting a liqueur into the chocolate pots de crème before they are completely set.

The broccoli soup could be made with fresh broccoli, but we do not include that as a possibility because of all the preparation time involved in peeling the skin from a bunch of broccoli. As long as you don't overcook the frozen broccoli, you will achieve good broccoli flavor and coloration. The greenest color will be obtained if you use broccoli flowerettes, but these can be hard to find. If you use broccoli spears, you will have the extra step of cutting up the broccoli for the food processor, but it really isn't time consuming if you do it with scissors right in the saucepan. Some people may own a knife that cuts through frozen foods, in which case they can cut up the frozen packages into eighths before cooking.

Making the chocolate pot de crème will take you back to when you baked your first cookies or assembled your first bread-and-butter sandwich—it's easy and fun! The idea of injecting a liqueur into each dessert is borrowed from the English, who often inject liqueurs into whole fruits with a hypodermic syringe. We have substituted an eye dropper, which works just as well; it can be purchased in a drugstore. Pot de crème pots with their little lids are nice dishes to own even though they have pretty much a single purpose. You can also use small ramekins, custard cups, or demitasse coffee cups. What you want is a receptacle that holds about ⅓ cup of liquid; and it has to have depth for the injection of liqueur to work.

The main course of chicken and noodles is a beautiful blend of the foods one associates with cold-weather months, textures ranging from soft to bitey, and warm colors. The apple, celery, and nut topping can be made the afternoon of the party and held for later warming up. Be sure you select apples with red, red skins. For additional color, you could use the greenest part of the celery stalks, in which case you might need three stalks, since you'll be cutting away the whiter, fatter ends.

The chicken dish should not be made much earlier than shortly before the party begins, and the noodles not too long before that. Though we usually advocate at-table serving of the main course, we think the individual plates here will be more attractive if you arrange them in the kitchen. You will have more control over topping the chicken with an effective portion of the apple mixture, much as it would be served to you in a fancy restaurant. If you serve at the table, it will be hard to spoon up the chicken without the apple mixture getting sort of lost in the shuffle. However, if you want to serve at the table, a pretty presentation would be to mound the noodles around the outside of a large, warm platter, pile the chicken and sauce in the middle and spread the apple mixture over the chicken. Or serve the noodles separately in a warm bowl.

A medium-dry white wine with fruity overtones goes well with the distinctive flavors of the broccoli soup, the paprika-laced noodles, and the topping on the chicken. Try a German Riesling from Bernkastel, a California Johannisberg Riesling, or a nice Chenin Blanc from the same state.

Broccoli–Cheese Soup

6 servings

2	*tablespoons butter*
1	*medium onion, coarsely chopped*
1	*small clove garlic, halved*
2	*10-ounce packages frozen broccoli spears* OR *chopped broccoli*
¼	*teaspoon oregano*
	Salt and freshly ground black pepper to taste
½	*cup water*
½	*cup dry white wine*
½	*cup sharp Cheddar cheese, grated*
3½	*cups chicken broth* OR *chicken stock*
¼	*to* ½ *cup heavy cream*

In a large saucepan, melt the butter over low-medium heat and sauté the onion and garlic until tender; do not let brown. Add the broccoli, oregano, salt, pepper, water, and wine, and bring to a boil over high heat, separating the broccoli with a fork. Cover the saucepan, reduce the heat to a simmer and cook until barely tender, about 5 minutes. Off the heat, cut the broccoli into 2-inch pieces (use scissors so you don't have to take the broccoli out of the pan).

To the container of an electric blender or a food processor fitted with the steel blade add the broccoli and the contents of the saucepan, along with the cheese; process until you have a smooth purée (this will have to be done in 2 or 3 batches). Return the broccoli purée to the saucepan and stir in the chicken broth. Reheat the soup over low heat, stirring occasionally, to let the flavors blend, about 15 minutes; do not let boil. *At this point, the soup can be held off the heat for 3 to 5 hours, or it can be refrigerated, covered, for 2 to 3 days.*

Shortly before serving, reheat the soup over low-medium heat. Stir in the cream, taste for seasoning, and reheat again without letting the soup boil. Serve immediately.

Brandied Chicken with a Sauté of Apples, Celery, and Nuts

6 servings

Wash and core the apples but do not peel the skin; then cut them into a ½-inch dice. In a medium skillet, melt 3 tablespoons of the butter over medium heat and sauté the apples, celery, and nuts, tossing constantly, about 10 minutes. Remove from the heat and reserve.

Cut the chicken breasts into strips which measure approximately 1 by 2 to 3 inches; pat dry with paper towels. Season the flour with plenty of salt and some pepper, and dredge the strips in the flour until lightly coated; shake off excess flour.

In a large skillet, melt 2 tablespoons of the butter and 1 tablespoon of the oil over medium heat until the butter is bubbly. Sauté half the chicken until it is golden brown and cooked through, about 10 to 15 minutes. Off the heat, remove the chicken with a slotted spoon to a plate. Return the skillet to the stove, melt 2 more tablespoons of the butter and the remaining oil, and sauté the rest of the chicken. When the second batch of chicken is done, pour over the brandy and continue cooking until it is nearly evaporated. Off the heat, remove the chicken to the plate with the rest of the chicken.

In the same skillet, melt the remaining 1 tablespoon of butter over low heat and sauté the scallions until tender. Turn the heat to medium-high, add the chicken stock and wine and cook, scraping up the particles from the bottom of the skillet, until the liquid is reduced by half. Return the chicken to the skillet along with any accumulated juices. Add the cream to the skillet and cook over medium heat, stirring constantly, until the cream is reduced slightly and is thickened. Remove the chicken from the heat and taste the sauce to

2	*small tart apples*
8	*tablespoons (1 stick) butter*
2	*celery stalks, finely chopped*
⅓	*cup pecans OR walnuts, finely chopped*
2¼	*pounds boneless, skinless chicken breasts*
½	*to ¾ cup flour*
	Salt and freshly ground black pepper to taste
2	*tablespoons vegetable oil*
¼	*cup brandy*
¼	*cup shallots OR scallions (white part only), finely chopped*
1½	*cups chicken broth OR chicken stock*
½	*cup dry white wine*
1	*cup heavy cream*

correct seasoning. *At this point, the chicken can be held, loosely covered, for 1 to 2 hours.*

When ready to serve, warm up the chicken over low heat, taking care that the cream does not boil; or you can warm in a 325-degree oven, covered, for 20 to 30 minutes. Warm up the apple mixture and serve the chicken immediately with the apples, celery, and nuts spread on top.

Paprika–Poppy Seed Noodles

6 servings

1	*12-ounce package medium egg noodles*
6	*to 8 tablespoons butter, melted*
1	*tablespoon poppy seeds*
2	*teaspoons paprika*
	Salt and freshly ground black pepper to taste
¼	*cup milk* OR *light cream, warmed*

In a large kettle, bring to a boil 6 to 8 quarts salted water, to which you have added a little vegetable oil. Add the noodles and cook over high heat until they are barely tender, about 7 to 9 minutes. Drain the noodles in a colander and run cool water over them. Return to the kettle and toss with the butter, poppy seeds, paprika, salt, and pepper. Pour the noodles into a greased, deep 4-quart casserole. *At this point, the noodles can be held, covered, for 3 to 4 hours.*

About 45 minutes before serving, preheat the oven to 350 degrees. Pour the warmed milk or cream over the noodles, toss gently and reheat, covered, for 20 to 30 minutes. Serve immediately.

Chocolate Pot de Crème

6 servings

1	*6-ounce package semi-sweet chocolate morsels*
¼	*cup strong coffee*

In the top of a double boiler, melt the chocolate over simmering water, then stir in the coffee until smooth; remove from the heat. Beat the egg yolks until smooth and stir into the chocolate until blended.

In a medium mixing bowl, beat the egg whites until they form stiff peaks. Fold the egg whites into the chocolate until completely blended, making sure to stir up all the chocolate from the bottom of the pan. Pour the chocolate into pot de crème pots (or small, straight-sided ramekins or cups that hold about ⅓ cup of liquid). Place in the refrigerator for 15 minutes.

Remove the chocolate from the refrigerator and inject the liqueur as follows: Using a regular eye dropper or medicine dropper about 4 inches long, dip it into the liqueur* and squeeze the rubber top until you've taken about ¼ teaspoon into the glass tube. Stick the end of the eye dropper into the chocolate in the center of each pot de crème and squeeze the rubber top again to inject the liqueur into the chocolate; do *not* release your hold on the rubber top until you have completely extracted the dropper from the chocolate (this prevents you from drawing up chocolate into the dropper glass). If you have any chocolate clinging to the end of the dropper, wash it off with cold water before repeating the procedure for the rest of the pots de crème. Return the pots to the refrigerator for 3 to 4 hours. *At this point the dessert can be stored in the refrigerator, covered, for several days.*

When ready to serve, place a dollop of whipped cream topping on each dessert. If you whip your own cream, you may want to sweeten it with a little confectioners' sugar.

4 eggs, separated

About 1½ teaspoons orange liqueur (Grand Marnier, Curaçao, Cointreau)

Whipped cream topping OR *½ cup heavy cream, whipped*

---

*The easiest way to handle the liqueur is to pour a couple of ounces into a measuring cup with a pouring spout. When finished, just pour the excess liqueur back into its bottle.

Fillets of Sole with Tomato–Pernod Sauce
Pasta with Peas and Mushrooms
Green Salad with Vinaigrette Dressing
Orange Crème Brûlée

This is an elegant but easy menu for fish lovers who live where they can obtain fresh fish. Frozen fish really can't be substituted because the slightly more fishy taste of frozen products will fight with the supreme delicacy of the tomato sauce laced with just a soupçon of Pernod. We have elected not to provide a first course for this menu. First of all, the fish and the pasta are both filling and complex enough to constitute separate entrées; together, they make more than a meal. Also, fish tends to keep cooking after removal from the heat and lose its firm, succulent texture; so we want to serve it as soon as possible. Generally, we like to provide a first course at our dinner parties, but we bend this tradition on occasion when appropriate or necessary.

For those who are intimidated by the idea of fish for company, notice that the fish and part of the sauce can be assembled long before the party starts. The only last-minute detail you have to attend to is finishing off the sauce—a simple procedure that takes 15 minutes.

The pasta is a third or fourth cousin of that heavenly, northern Italian dish called "straw and hay," but without the addition of ham. Most people think of pasta as something to be whipped up while the kids are being called in to supper, but this dish can be made ahead and reheated by moistening it first with some cream. (Note: With the addition of a little more cheese and cream, plus some slivers of ham or chicken, if you want, this makes a first-rate dish to serve for a late-night supper after returning from the theater or a movie.)

The fish and the pasta can be served from the kitchen or at the table. The advantage of the latter is that any leftover pasta will be in plain sight inviting second helpings. Be sure you cook both the fish and the pasta in presentable baking dishes for bringing to the table. Spoon plenty of tomato-Pernod sauce over the fish portions—in fact, use it up; if the sauce floats into the pasta, so much the better.

The salad should definitely be served as a separate course between dinner and dessert. We don't always insist on this, but since there is no first course and it is only civilized to have a minimum of three acts at a company dinner, we urge you to give the salad some fanfare. If you wish, you can add some sieved egg, a sprinkling of chopped walnuts, or black olives to the greens. A strong argument for always serving a salad with a vinaigrette dressing as a separate course is to avoid the clashing tastes of vinegar and the wine you're drinking. Neither does the other any good whatsoever.

In our frenetic experimentation with desserts for this book (one of us doesn't particularly like desserts, the other has to watch her weight—it figures!), we created the orange crème brûlée by mistake. We were elated because the dessert is delicious, managing to be both refreshing and rich. The mandatory instruction to follow is to refrigerate the dessert overnight for at least 24 hours; otherwise the custard doesn't firm up sufficiently.

We would serve a fairly dry but not terribly complicated white wine with this dinner—perhaps a Soave, a reputable Chablis, or a Muscadet. There are a lot of delicate flavors involved here—peas and mushrooms, for example, and you *do* want the Pernod to be noticed. If you want to spend the money, another wine choice would be a Pouilly-Fumé.

Fillets of Sole with Tomato–Pernod Sauce

6 servings

2¼ *pounds fresh fillets of sole* OR *flounder*

8 *tablespoons (1 stick) butter, softened to room temperature*

¼ *cup fresh parsley, finely chopped*

3 *tablespoons shallots* OR *scallions (white part only), finely chopped*

Juice of ½ lemon

Salt and freshly ground black pepper to taste

¾ *cup dry white wine*

1 *tablespoon Pernod liqueur*

2 *tablespoons flour*

1 *cup heavy cream*

1 *16-ounce can Italian plum tomatoes, drained and finely chopped*

1 *teaspoon fennel seeds (optional)*

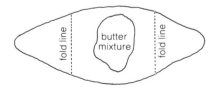

Lay the fish flat on paper towels with the skin side facing up and pat dry. In a small mixing bowl, blend 6 tablespoons of the butter, 2 tablespoons of the parsley, and the shallots. Put equal portions of the butter mixture in the center of each fish fillet, pressing down to flatten slightly. Sprinkle the fillets with the lemon juice and with a little salt and pepper. Fold up each fillet over the butter as though you were folding a business letter (see diagram). In a greased, shallow baking dish measuring about 9 x 13 x 2 inches, place the folded-up fillets, seam side down. Pour the wine and Pernod around the fish. *At this point, the fish can be stored in the refrigerator, covered, for 4 to 5 hours.* Let the fish come to room temperature for 45 to 50 minutes before cooking.

In a medium saucepan, melt the remaining 2 tablespoons of butter over low heat, then stir in the flour until smooth. Add the cream and cook over low heat until thickened, stirring constantly. Stir in the tomatoes and fennel seeds and simmer, uncovered, for 10 to 15 minutes. Season to taste with salt and pepper. *At this point, the sauce can be held for 3 to 4 hours until ready to finish.*

Preheat the oven to 400 degrees.

Cover the fish loosely with foil and bake for 15 minutes. Carefully remove the fish with a slotted spatula to a warm serving platter and keep warm while finishing the sauce.

Pour into the tomato-cream sauce ¾ cup of the wine liquid from the dish in which the fish cooked; bring to a simmer and cook over very low heat about 10 minutes. Pour the sauce over the fish, sprinkle with the remaining parsley, and serve immediately.

Pasta with Peas and Mushrooms

6 servings

Cook the peas according to the package directions, but do not continue cooking after the water has returned to a boil and the peas are separated; drain and reserve.

In a large skillet, melt 4 tablespoons of the butter over low-medium heat and sauté the mushrooms. When the juice released by the mushrooms starts to cook down, add the scallions, garlic, and parsley to the skillet, and continue cooking until the scallions are tender. Reserve.

In a large kettle, bring to a boil 6 quarts salted water, to which you have added a little vegetable oil. Add the noodles and cook over high heat until they are barely tender, about 5 minutes. Drain the noodles in a colander or large sieve and run cool water over them.

In a large mixing bowl, place the noodles and vegetables and toss gently with the remaining butter, cheese, salt, and pepper. Spoon the pasta dish into a greased, deep 3- or 4-quart casserole. *At this point, the dish can be held, covered, for 3 to 4 hours.*

About 45 minutes before serving, preheat the oven to 350 degrees.

Pour the cream over the pasta and bake, covered, for 30 minutes, until the dish is heated through. Serve immediately.

1   10-*ounce package frozen peas*

8   *tablespoons (1 stick) butter, softened to room temperature*

12 *ounces fresh mushrooms, sliced*

¼   *cup scallions with part of green tops, finely chopped*

1   *clove garlic, finely chopped*

¼   *cup fresh parsley, finely chopped*

1   *12-ounce package* fine *egg noodles*

½   *cup Parmesan cheese* OR *Romano cheese, grated*

   Salt and freshly ground black pepper to taste

¼   *cup half-and-half cream* OR *light cream, warmed*

Green Salad with Vinaigrette Dressing

6 servings

2 to 3 *heads soft lettuce (Boston, leaf, salad bowl, Bibb and the like)*

4 to 5 *radishes, thinly sliced*

Salt and freshly ground black pepper to taste

2 *tablespoons red wine vinegar*

6 *tablespoons olive oil* OR *a combination of olive and vegetable oil*

2 to 3 *tablespoons fresh parsley, finely chopped*

½ *teaspoon chervil (optional)*

Wash the lettuce and thoroughly dry; tear into bite-size pieces. Place the lettuce and radishes in a lidded, plastic container lined with paper towels or in a plastic bag twisted closed; refrigerate.

In a small mixing bowl or a jar with a tight-fitting lid, combine the salt, pepper, and vinegar. Add the oil, beating it in thoroughly with a wire whisk if using a bowl; or shaking the ingredients together vigorously in a jar. *At this point, the lettuce and salad dressing may be held for several hours.*

Shortly before serving, place the lettuce in a salad bowl. Mix the salad dressing again as you did before, pour it over the lettuce, and toss until well coated. Sprinkle the parsley and chervil over the lettuce and toss again. Serve on salad plates.

Orange Crème Brûlée

6 to 8 servings

2 *16-ounce cans mandarin oranges, drained*

2 *tablespoons orange liqueur (Grand Marnier, Curaçao, Cointreau)*

4 *egg yolks*

1 *tablespoon granulated sugar*

In a 10-inch quiche pan 1¼-inch deep, arrange the oranges; spoon the liqueur over them.

In a small mixing bowl, beat the egg yolks; add the granulated sugar and continue beating until satiny smooth.

In a medium saucepan, heat the cream just to boiling (small bubbles will appear on the surface). Remove from the heat and whisk a small amount of the cream into the egg yolks, using a rapid motion so that the yolks and cream won't curdle. Pour the egg yolk mixture into the cream, stirring rapidly. Return the cream to the stove and cook over low heat, stirring constantly, until the sauce thickens and coats the back of a spoon; this will take about 10 minutes. Cool the sauce by immersing the pan in some cold water for a few minutes. Then pour the sauce over the oranges and refrigerate at least overnight. *At this point, the dessert can be stored in the refrigerator, covered, for 1 to 2 days.*

Preheat the oven to BROIL.

In a small mixing bowl, combine the brown sugar and coconut and sprinkle over the top of the dessert, patting it down to form a solid topping. Place the crème brûlée 6 inches from the heat and broil until the sugar has caramelized, about 2 minutes (watch carefully to prevent burning the coconut). Serve immediately.

2 *cups heavy cream*

½ *cup light brown sugar, packed*

½ *cup coconut, shredded*

Clam and Chicken Consommé
Fish Fillets Layered with Eggplant, Spinach, and Cheese
Carrots Marsala
After—Dinner Drink Mousse

When we took away the eggplant from our moussaka recipe, (page 132), we vowed we would not exclude that noble vegetable altogether from the book. But we admit we didn't expect eggplant to turn up as the foundation for a rather unusual fish dish. This is a menu for those who appreciate seafood and food that is packed with vitamins, but it also appeals to the epicure who would float cream in his consommé, spice up carrots with a dash of Marsala wine and conclude his dinner by polishing off a mousse laced with a liqueur.

When you make the clam and chicken consommé for the first time, you'll wonder that anything looking so bland can taste so good. No question that clam juice and chicken broth are colorless liquids, but when they are heated up together and topped with a big mound of horseradish-flavored whipped cream, they add up to a unique and quite bracing soup. To give visual interest, we sprinkle the cream with some parsley.

The fish layered with eggplant, spinach, and cheese is essentially a meal-in-one dish. The magic of combining ingredients not normally connected with each other works here to produce an entrée that will be loved by haters of fish, spinach, or eggplant. When shopping for the fish, look for fresh fillets of similar thickness. You can make the dish with frozen fillets of flounder, but we don't recommend this because frozen fish is often inferior to the fresh; however, we don't completely discourage you from trying it.

A fish entrée can appear rather pallid on a plate, but what happens with this treatment is that as the cheese melts down through the various layers, the spinach is exposed to color the dish an inviting forest green. We direct you in the recipe to serve the fish immediately upon removal from the oven, but actually you can hold it in reserve while enjoying the consommé, because the cheese and crumb topping acts to seal heat in the dish for a number of minutes.

To accompany the fish we have created a ridiculously simple recipe for carrots in which they get tossed and steamed in a little butter, thyme, and Marsala—all in a matter of a few minutes to preserve flavor, color, and texture. The bright orange of the vegetable really sets off the green and white colors in the entrée. The wine can be omitted if you don't have any on hand and don't want to go to the trouble of buying some; the carrots cooked with only the butter and thyme are delicious. In fact, we often cook them this way for ordinary dinners.

Have fun with the mousse. We created it for people who have a cabinet full of bottles of liqueurs which are gathering dust because no one drinks them anymore (at least that has been our experience). Actually, we wanted to come up with a recipe that could be varied according to whatever liqueurs you have on hand, or according to your personal liqueur preference or perhaps that of an honored guest. You can put any desired single liqueur or combination of liqueurs into the mousse, as long as the total measurement is one-half cup.

The preferred wine for this dinner is a medium or full dry white. We would stay with the California wines—a Chablis, Sauvignon Blanc, or Chardonnay.

Clam and Chicken Consommé

6 servings

3   8-ounce bottles clam juice

3   cups chicken broth OR chicken stock

    Celery salt to taste

¾   cup heavy cream

2   to 3 tablespoons horse-radish

¼   cup fresh parsley, finely chopped

Into a large saucepan, pour the clam juice and chicken broth and simmer, uncovered, until the flavors are blended, about 20 minutes. Add the celery salt to taste. *At this point, the consommé can be held off the heat for 3 to 5 hours.*

In a medium mixing bowl, whip the cream to stiff peaks and stir in the horseradish; refrigerate for 1 to 2 hours.

Shortly before serving, reheat the consommé to piping hot without letting it boil. Serve the consommé in warm cups or small bowls with a large dollop of the whipped cream sauce and a sprinkling of the parsley on top.

Fish Fillets Layered with Eggplant, Spinach, and Cheese

6 servings

1   large eggplant, about 1½ pounds

½   cup dry white wine

2   teaspoons basil

½   teaspoon garlic powder

    Salt and freshly ground black pepper to taste

1   10-ounce package frozen leaf spinach OR chopped spinach

Preheat the oven to 350 degrees.

Wash the eggplant, slice off the ends (but do not peel the skin), and slice lengthwise into ¼-inch-thick slices. In a shallow baking dish measuring about 12 x 20 x 2 inches, crowd the eggplant in a single layer (the eggplant will shrink in the cooking) and pour over the wine and ½ cup cold water. Sprinkle the eggplant with 1 teaspoon of the basil, ¼ teaspoon of the garlic powder, and salt and pepper to taste. Bake, uncovered, for 20 to 25 minutes, until tender. Remove the eggplant from the liquid with a slotted spatula and drain on paper towels. Reserve the liquid in the baking dish and let cool.

In a medium saucepan, cook the spinach according to the package directions until barely tender, breaking it up with a fork as it cooks to hasten the process. Drain the spinach in a sieve or colander and run cold water over it. Using your hands, squeeze out all the moisture from the spinach and reserve.

Arrange the fish fillets in the baking dish in which you cooked the eggplant and dot with about 2 tablespoons of the butter. Place the eggplant on top of the fish and dot with another 2 tablespoons butter. Spread the spinach on top of the eggplant and dot with another 2 tablespoons butter. Place enough Monterey Jack cheese on top of the spinach to completely cover the dish. *At this point, the fish can be stored in the refrigerator, covered, for several hours.* Let the dish come to room temperature for 30 to 45 minutes before cooking.

Preheat the oven to 350 degrees.

In a medium skillet, melt the remaining 3 tablespoons of butter over low heat. Off the heat, stir the bread crumbs into the butter along with the remaining basil, garlic powder, and the celery salt. When cool, stir in the Parmesan cheese.

Bake the fish for 20 minutes, uncovered. Remove the dish from the oven and turn the oven on to BROIL. Sprinkle the bread crumb mixture over the dish and place under the broiler, about 3 inches from the heat. Broil until brown and bubbly, about 2 minutes. Serve immediately.

2½ *pounds fresh fillets of flounder* OR *sole* OR *whitefish*

9 *tablespoons butter*

¼ *-inch-thick slices of Monterey Jack cheese* OR *Provolone cheese to cover the dish*

1½ *cups fresh bread crumbs*

½ *teaspoon celery salt*

¼ *cup Parmesan cheese* OR *Romano cheese, grated*

Carrots Marsala

6 servings

8 to 10 *carrots, about*
   1¼ pounds

3 *tablespoons butter*

½ *teaspoon thyme*

   Salt and freshly ground
   black pepper to taste

3 *tablespoons Marsala*
   wine

Trim the ends of the carrots and scrape them. In a food processor fitted with the shredding disk, or with a hand grater, grate the carrots. *At this point, the carrots can be stored in the refrigerator, covered, for several hours.*

In a large skillet, melt the butter over low heat and add the thyme. Add the carrots and toss to coat them thoroughly with the butter. Season with salt and pepper and dribble on the Marsala. Cover the carrots and cook over very low heat for 5 to 10 minutes. Off the heat, toss again and keep warm during the soup course.

After–Dinner Drink Mousse

6 servings

4 *eggs*

   Scant ⅔ cup sugar

½ *cup cold water*

1 *package unflavored*
   gelatin

½ *cup liqueur, well*
   chilled *

1¼ *cups heavy cream*

   Grated chocolate for
   garnish (optional)

In the top of a double boiler, break the eggs and beat them well; add the sugar and continue beating until satiny smooth. Add the cold water and gelatin and stir to blend; let this mixture stand for a few minutes to soften the gelatin. Bring a little water to a boil in the bottom of the double boiler, then reduce the heat to simmer. Set the egg mixture over the water and cook, stirring constantly, until the gelatin is completely dissolved. Pour the egg mixture into a large mixing bowl and stir in the chilled

*For a brandy Alexander mousse, use 4 tablespoons brandy, 4 tablespoons brown crème de cacao; for a grasshopper mousse, use 6 tablespoons green crème de menthe, 2 tablespoons white crème de cacao. Or you can flavor the mousse with ½ cup of a single favorite liqueur or cordial such as Amaretto, crème de cassis, Grand Marnier, Galliano, etc.

liqueur, then place in the refrigerator until partly set (this will take about 1 hour).

In a large mixing bowl, whip the cream to stiff peaks and fold into the liqueur mixture until everything is thoroughly blended. (Note: If the liqueur mixture has jelled so much that it isn't going to fold into the cream without lumps, stir it up with an electric beater on the "stir" or "mix" setting until it is smooth, then proceed to fold in the whipped cream.) Chill the mousse until set, about 4 to 6 hours. *At this point, the mousse can be stored in the refrigerator, covered, for 1 to 2 days.*

When ready to serve, spoon the mousse into individual dessert dishes and sprinkle some grated chocolate over each portion, if you wish.

Curried Carrot Soup
Shish Kebab of Sirloin, Peppers, Onion, and Banana with Peanut Butter Sauce
Parslied Rice
Coffee Ice Cream with Coffee Liqueur

This is one of the most unusual menus in the book, yet it is extremely simple to prepare and manage. If you were to encounter an item like peanut butter sauce on a restaurant menu, you might very well pass it over with a resounding "yuk." Most of us love peanut butter or may even be addicted to it on bread or crackers, but to imagine it as an essential ingredient in a main dinner course when company's coming—well, that seems as bizarre as serving raw fish. Yet the idea for this incredibly delicious and exotic shish kebab comes from one of New York's more exotic restaurants— a dark, smoky, somewhat primitive hole-in-the-wall in Greenwich Village called Chumley's. When we lived in the Village in our youth, we thought that dining at Chumley's—with its initial-carved wooden tables and yellowing prints of book jackets on the walls—was the epitome of the bohemian life. One had to *know* about Chumley's to eat there because no exterior sign of a restaurant existed. At any rate, we are grateful to Chumley's for giving us the idea of spicing up a shish kebab with a sauce laced heavily with one of America's favorite foods. Believe us, your guests will *love* it.

The curried carrot soup is also a conversation piece and will be very popular with everyone except those poor souls who don't like curry. The soup is a gorgeous shade of orange—looks wonderfully inviting with the flecks of parsley on top as your guests sit down to eat. The only cautionary note about the soup is to make certain the carrots are completely tender before you purée them in the food processor or blender; otherwise, you'll end up with some undesirable chunks in the finished product.

You will pay a good price for the boneless sirloin, but you should splurge here because you want tender meat; and besides, the rest of the menu is relatively inexpensive. You may need to buy two steaks, each about 1½ inches thick. If there's fat on the steaks, allow for the fact that you're going to have to cut it off later, and buy a little more than 3 pounds of meat. As for the vegetables, if you can't find a red pepper, buy another green pepper, or if the red color is important to you, you can substitute one of those rather flavorless hothouse tomatoes for the red pepper. Be sure to select an underripe banana because a ripe one will fall right off the skewers when being broiled.

The skewers should be 18 inches long and strong. Some have wooden handles, which is nice because then you don't need a hot pad to turn them. You can thread the skewers in a random pattern because you're not bringing them to the table. However, it is important to alternate the meat with the peppers, onion, and banana rather than sticking all the meat on the same skewers; this insures better overall cooking of the meat. You will need a total of six skewers.

Unfortunately, while everything else in this menu can be prepared completely ahead of time, you will have to cook the shish kebab while guests are sipping their last drinks. But the broiling is a snap—just keep an eye on the clock and turn every 5 minutes—and you would be in the kitchen anyway, warming up the soup and rice. Remember to cut up the vegetables earlier in the day; only the banana has to wait to the last minute.

When the shish kebab is done, remove the meat and other ingredients immediately to a warm serving platter and cover tightly with heavy-duty foil to keep everything warm while the soup is being consumed; don't return the shish kebab to the oven because this would dry it out. If you own an electric hot tray, you can place the platter on it, but the meat should stay warm regardless as long as you cover it with the heavy-duty foil. Add lemon wedges to the shish kebab platter and bring it to the table, along with the rice in a decorative bowl and the peanut butter sauce in a small bowl or gravy boat. Spoon peanut butter sauce generously over each individual portion of shish kebab as you serve it, telling guests to squeeze lemon juice over everything; the rice goes on the individual plates alongside the shish kebab.

There is probably no simpler or nicer dessert than ice cream with a liqueur poured over it. One of our favorites is coffee ice cream of excellent quality with one of the well-known liqueurs with a matching flavor. You might consider serving some kind of chocolate cookie with the ice cream, as the flavors of coffee and chocolate are pleasant combinations too.

The richness of the dinner's main course deserves a truly sturdy, full-bodied red wine to go with it. We'd vote for a Zinfandel, a Barbera or, from France, a Saint-Emilion.

Curried Carrot Soup

6 servings

8	to 10 *medium carrots*
3	*tablespoons butter*
1	*large onion, coarsely chopped*
1½	*teaspoons curry powder*
	Salt and freshly ground black pepper to taste
5	*cups chicken broth* OR *chicken stock*
1	*1 x 2-inch strip orange zest*
½	*cup orange juice*
¼	*cup dry sherry*
2	*tablespoons fresh parsley* OR *chives, finely chopped*

Trim the ends of the carrots, scrape them, and cut into 1-inch pieces; if the carrots are fat, cut in half lengthwise before cutting into pieces.

In a large saucepan, melt the butter over low-medium heat and sauté the onion until tender; stir in the curry powder, salt, and pepper. Add the carrots, 1 cup of the chicken broth, the orange zest and orange juice, cover and simmer for 30 minutes, or until the carrots are tender.

In an electric blender or food processor fitted with the steel blade, purée the carrot mixture until smooth; this will have to be done in 2 or 3 batches. Return the carrot mixture to the saucepan and add the remaining chicken broth and the sherry. Reheat the soup over low heat for about 15 minutes to blend the flavors, stirring occasionally; taste to correct seasoning. *At this point, the soup can be held off the heat for 3 to 5 hours, or it can be stored in the refrigerator, covered, for 2 to 3 days.*

Shortly before serving, reheat the soup over low-medium heat until it is piping hot without letting it boil. Serve in warm bowls or cups with the parsley or chives sprinkled on top.

Shish Kebab of Sirloin, Peppers, Onion, and Banana with Peanut Butter Sauce

6 servings

To make the peanut butter sauce: In a medium saucepan, melt the butter over low-medium heat and sauté the onion and garlic until tender; add the ginger and bay leaf. Add the beef broth and bring just to a boil, then lower the heat and stir in the peanut butter, tomato paste, honey, salt, and hot pepper sauce until everything is well blended and smooth. Simmer, uncovered, for 15 to 20 minutes, stirring occasionally. Remove the sauce from the heat and let it cool slightly; discard the bay leaf. In an electric blender or food processor fitted with the steel blade, purée the sauce until smooth. *At this point, the peanut butter sauce can be cooled completely and stored in the refrigerator, covered, for 1 week.*

Pat the steak dry with paper towels. Trim the meat of any fat and cut into 2-inch cubes; you should have 4 cubes of meat per person.

In a small mixing bowl, combine the garlic, cumin, salt, pepper, and soy sauce, then whisk in the vegetable oil until well blended. In a shallow dish big enough to hold the steak in a single layer, place the cubes of meat, pour over the marinade, and turn to thoroughly coat. Marinate for at least 3 hours, turning occasionally. *At this point, the steak can be stored in the refrigerator for several hours.* Let it come to room temperature for 1 hour before cooking.

Peanut butter sauce

2	tablespoons butter
1	medium onion, coarsely chopped
2	cloves garlic, coarsely chopped
¼	teaspoon ground ginger
1	bay leaf
1½	cups beef broth OR beef stock
½	cup smooth peanut butter
1	tablespoon tomato paste
1	tablespoon honey
	Salt to taste
	Dash hot pepper sauce
3	pounds boneless sirloin steak
2	cloves garlic, finely chopped
1	teaspoon ground cumin
	Salt and freshly ground black pepper to taste

2 tablespoons soy sauce

½ cup vegetable oil

1 large green pepper

1 large red pepper

1 large onion OR 6 small white onions about 1½" in diameter

1 semiripe banana

1 lemon, cut into 6 wedges

When ready to cook, preheat the oven to BROIL.

Reheat the peanut butter sauce over low heat and keep warm while broiling the shish kebab; do not let the sauce boil. If the sauce is too thick, add a small amount of beef broth or water.

Wash and seed the peppers and cut into 6 squares. If using a large onion, cut it into 6 pieces. Cut the banana into 6 pieces. Thread the steak, peppers, onion, and banana on 6 18-inch metal skewers, alternating the cubes of meat with the other ingredients; brush the peppers, onion, and banana with the marinade.

Place the skewers on your broiling pan and broil 6 inches from the heat for approximately 5 minutes on each side, turning the skewers clockwise 3 or 4 times and brushing the food with leftover marinade or with oil. The total cooking time is about 15 minutes, depending on the desired degree of doneness; good meat such as sirloin should be pink in the center when done. Remove food from skewers and serve equal portions on individual plates with the peanut butter sauce poured over all. Place a wedge of lemon on each plate for squeezing over the shish kebab. Serve immediately.

Parslied Rice

6 servings

1½ cups long-grain white rice

   Salt to taste

4 to 6 tablespoons butter

2 cups cold water

In a large saucepan, put the rice, salt, 1 tablespoon of the butter, water, and beef broth; cover and bring to a boil, stirring occasionally. Lower heat and simmer, covered, until the rice is cooked and the liquid is absorbed, about 15 minutes. Remove from the heat and keep covered. *At this point, the rice can be held for 2 to 3 hours.*

About 30 minutes before serving, melt the remaining butter and toss gently with the rice, parsley, and the optional almonds until everything is well blended. You can reheat the rice in a 350-degree oven for 15 to 20 minutes, covered. Or you can add ¼ cup tepid water to the rice, cover, and reheat over low heat on the top of the stove for 15 minutes. Serve immediately in a warm bowl.

1 *cup beef broth* OR *beef stock*

½ *cup fresh parsley, finely chopped*

½ *cup slivered almonds (optional)*

Coffee Ice Cream with Coffee Liqueur

6 servings

Spoon the ice cream into individual dessert dishes and pour the liqueur over each serving. If desired, garnish each serving with a grating of chocolate.

1 *quart coffee ice cream of good quality*

6 *tablespoons coffee liqueur (Kahlúa, Tia Maria, etc.)*

Grated chocolate for garnish (optional)

Sherried Consommé
Braised Smoky Beef Brisket
Scalloped Potatoes with Garlic and Cheese
Spinach Salad
Cranberry–Orange Sherbet

A brisk morning in fall or a bone-chilling winter afternoon can cause visions of meat and potatoes to dance in a hostess's head. While we believe that meat (usually beef) and potatoes are the bulwarks of far too many meals in this country, we can accept the appeal of these staples when they are concocted with unusual or elegant touches. Thus we offer the uncommon cut of beef brisket which is marinated in liquid smoke, herbs, and spices, plus a recipe for scalloped potatoes that raises this mundane dish to more respectable heights.

This menu requires a little more advance work than most, but you'll have everything well under control by the time the doorbell rings. The dessert has to be made at least one day in advance of your party, and of course could be made weeks earlier. The cranberry-orange relish used in the dessert is marketed under the name of Cranorange relish™ and is produced by a well-known company specializing in cranberry products. We recommend that you purchase a good quality of sherbet to be sure of its richness and density. The combination of red and orange in this dish gives it a festive appearance; the chopped nuts swirled into the sherbet provide an unexpectedly pleasant crunch in the texture.

A beef brisket is still unusual enough to often require ordering it from your butcher a few days ahead of time, although he will have no trouble obtaining it for you. Several years ago the key ingredient of liquid smoke was hard to find, but in our recent experience most supermarkets carry bottles of it or will stock it upon request. When purchasing the barbecue sauce for the brisket, make sure it is the *plain* variety, with no added flavorings such as "smoke."

We think it is important to call your attention to the fact that the brisket must marinate overnight; nothing is more frustrating than to read such a direction in a recipe when it's too late! The cooking of the meat takes a long time, too, so be sure to allow for this as you plan your day. The aroma that fills the house when this meat is in the oven is mouthwatering, so be prepared for guests to be instantly hungry when they arrive.

The scalloped potatoes are made more complex than most recipes for this dish by sprinkling garlic on each layer and using cream instead of milk. And because we grate our potatoes instead of slicing them, they seem to absorb more of the cream as they cook, becoming in the end a silky, smooth amalgam of garlic, cheese, and cream.

If you don't have two ovens, you are going to have a problem cooking the meat and potatoes together, because they cook at different temperatures. What we suggest is that you cook the potatoes in the hour before you start the brisket. Keep them well-covered with foil at room temperature until the brisket is done. Then pop the potatoes back into the oven at 375 degrees—still covered—and cook until heated through.

On the morning of the party, you can get the salad prepared in part by making the dressing (actually, this can be made a day or two earlier), frying the bacon (cook extra for breakfast), and cleaning the spinach. The sherried consommé simmers while you and your guests enjoy their drinks; there's no preparation and no attentiveness necessary for this very simple first course, which nevertheless sets the right mood for the food to come.

A hearty meat-and-potatoes dinner calls for an unpretentious jug of a hearty red wine. This could be a Burgundy, a Chianti, or any red table wine you like.

Sherried Consommé

6 servings

3	11-*ounce cans beef consommé, undiluted*
1½	*cups water*
1½	*cups dry sherry*
6	*thin slices lemon*
2	*tablespoons fresh parsley, finely chopped*

In a large saucepan, stir together the consommé, water, and sherry. Heat the soup to a simmer, then lower the heat to just below simmer and maintain that temperature for 30 to 45 minutes; do not let the soup boil. When ready to serve, place the lemon slices in warm soup cups or bowls and pour the consommé over them. Sprinkle the parsley over the lemon slices (they'll float to the surface) and serve immediately.

Braised Smoky Beef Brisket

6 servings

1	*4-pound fresh beef brisket*
2	*ounces liquid smoke*
¼	*teaspoon celery seeds*
1	*clove garlic, finely chopped*
1	*onion, sliced*
2	*teaspoons Worcestershire sauce*
	Salt and freshly ground black pepper to taste
6	*ounces barbecue sauce*
¼	*cup fresh parsley, finely chopped*

The evening before your party, place the beef brisket in a shallow baking dish large enough to hold it; don't worry about forcing the meat in to fit because it will shrink in the long cooking. Sprinkle the brisket with the liquid smoke, celery seeds, and garlic; cover the top with the onion slices. *At this point, the brisket must be stored in the refrigerator overnight until ready to cook.*

Preheat the oven to 275 degrees. (Note: The brisket requires a total of 6½ hours from oven to table, so be sure to allow plenty of cooking time!)

Remove the onion slices from the brisket and sprinkle over it the Worcestershire sauce, salt, and pepper; replace the onion slices. Cover the dish loosely with aluminum foil and bake for 5 hours. Remove the foil, pour the barbecue sauce over the brisket and cook, uncovered, for 1 hour. Remove the brisket from the oven and let it sit in the juices for 30 minutes; keep warm by covering with the aluminum foil.

When ready to serve, place the brisket on a warm serving platter and slice. Pour over the sauce, sprinkle with the parsley, and serve immediately.

Scalloped Potatoes with Garlic and Cheese

6 to 8 servings

Preheat the oven to 350 degrees.

In a small mixing bowl, combine the cheese and garlic.

Try to pick potatoes of uniform size. Wash the potatoes. In a large saucepan, bring to a boil enough salted water to cover the potatoes; add the potatoes and simmer, covered, until barely tender, about 7 to 10 minutes. Drain the potatoes, and when cool enough to handle, peel away the skin and grate on the coarse side of a hand grater or in a food processor fitted with the shredding disk. Grate the potatoes in batches of three, layering one batch of potatoes in the casserole before grating the next batch. It is important to layer the potatoes this way so they don't turn gray.

Place the first third of your grated potatoes in a greased, deep 2½-quart casserole. Sprinkle generously with salt and pepper and a third of the garlic-cheese mixture, then slowly pour just enough of the cream down the sides of the dish to cover the potatoes. Repeat the grating and the layering in this manner for 2 more layers, ending with cheese on the top. The cream should come up to about two-thirds of the potatoes; if you do not have enough cream, finish with whole milk. Dust some paprika over the top of the dish.

Bake the potatoes for 30 minutes, covered,

2 *cups sharp Cheddar cheese, grated*

1 *large clove garlic, finely chopped*

6 to 8 *medium red (new) potatoes, about 2½ pounds*

Salt and freshly ground black pepper to taste

About 1 pint whipping cream

Paprika

then remove the cover and bake for another 20 to 30 minutes, until the cream is absorbed and the top is golden brown and bubbly. Remove from the oven. *At this point, the potatoes can be held, covered, for 3 to 4 hours.*

About 30 minutes before serving, preheat the oven to 375 degrees and reheat the potatoes, covered, for 15 to 20 minutes until heated through. Serve immediately.

Spinach Salad

6 servings

4	*slices bacon*
1½	*pounds loose fresh spinach* OR *1 10-ounce bag fresh spinach*
½	*pound fresh mushrooms, thinly sliced*

Dressing

½	*teaspoon dry mustard*
⅛	*teaspoon sugar*
	Salt and freshly ground black pepper to taste
1	*clove garlic, halved*
2	*tablespoons cider vinegar*
1	*tablespoon white wine*
1	*teaspoon soy sauce*
½	*cup olive oil* OR *a combination of olive and vegetable oil*

In a medium skillet, fry the bacon over medium heat until crisp. Drain well on paper towels, and when cool enough to handle, crumble into small pieces; reserve.

Wash the spinach and break off the stems. Dry the leaves thoroughly and tear into bite-size pieces. Place the leaves in a lidded container lined with paper towels, or seal them in a plastic bag. *At this point, the spinach can be stored in the refrigerator for several hours.*

In a medium mixing bowl, prepare the dressing by combining the mustard, sugar, salt, pepper, and garlic. Stir in the vinegar, wine, and soy sauce, then whisk in the oil until everything is well blended. *At this point, the dressing can be held for several hours; or it can be stored in the refrigerator, covered, for 1 to 2 days.* If the dressing becomes too thick in the refrigerator, thin it with a little white wine.

Shortly before serving, put the spinach in a large salad bowl and top with the bacon and the mushrooms. Discard the garlic from the salad dressing and whisk the dressing again until it is well mixed. Pour it over the spinach and toss until the spinach leaves and the mushrooms are thoroughly coated. Serve on individual salad plates.

Cranberry–Orange Sherbet

Into a large mixing bowl, spoon the sherbet and let it soften slightly. Mix in the cranberry-orange relish and walnuts until thoroughly blended. Spoon the sherbet into a plastic container and freeze until firm, about 24 hours. *At this point, the sherbet can be stored in the freezer, covered, for 2 to 3 months.* Remove from the freezer 10 to 15 minutes before serving.

1   *quart orange sherbet*

1   *cup cranberry-orange relish*

½   *cup walnuts, finely chopped*

Spinach Soup
  Meat and Zucchini Moussaka
    Vegetable Salad
    with Feta Cheese Dressing
      Toasted Pocket Bread
        Fig Whip

When we decided to write this book, the second rule we established after "quick and easy menus" was "no casseroles or stews" for the main course. Without any difficulty or temptation, we have managed to abide by these rules, except for a vegetarian casserole (see p. 160) and the Greek moussaka presented here. We happen to be partial to moussaka, enjoying its light and airy layers of meat, vegetables, and cheesey custard much more than its ponderous Italian counterpart, lasagna. And we wanted to tuck in a somewhat ethnic menu somewhere, although our considerable experimentations with a moussaka have resulted in a rather personalized—Americanized?—dish. Our variations include the use of zucchini instead of eggplant, an idea we picked up from a close friend, Daphne Metaxis Hartwig, who has written a Greek cookbook; this substitution saves time and gives the dish a more interesting texture.

The moussaka does take a little time to prepare even without the eggplant, but it—along with everything else in the menu except the toasted bread—can be made at least a day in advance. In fact, the flavor of moussaka actually improves if it is allowed to stand for a day, so we recommend putting together the dish and baking it the night before or early in the morning the day of the party. You should have no trouble locating ground lamb. Most grocery stores carry it in the form of lamb patties; if you don't find any, ask the butcher for it. The moussaka can be made entirely with ground beef, but a special taste will be missing. Speaking of taste, we like the tangy flavor of dry curd cottage cheese in the moussaka better than the blander ricotta cheese, although the latter is considered more authentic.

We start the meal with a very light and very pretty soup—as green as Ireland's countryside. We have never encountered anyone who didn't polish it off, including people who normally shun spinach. Notice that during the time it takes to eat the soup course, the moussaka is "settling" after being removed from the oven; this facilitates cutting it into squares.

The distinctive ingredient in our vegetable salad is feta cheese, a Greek standby. We find it readily available in the East, frequently to be found in the produce department near the lettuce. If you should have trouble finding feta cheese, you can substitute some form of blue cheese like Roquefort (we happen to like blue cheese just as well as the feta in the salad). The combinations in the salad can be varied, if necessary; for example, you could omit the green beans and add more carrots. And we can't stress enough the importance of blotting away all the moisture from your cooked vegetables; otherwise, you will end up with a runny, watery salad dressing.

The pocket bread which has recently become popular for sandwiches has origins in the Mediterranean. We have come up with a treatment that makes it a tasty yet still authentic accompaniment to moussaka and salad. Generally, you will find two sizes of pocket bread in supermarkets—one about 3 or 4 inches in diameter and the other about 5 or 6 inches. The larger size is preferable because you can cut the bread into manageable strips. You can't do much with the smaller bread except pull it apart and serve as is.

The fig whip recipe has been in one of our family's recipe boxes for several generations. It is about as close to heaven as you can get in terms of richness. We can't imagine a better way to indulge in figs.

Except for the elegant dessert, this is an unpretentious, robust meal which calls for a straightforward red wine such as a Burgundy, a Barbera, or some other red table wine put out by a reputable firm. To carry through the Greek theme, you could offer a popular and good Greek table wine called Demestica.

Spinach Soup

6 servings

2	*10-ounce packages frozen chopped spinach*
6	*cups chicken broth* OR *chicken stock*
⅛	*teaspoon ground nutmeg*
	Salt and freshly ground black pepper to taste
2	*teaspoons red wine vinegar*
2	to 3 *tablespoons butter*

In a large saucepan, cook the spinach according to the package directions until barely tender; do not overcook. Drain the spinach in a sieve, pressing out all excess liquid with the back of a large spoon.

In the same large saucepan, heat the chicken broth just to boiling. In an electric blender or food processor fitted with the steel blade, place the spinach with 1 or 2 cups of the chicken broth and purée until smooth (this will have to be done in 2 or 3 batches). Return the puréed spinach to the saucepan and season with nutmeg, salt, and pepper. *At this point, the soup can be held off the heat for 3 to 5 hours.*

Shortly before serving, reheat the soup to piping hot without letting it boil. Stir in the vinegar and butter, and taste to correct seasoning. When the butter has melted, serve immediately in warm bowls or cups.

Meat and Zucchini Moussaka

6 to 8 servings

2	*tablespoons butter*
2	*medium onions, finely chopped*
2	*cloves garlic, finely chopped*
1	*pound ground chuck*
¾	*pound ground lamb*
1	*6-ounce can tomato paste*

In a large skillet, melt 2 tablespoons butter over low heat and sauté the onions and garlic until tender; do not brown. Spoon the contents of the skillet into a bowl and reserve.

There should be enough butter left on the bottom of your skillet for browning the meat; if not, you can add just enough oil to cover the surface. Increase the heat to medium and brown the beef and lamb, breaking the meat up into small pieces as it cooks. When the meat has lost its pink color, drain off all the fat (this is especially important with lamb fat). Scrape the onion mixture into the meat, and add to the skillet the tomato paste, parsley, cinnamon, ground cloves, salt, pepper, water, and wine. Cook the meat mixture over low heat, uncovered, stirring occasionally, until the liquids have been absorbed. Let the meat cool. Beat the 2 eggs and add to the meat, along with the sesame seeds and ¼ cup of the Parmesan cheese.

Wash the zucchini, trim off the ends (but do not peel the skin), and slice lengthwise into ¼-inch slices. In a greased 9 x 13 x 2-inch shallow baking dish, arrange half the slices over the bottom of the dish and top with half the meat mixture. Layer the rest of the zucchini slices in the dish and cover with the rest of the meat.

Preheat the oven to 375 degrees.

To prepare the sauce: In a medium saucepan, melt 4 tablespoons butter over low heat. Off the heat, stir in the flour until smooth. Slowly pour in the warm milk, stirring constantly. Return the sauce to the heat and cook, stirring constantly, until thickened. Remove from the heat and add the salt.

Beat the 3 eggs with a whisk until really frothy. Spoon a little bit of the sauce into the eggs, whisking constantly, then add the eggs to the sauce and stir until blended. Return the sauce to the stove, stir in the ricotta cheese, and continue stirring over very low heat until the cheese has melted (cottage cheese won't melt entirely). Pour the sauce over the meat, using a fork carefully along the sides of the dish to let the sauce trickle down through the layers, filling up the air spaces. Sprinkle the remaining Parmesan cheese over the top and sprinkle the surface with a little paprika. Bake for 1 hour.

At this point, the moussaka can be cooled completely and refrigerated, covered, overnight; or it can be held at room temperature for several hours. If the moussaka has been refrigerated, let it come to room temperature for 45 to 60 minutes before reheating in a 350-

¼ *cup fresh parsley, finely chopped*

¾ *teaspoon cinnamon*

¼ *teaspoon ground cloves*

1 *teaspoon salt*

Freshly ground black pepper to taste

2 *tablespoons water*

¼ *cup dry red wine*

2 *eggs*

⅓ *cup sesame seeds*

¾ *cup Parmesan cheese* OR *Romano cheese, grated*

4 *medium to large zucchini, about 2½ pounds*

Paprika

Sauce

4 *tablespoons butter*

3 *tablespoons flour*

2 *cups milk, warmed*

½ *teaspoon salt*

3 *eggs*

1 *cup ricotta cheese* OR *small, dry curd cottage cheese*

degree oven for 30 to 45 minutes. If held at room temperature, reheat the moussaka for 20 to 30 minutes. Let the moussaka stand for 10 minutes before cutting into squares and serving.

Vegetable Salad with Feta Cheese Dressing

6 to 8 servings

½ *pound fresh green beans*

2 *carrots*

1 *10-ounce package frozen peas, thawed*

1 *16-ounce can chickpeas (garbanzo beans), drained*

1 *green pepper*

Dressing

1¼ *cups mayonnaise*

½ *cup feta cheese* OR *blue cheese, crumbled*

2 *teaspoons lemon juice*

2 *tablespoons fresh parsley, finely chopped*

⅛ *teaspoon cayenne pepper*

   Salt to taste

6 *to 8 lettuce leaves*

Break off the stem end of the beans and snap them into approximately 2-inch lengths. Trim the ends of the carrots, scrape them, and cut into a ½-inch dice. In a large saucepan, bring to a boil 3 to 4 quarts salted water and plunge in the beans and carrots. Cover until the water returns to the boil, uncover and boil for no more than 3 to 5 minutes, until the vegetables are barely tender.

While the beans and carrots are cooking, place the peas in a colander. When the beans and carrots are done, pour them into the colander along with the boiling water, which will cook the peas sufficiently for the salad. Run cold water over the vegetables to cool quickly.

Dry the cooked vegetables and the chickpeas *thoroughly* on paper towels. Wash and seed the green pepper and cut into a ½-inch dice. Put all the vegetables into a large bowl.

In a medium mixing bowl, prepare the dressing by combining the mayonnaise, cheese, lemon juice, parsley, cayenne pepper, and salt; pour over the vegetables and gently stir to blend. *At this point, the salad can be stored in the refrigerator, covered, for 1 day.* Serve on individual lettuce leaves.

Toasted Pocket Bread

Makes 24 bread strips

Stack the breads and cut through the middle with a bread knife; then cut off the rounded sides so you are left with 2 stacks of strips, each measuring about 2 x 6 inches (see diagram). Gently separate each attached strip either with your fingers or a bread knife, ending up with 24 strips of bread. Butter the strips on the rough side and sprinkle the cumin over the butter. *At this point, the strips can be wrapped in foil or sealed in plastic wrap and refrigerated for 1 day.* Let come to room temperature for 1 hour before cooking.

Preheat the oven to BROIL.

Place half the bread strips, buttered side up, on an ungreased cookie sheet and broil 6 inches from the heat for 2 to 3 minutes, watching constantly. Repeat the procedure with the remaining bread strips. Serve the bread strips immediately in a cloth-covered bread basket. Or you can let the strips cool, store them in a covered container for up to 2 days, and when ready to use, reheat in foil at 350 degrees for 20 minutes.

6 *pocket breads (also called pita), 5 to 6 inches in diameter*

5 *to 6 tablespoons butter, softened to room temperature*

4 *teaspoons ground cumin*

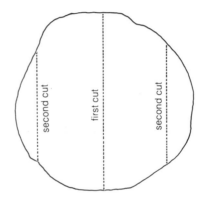

Fig Whip

6 to 7 servings

In a medium saucepan, place the figs, sugar, and enough water to barely cover, about 1 cup. Bring to a boil, then lower the heat and simmer, covered, until the figs are tender, about 45 minutes.

In a food processor fitted with the steel blade, purée the figs and the cooking liquid until fairly smooth; you can also mash the figs by hand or purée through a food mill. Scrape

4 *to 6 ounces dried figs*

½ *cup sugar*

½ *tablespoon unflavored gelatin*

½ *teaspoon almond extract*

1 *cup heavy cream*

the figs into a large mixing bowl and let cool. Dissolve the gelatin in about 2 tablespoons of cold water and add to the figs. Stir in the almond extract.

In a large mixing bowl, whip the cream to stiff peaks and fold into the figs until thoroughly blended. Chill the dessert until firm, about 4 to 6 hours. *At this point, the fig whip can be stored in the refrigerator, covered, for 1 to 2 days.*

Salmon Bisque
  Veal Scallopini with
  Mustard and Marsala
    Mushroom Risotto
      Buttered Green Beans
_____*Brandied Fruit Compote*

We believe this is a flawless dinner with which only a vegetarian could find fault. Opening with the rose-colored salmon soup flecked with the green of dill and pepper and closing with a very pretty, bright, brandy-spiked fruit compote, the dinner is one of two in the book featuring veal. For a while we were going to include only one veal recipe in the book, but then we realized that ever since the price of veal hit the rafters several years ago, people are ordering more veal when they eat in restaurants. We decided that people love veal, they're just boycotting it for home consumption. This could be because when someone pays through the nose for veal, he or she wants to be sure of not only getting a good piece of meat but also of knowing how to cook it. When in doubt about either of these criteria, people put their trust in restaurants.

We have taken the guess work out of dealing with veal at home. Of course we can do nothing about its cost, but we figure you're not going to mind spending money on certain friends, especially when you can translate expenditure into a gemlike yet foolproof meal. Veal scallopini usually gets cooked very quickly and must be eaten immediately; also, it is cooked as a flat piece of meat, which means cooking two or three batches when you're feeding six people, because all of the meat can't fit into one skillet. We have changed this standard procedure by shaping the veal into compact rolls which fit in a single skillet, and cooking them in a delectable Marsala sauce for about half an hour; this not only insures tenderizing even a carelessly cut piece of veal, it also means that the veal can stand in the sauce during the entire cocktail hour. In fact, the only demanding routine you need to perform in the kitchen before dinner is tossing the beans in some butter to warm them up.

A word about buying the veal. If you are on good terms with

your butcher and trust him, let him know your needs in advance of the day of your purchase. Tell him you would like 12 veal scallops (this is a thin cut taken from the leg of a calf), each measuring approximately 3 to 4 inches by 8 to 10 inches; the total weight should be 2 pounds (if the butcher's habit is to slice veal quite thin, you will end up with more than 12 scallops). If you have to buy the veal in prewrapped packages, chances are that you will get a mixed bag of good-sized pieces and little dinky pieces; the latter can be rolled up, but they have a tendency to dry out while cooking.

One variation on the risotto we want to mention is to omit the mushrooms, and instead stir in ¼ teaspoon of saffron at the end of the cooking. This gives the rice a rich golden color, and of course the recipe is made easier because there's no cleaning and sautéing of mushrooms. The problem with saffron is that it's horrendously expensive unless you can find a bargain at a health food store or gourmet food shop.

The green beans are a part of this menu mostly for a touch of green on individual dinner plates. However, the meal is filling enough without a vegetable, so if you want to omit the beans to save work and time, please do.

You can present this meal in one of two ways. The veal rolls can go on a small platter by themselves, with the rice being served perhaps from the casserole dish in which you placed it on reserve; the beans, too, would be served in a separate bowl. This presentation helps keep the rice warm for those who come back for second helpings. Another way is to mound the rice in the middle of a large serving platter (you could keep some of the rice in the oven for seconds) and arrange the veal rolls around the rice; this approach is somewhat more dramatic. A divided platter, if you have one, would work well here, too.

The only thing that really needs to be said about the fruit compote is to use a good quality of brandy—not some cheap variety you keep in the pantry for cooking purposes. The compote is delicious all by itself, but for color and taste contrasts, consider topping each serving with some sour cream or regular cream; or if you have the time to make it, some crème fraîche would be even better.

The wine to go with this particular treatment of veal can be practically any light or medium red which you happen to like. One of our favorites with the meal is a Côtes-du-Rhône.

Salmon Bisque

In a large saucepan, melt 4 tablespoons of the butter over low-medium heat and sauté the onion and green pepper until tender. Off the heat, stir the flour into the vegetables until smooth, then add the chicken stock and the milk and stir until smooth. Return the saucepan to the stove and cook over low heat, stirring constantly, until slightly thickened. Season with the dillweed, salt, and pepper.

Remove any bone or gray skin from the salmon. In an electric blender or food processor fitted with the steel blade, place the salmon and the contents of the saucepan and purée until smooth; this will have to be done in 2 or 3 batches. Return the bisque to the saucepan and reheat over low heat to let the flavors blend, about 15 minutes; stir occasionally. *At this point, the bisque can be held off the heat for 3 to 5 hours, or it can be stored in the refrigerator, covered, for 2 to 3 days.*

Shortly before serving, reheat the bisque over low-medium heat until it is piping hot. Stir in the cream, taste for seasoning, and reheat again without letting the bisque boil. Stir in the remaining 2 tablespoons butter until it melts and serve immediately with a sprinkle of dill on top.

6 *tablespoons butter*

1 *small onion, finely chopped*

⅓ *cup green pepper, finely chopped*

4 *tablespoons flour*

2 *cups chicken broth* OR *chicken stock*

2 *cups whole milk*

½ *teaspoon dillweed*

Salt and freshly ground white pepper to taste

1 *16-ounce can* red *salmon, drained*

½ *cup heavy cream*

Veal Scallopini with Mustard and Marsala

6 servings

2	to 2¼ *pounds veal scallops, cut thin*
	About 2 tablespoons Dijon mustard
	Salt and freshly ground black pepper to taste
	Flour for dredging
3	*tablespoons butter*
3	*tablespoons vegetable oil* OR *a combination of vegetable and olive oil*
1	*medium onion, finely chopped*
½	*teaspoon oregano*
¼	*teaspoon thyme*
1	*bay leaf*
1	*1 x 2-inch piece lemon peel*
¾	*cup beef broth* OR *beef stock*
¾	*cup Marsala wine*
1	*egg yolk*
2	*tablespoons heavy cream*
¼	*cup fresh parsley, finely chopped*

Dry the veal on paper towels and flatten with the heel of your hand or with a meat pounder; it's a good idea to do this on a piece of waxed paper on a cutting board. Spread one side of each veal scallop with ¼ to ½ teaspoon of mustard, depending on the size of your scallop; you want a thin coating. Sprinkle the scallops with salt and pepper. Roll up each scallop and tie in the middle with fine kitchen string; or you can secure the scallops with toothpicks as long as you break off any protruding ends. Dredge each rolled-up scallop in the flour and shake off any excess. You should have at least 2 scallops per person.

In a large skillet, melt the butter and oil over medium heat and when the foam has subsided, add the veal and brown until golden on all sides; you will probably have to do this in 2 batches. Lower the heat, add the onion and herbs to the skillet, and cook until the onion is tender. Add the lemon peel, beef broth, and Marsala and simmer, covered, for 20 minutes, basting and turning the veal rolls often. Off the heat, remove the bay leaf and lemon peel. Cut away the kitchen string or extract the toothpicks (the latter is slightly more difficult, which gives an advantage to using kitchen string). *At this point, the veal can be held, covered, while the guests enjoy their drinks.*

Shortly before serving, reheat the veal over low heat. In a small mixing bowl, beat the egg yolk and beat in the cream. Spoon a little of the veal sauce into the egg mixture, whipping it very fast so nothing curdles. Slowly add the egg mixture to the sauce in the skillet, stirring constantly until the sauce is thickened. Serve the veal rolls with the sauce spooned over and parsley sprinkled over all.

Mushroom Risotto

In a large skillet, melt 3 tablespoons of the butter over low-medium heat and sauté the mushrooms until tender; remove from the heat and reserve.

In a large saucepan, melt 3 tablespoons of the butter over low-medium heat and sauté the onion until tender. Add the rice and continue to sauté for about 3 minutes, making sure the rice is thoroughly coated with the butter. Pour in the chicken broth, bring to a boil, then lower the heat and simmer the rice, covered, until it is cooked and the liquid is absorbed, about 20 to 25 minutes. Off the heat, stir in the mushrooms, saffron, cheese, and the remaining 2 tablespoons butter. *At this point, the rice can be held, covered, for 2 to 3 hours.*

About 30 minutes before serving, preheat the oven to 350 degrees.

Add about ¼ cup tepid water to the risotto and toss gently. Spoon into a greased, deep 2½- or 3-quart casserole and reheat the risotto, covered, for 15 to 20 minutes. Serve immediately.

8	*tablespoons (1 stick) butter*
12	*ounces mushrooms, thinly sliced*
1	*medium onion, finely chopped*
1½	*cups long-grain white rice*
3	*cups chicken broth* OR *chicken stock*
¼	*teaspoon saffron* OR *tumeric (optional)*
¼	*cup Parmesan cheese* OR *Romano cheese, grated*

Buttered Green Beans

Snap off the stem end of the beans and break into approximately 2-inch lengths. In a large kettle, bring 4 to 5 quarts salted water to a boil, plunge in the beans, cover until the water returns to a boil and then cook, uncovered, for 5 to 7 minutes, until barely tender. Drain in a colander and run cold water over the beans. Pat the beans dry on paper towels. *At*

1½	*pounds green beans*
4	*to 6 tablespoons butter*
	Salt and freshly ground black pepper to taste

this point, the beans can be held for several hours or they can be refrigerated, covered, for 1 day. Let the beans come to room temperature for 45 to 60 minutes before reheating.

In a large skillet, melt the butter over medium heat until bubbly. Add the beans, salt, and pepper, and sauté gently over low-medium heat, tossing constantly, until the beans are completely heated through. Cover the beans to keep warm while enjoying your salmon bisque. When ready to serve, place in a warm serving bowl and pour on the butter.

Brandied Fruit Compote

6 servings

4	*ounces dried apricots*
¾	*cup light brown sugar, packed*
3	*ounces brandy*
6	*ounces dried, pitted prunes*
1	*16-ounce can sliced cling peaches, drained*
6	*to 8 tablespoons sour cream* OR *heavy cream (optional)*

In a 2-quart bowl or deep dish, layer the apricots; sprinkle over the fruit ¼ cup of the brown sugar and 1 ounce of the brandy. Arrange the prunes over the apricots and sprinkle over them another ¼ cup of the sugar and 1 ounce of the brandy. Place the peaches over the prunes and add the remaining sugar and brandy over all. Do not stir or toss the layers of fruit.

Refrigerate the compote, covered, for a minimum of 1 day. At the end of a day, you can stir the fruit. *At this point, the compote can be stored in the refrigerator for 1 to 2 weeks.* The longer it sits in the refrigerator, the tastier it will be.

Serve the compote in dessert dishes with a dollop of sour cream on each serving, if desired.

Cream of Lima Bean Soup
Roast Loin of Pork with Onion Stuffing
Green and Yellow Squash with Dill
Raspberry–Amaretto Sundae

When we were growing up, the fancy meal of the week was dished up right after church on Sunday and usually featured something special and relatively expensive such as a ham, leg of lamb, or pork roast. These meats were cooked in a most straightforward manner—some brown sugar on the ham, and salt and pepper on the others which, unless the meat got overcooked, yielded the unadorned flavor of the meat along with some delicious pan gravy. Even after we learned to cook and began entertaining in our own homes, we often served those standbys of long-ago Sundays—especially leg of lamb and pork roast seasoned with things like garlic, thyme, and rosemary. Unfortunately, over the last several years a leg of lamb has become almost unaffordable, and most pork has become as dry and tough as a brand-new baseball mitt. While we regretfully excluded the leg of lamb from our book, we decided to rise to the challenge of how to put a little bit of tenderness back into a pork roast. Our solution: a mild and delectable onion stuffing that imparts moistness to the meat while not detracting at all from its flavor.

Boneless pork roasts are rolled just once and tied. If you were to take such a roast home and untie it, you'd have a fairly small and very chunky piece of meat lying in front of you, completely inappropriate for stuffing. What you want to do when you have picked out your 4-pound roast is hand it to the butcher and tell him to butterfly it. This means he will cut clear through the middle of the meat almost to the other side, a procedure which doubles the surface of the meat when you lay it out flat. It doesn't hurt to caution the butcher not to cut the pork all the way through, and not to cut any holes in the meat while doing the butterflying.

Most of us think of lima beans as a pretty boring vegetable unless accompanied by corn, but when baby limas are combined with sage, garlic, cream, and a dash of vinegar, they constitute a marvelous soup, one that goes especially well before our pork roast. While regular lima beans could be used, we have found that the skins do not purée as thoroughly in the food processor as do the baby limas; this results in a soup that has more texture than is desirable. In fact, if you use regular lima beans, you probably should force them through a sieve or a food mill to get rid of the skins instead of using the food processor or electric blender (the food processor is really the best appliance for this recipe). Our directions call for using popcorn or parsley as a garnish, but the former is far more attention-getting and tastes great with the soup. So think about making a batch of popcorn for the kids prior to your party, and reserving some to float on the surface of each serving of soup.

The squash must be cooked just before sitting down to the soup course; if you cook it in advance and hold, it will be tasty but limp. What you can do to save time in the kitchen is slice the squash shortly before your guests arrive. However, cut squash secretes a lot of juice which you want to get rid of before cooking. Therefore we suggest that as you slice the squash, you spread the slices on paper towels, layering one towel on top of the other, and placing everything in some kind of container to put in the refrigerator.

We like to use the food processor's ⅛-inch slicer disk to cut the squash. This yields paper-thin slices which cook very fast and take on a more buttery flavor than thicker slices; also, you don't need to use as much butter. However, the ⅛-inch disk is a special attachment which we're not going to insist you run out and buy; so if you don't own it, the regular slicer attachment or a hand grater is acceptable. You might need to increase the butter by a tablespoon, though.

Amaretto has become such a popular liqueur that we decided to feature it in a dessert. As you probably know, Amaretto derives its flavor from almonds, so we have capitalized on that fact by stirring lots of sliced almonds into the raspberry sherbet concoction, which gives it a wonderful and quite unexpected texture of crunchiness. The liqueur itself is an ingredient both in the sherbet and the sauce. This is one of the book's most visually appealing desserts, with the deep red sauce of the raspberries spilling over the bricks of vivid pink sherbet.

A young red wine goes well with pork flavored with onion— perhaps a Beaujolais from France (especially a Fleurie), a California Zinfandel, or Italy's Valpolicella.

Cream of Lima Bean Soup

6 servings

In a large saucepan, melt the butter over low-medium heat and sauté the onion and garlic until tender; stir in the sage, salt, and pepper. Add the lima beans and 1 cup of the chicken broth; bring to a boil over high heat while separating the beans with a fork. Cover the saucepan, reduce the heat to a simmer, and cook until tender, about 10 to 15 minutes.

In a small mixing bowl, beat together the cream and vinegar. In the container of an electric blender or a food processor fitted with the steel blade, put the bean and cream mixtures and the 4 tablespoons of parsley; purée until smooth (this will have to be done in 2 or 3 batches). Return the lima bean purée to the saucepan and stir in the remaining chicken broth. Reheat the soup over low heat, stirring occasionally, about 15 minutes, to let the flavors blend; do not let boil. Taste to correct the seasoning. *At this point, the soup can be held off the heat for 3 to 5 hours, or it can be refrigerated, covered, for 2 to 3 days.*

Shortly before serving, reheat the soup over low-medium heat until it is piping hot, but do not let it boil. Serve immediately with some popcorn floated on top, or with a little parsley sprinkled over each serving.

2 *tablespoons butter*

1 *medium onion, coarsely chopped*

1 *clove garlic, halved*

2 *teaspoons sage*

Salt and freshly ground black pepper to taste

2 *10-ounce packages frozen* baby *lima beans*

4 *cups chicken broth* OR *chicken stock*

1 *cup light cream*

2 *tablespoons red wine vinegar*

4 *tablespoons fresh parsley, finely chopped*

Popcorn OR *parsley for garnish*

Roast Loin of Pork with Onion Stuffing

6 servings

3½	to 4 *pound boneless pork roast, loin end*
4	*tablespoons butter*
2	*medium onions, finely chopped*
1½	*cups fresh bread crumbs*
½	*cup Gruyère cheese* OR *Swiss cheese, grated*
¼	*cup fresh parsley, finely chopped*
½	*tablespoon chili powder*
	Salt and freshly ground black pepper to taste
2	*egg yolks, beaten*
	About 3 tablespoons heavy cream
¼	*cup dry vermouth* OR *dry white wine*
	Paprika

Ask your butcher to butterfly the pork roast and caution him not to make any holes in the meat. He will probably retie the roast with string, in which case you will have to remove the string at home.

In a medium skillet, melt the butter over low-medium heat and sauté the onions until tender; let the onions cool. Stir into the onions the bread crumbs, cheese, 3 tablespoons of the parsley, chili powder, salt, pepper, and egg yolks; blend thoroughly. Add the cream a little at a time, until the stuffing has a thick but spreadable consistency.

Pat the pork roast dry with paper towels and season both sides with salt and pepper. Spread the onion stuffing evenly over the underside of the roast to about 1 inch of the edge. Roll up the roast like a jelly roll and tie securely in several places with kitchen string. *At this point, the roast can be stored in the refrigerator for 2 to 3 hours.* Let it come to room temperature for 50 to 60 minutes before cooking.

Preheat the oven to 325 degrees.

Place the pork roast in a roasting pan (put a rack on the bottom if the pan doesn't have a built-in rack or tree pattern) and rub the surface with the vermouth. Sprinkle the top of the roast with more salt and pepper, and dust with a little paprika. Cook the roast, uncovered, for approximately 2½ hours, or 40 minutes per pound. Let the roast stand for 15 to 20 minutes before carving.

When ready to serve, place the pork roast on a warm serving platter and remove the string. Carve the roast into ¾-inch-thick slices and garnish with the remaining parsley.

Green and Yellow Squash with Dill

6 servings

Wash the zucchini and yellow squash and trim away the ends, but do not peel the skin. Using a food processor fitted with the slicing disk, the side of a hand grater, or a very sharp knife, slice the squash into very thin rounds, about ⅛-inch thick, if possible (the ⅛-inch slicing disk attachment for the food processor works best here; it usually has to be purchased as a special attachment).*

In a large skillet, melt the butter and oil over medium heat and when the foam has subsided, lower the heat and sauté the garlic quickly until tender but not browned. Add the squash, dill, salt, and pepper, and toss to coat the squash with the butter and oil. Continue tossing and cooking until barely tender, about 10 minutes. Off the heat, cover and keep warm during the soup course. Spoon into a warm bowl and serve immediately.

* If you cannot slice the 2 squashes as thin as ⅛-inch, you'll need to buy a little more squash—about 1½ pounds of each variety.

1 *pound zucchini*

1 *pound yellow squash*

3 *tablespoons butter*

3 *tablespoons olive oil*

1 *large clove garlic, finely chopped*

2 *teaspoons dillweed*

Salt and freshly ground black pepper to taste

Raspberry–Amaretto Sundae

6 servings

In a large mixing bowl, combine the sherbet, almonds, sugar, and Amaretto until thoroughly blended. In another large mixing bowl, whip the cream to stiff peaks and fold into the sherbet mixture until completely blended; you should not see any streaks. Pour the sherbet

1 *pint red raspberry sherbet, slightly softened*

½ *cup sliced almonds*

¼ *cup confectioners' sugar*

¼ cup Amaretto liqueur

1 cup heavy cream

Sauce

1 10-ounce package frozen red raspberries, thawed

1 teaspoon lemon juice

1 teaspoon cornstarch

3 tablespoons Amaretto liqueur

into a 4 x 8 x 3-inch loaf pan and freeze for 1 day (if you do not have a loaf pan in this size, you can pour the sherbet into any freezer container, but you will have to serve the dessert in scoops instead of in slices). *At this point, the sherbet can be stored in the freezer, covered, for 1 to 2 months.*

The sauce should be made several hours in advance of serving, and it can be made several days before your party. Drain the juice from the berries into a small saucepan; reserve the berries. Add the lemon juice to the raspberry juice and bring to a boil. Blend the cornstarch with about 1 tablespoon of cold water and pour this into the raspberry juice; stir until thickened. Off the heat, return the berries to the thickened raspberry juice and stir in the Amaretto. *At this point, the sauce can be held for several hours; or it can be stored in the refrigerator, covered, for several days.* Let the sauce come to room temperature for 30 to 45 minutes before serving.

When ready to serve, slice the sherbet into 6 slices and place on individual dessert plates. Pour a little of the raspberry sauce onto each portion and serve immediately.

Sauerkraut Salad
Ham Poached
in Cider with Madeira Sauce
Spinach and
Escarole Baked with Cheese
Banana Pudding
with Hot Rum–Butter Sauce

Many years ago, when we were just beginning to learn what good food was all about, one of us was invited to dinner at the apartment of a successful writer friend who served a main course of meat loaf. We didn't know whether to be shocked at the gaucheness of such a choice or impressed by the friend's boldness—after all, it *was* an excellent meat loaf. Obviously, that meat loaf was a memorable meal, a sure tribute to our friend's imagination and talent. Thus, the recollection of that long-ago dinner has encouraged us to build a menu around another rather pedestrian food—ham.

This is no ordinary ham, however. What happens to the meat in the cooking causes it to achieve new heights of gustatory excitement. First, the thick slice of ham is poached for over an hour in a bath of fresh apple cider. This treatment rids the ham of that extra bit of saltiness that usually keeps one swilling water far into the night. What remains is a truer ham flavor tinged with the sweet bitiness of apples. Next, a wonderfully rich sauce is produced by combining the poaching liquor with tomato paste, heavy cream, and Madeira wine. The ham is then sliced into strips and covered with generous quantities of the sauce. Your guests will not believe that ham can be such a pleasure to eat until they have tried your recipe.

The first course, sauerkraut salad, is a curiosity piece which we adapted from a similar appetizer at a wildly popular seafood restaurant in our area. There are crocks of the salad on every table in the restaurant for diners to eat while sipping cocktails. You might want to serve plain or sesame-coated breadsticks with the salad, or crackers flavored with poppy seeds or caraway seeds. The salad keeps for a long time in the refrigerator, seeming to improve in taste as it ages.

The dinner plate in this menu is a treat for the eyes because beside the rosy-red ham in its velvety sauce sits the deep green square of baked spinach and escarole. The latter dish combines two extremely nutritious vegetables with a blend of two cheeses and sour cream, plus the notable seasonings of celery salt and nutmeg. The overall tanginess of these ingredients is the perfect foil to the rich, vaguely sweet ham. The ham's sauce also tastes delicious with the vegetables.

All we need to say about the dessert of banana pudding with a hot sauce composed of rum and butter is that diners will loosen their belts or want to go for a walk after they've consumed it.

Most people think rosé wine is the only wine to be drunk with ham, but we don't believe there is ever only one wine to go with a particular food. Anyway, this ham dish would not marry well with most rosés. We suggest a fairly young red wine from France such as a Beaujolais, a Volnay, or a Côtes-du-Rhône. Or if you want to stick with American wines, try a Ruby Cabernet or a Gamay Beaujolais. Italy's Valpolicella would be a fine choice, too.

Sauerkraut Salad

6 to 8 servings

In a large colander, place the sauerkraut and squeeze out all the juice; you will have to use your hands for this. In a large mixing bowl, place the sauerkraut, onion, green and red pepper, and carrot.

In a small mixing bowl, whisk together the sugar, vinegar, and vegetable oil; pour over the sauerkraut and toss to thoroughly blend. *At this point, the salad must be stored in the refrigerator, covered, for a minimum of 2 days, or for as long as 1 week; toss occasionally.* When ready to serve, toss the salad again and serve on individual salad plates with melba toast rounds or breadsticks.

1	*2-pound package fresh sauerkraut, drained*
¼	*cup onion, finely chopped*
¼	*cup green pepper, finely diced*
¼	*cup red pepper, finely diced*
¼	*cup carrots, grated*
¼	*cup sugar*
¼	*cup white vinegar*
1½	*tablespoons vegetable oil*

Ham Poached in Cider with Madeira Sauce

6 servings

Pat the ham dry with paper towels and make ¼-inch slashes around the edge of the ham with a sharp knife, about every 3 inches; this will prevent the ham from curling up while cooking. In a large skillet, place the ham and arrange the onion slices on top. Pour in enough apple cider to reach the top of the ham. Bring the cider to a boil, then lower the heat and simmer, covered, for 1¼ hours. Measure out 1½ cups cider liquid for the sauce and reserve; discard the onion. *At this point, the ham can be held warm in the remaining liquid, covered, for 1 to 2 hours.*

1	*ham slice, about 2½ inches thick and weighing 3 pounds*
1	*large onion, sliced*
	Fresh apple cider to cover
4	*tablespoons butter*
4	*tablespoons flour*
1	*tablespoon tomato paste*

3 tablespoons Madeira
   wine

½ cup heavy cream

3 tablespoons fresh par-
   sley, finely chopped

In a medium saucepan, melt the butter over low heat. Off the heat, stir in the flour until smooth, then stir in the tomato paste until smooth. Return the saucepan to the heat and slowly pour in the cider liquid, stirring constantly, until the sauce is thickened. Stir in the Madeira and cream and heat through, but do not allow to boil.

Shortly before serving, reheat the ham in the skillet liquid over low-medium heat until piping hot. Remove the ham with a slotted spatula to a warm serving platter and slice the ham on the diagonal into thin slices. Pour the Madeira sauce over the ham and garnish with the parsley.

Spinach and Escarole Baked with Cheese

6 servings

2 10-ounce packages fro-
   zen chopped spinach

1 medium head escarole
   lettuce

1 medium onion, finely
   chopped

2 cups ricotta cheese OR
   small, dry curd cottage
   cheese

½ cup sour cream

½ cup Parmesan cheese
   OR Romano cheese,
   grated

2 eggs, lightly beaten

2 tablespoons horseradish

In a large saucepan, cook the spinach in 1 cup boiling, salted water until it is thawed, breaking it up with a fork as it cooks to hasten the process. Drain the spinach in a sieve or colander and run cold water over it. Using your hands, squeeze out all the moisture from the spinach and place in a large mixing bowl.

Wash the escarole leaves, break in half, and place in the same saucepan in which you cooked the spinach; don't shake the water off the leaves. Place the escarole over medium-high heat and cook until it is wilted, stirring up the leaves from the bottom as they wilt; this will take about 3 minutes. Drain the escarole in a colander and run cold water over it. Using your hands, squeeze out all the moisture from the escarole and add to the spinach.

To the spinach and escarole, add the onion, ricotta cheese, sour cream, Parmesan cheese, eggs, horseradish, lemon juice, celery salt, nutmeg, salt, and pepper; stir everything gently to thoroughly blend. Spoon the mixture into a greased, shallow 8 x 11 x 2-inch baking dish and smooth over the top. *At this point, the dish can be stored in the refrigerator, covered, for several hours.* Let the dish come to room temperature for 30 to 45 minutes before cooking.

Preheat the oven to 350 degrees.

Bake the spinach and escarole for 40 to 50 minutes, or until a toothpick inserted in the center comes out clean. Cut into squares and serve immediately.

2	*teaspoons lemon juice*
½	*teapoon celery salt*
⅛	*teaspoon nutmeg*
	Salt and freshly ground black pepper to taste

Banana Pudding with Hot Rum–Butter Sauce

6 servings

Preheat the oven to 450 degrees.

In a food processor fitted with the steel blade, place the bananas, sour cream, granulated sugar, flour, eggs, and lemon juice, and process until smooth (you can also blend the ingredients together by hand, mashing the bananas first with a fork). Put the banana mixture into a greased, 9-inch pie plate.

Bake the pudding for 10 minutes at 450 degrees, then reduce the heat to 350 degrees and bake for 30 minutes longer, or until a toothpick inserted in the center comes out clean. Let the pudding cool. *At this point, the pudding can be held at room temperature for 5 to 6 hours, or it can be refrigerated, covered, for 1 day.*

In a small bowl or cup, blend the cornstarch with 2 tablespoons of water. In a medium saucepan, melt the butter over low heat. Add the brown sugar and the ½ cup of water,

4	*very ripe bananas*
1	*cup sour cream*
⅔	*cup granulated sugar*
2	*tablespoons flour*
2	*eggs, well beaten*
1½	*teaspoons lemon juice*

Sauce

1	*tablespoon cornstarch*
4	*tablespoons butter*
½	*cup light brown sugar, packed*
½	*cup water*
¼	*cup dark rum*

and bring just to a boil; remove from the heat and stir in the cornstarch. Return to the heat and cook until thickened. *At this point, the sauce mixture can be cooled and stored in the refrigerator, covered, for several days.*

Just before serving, reheat the sauce mixture over medium heat, stirring; then add the rum and stir to blend. Cut the pudding into pie-shaped wedges and pour the hot rum-butter sauce over each serving.

4

A Pair of Vegetarian Dinner Party Menus

Melon Soup
  Minestrone Casserole
    Beer and Dill Bread
      Green Bean,
      Cheese, and Olive Salad
        Summer Fruits in Soft Custard

While we don't expect our book to be a big seller to vegetarians, we do believe we have created a couple of inspired vegetarian menus which will gain a new respect and enthusiasm among the uninitiated for what is often perceived to be a bland diet. These were difficult menus for us to plan inasmuch as we, too, thought that vegetarian cuisine consisted largely of soy beans, tofu, and brown rice.

A menu can be a work of art, and we think our summertime vegetarian dinner menu is worthy of such a florid description. For one thing, the fruits of a summer garden or farmers' market are represented in every course, from soup to dessert. This bestows upon the cook a sense of accomplishment for having utilized so fully what is at hand. Still, a random harvest or well-stocked produce counter do not preclude an attractive, memorable meal on the table. Color, taste, and texture have to come into play and balance each other. And there should be a few agreeably unexpected combinations.

Our vegetarian dinner begins with one of the prettiest and most refreshing soups we've ever tasted, a melon soup that is the essence of melon flavor, but with some interesting additions which lend subtlety and complexity. Most recipes for melon soup either call for chicken broth (can't use it in a vegetarian dish) or are far too sweet. Our recipe is just the melon, some citrus juice and then—surprise!—a splash of vodka. No one will realize there is vodka in the soup unless you tell, but its presence seems to cut sweetness while heightening flavor. White bowls show off the soup's orange-green color to best advantage. If you want to garnish each bowl, consider two or three melon balls or a sprig of fresh mint, but this really isn't necessary.

We advise you to buy the cantaloupe and honeydew several

days in advance, to give them ample time to ripen. If they should rapidly reach the point at which you need to cut them open, go ahead and make the soup at the same time. We indicate in the recipe that the soup can be refrigerated for 2 to 3 days, but we've stored it for up to a week with no bad effects; the soup can also be frozen. You can substitute another cantaloupe for the honeydew if the latter is unavailable, although the different flavor of honeydew makes for a more interesting soup. You can also substitute another orange melon, such as Persian or musk, for the cantaloupe.

The minestrone casserole will have everyone clamoring for the recipe—at least that has been our experience. Most people can't believe so many vegetables together can taste and look so good! There is no trick to making it; in fact, the preparation is kind of fun. The only insiders' tips we can pass along are: Be sure to taste to correct seasoning because the dish usually needs more salt; and do try to use Gruyère cheese or at least an aged or imported Swiss with some flavor, such as Emmethal. Most Swiss cheeses available in this country are disappointing, which is why we use the more expensive but far more interesting Gruyère. Swiss cheeses keep for a long time under refrigeration.

Accompanying the minestrone casserole is a delicious beer bread which is well-seasoned with dillweed. If you don't grow your own dill, look for the fresh herb in farmers' markets or at roadside produce stands. Otherwise, dried dill is a perfectly fine substitute. We use a regular beer in this recipe rather than low-calorie beer because we think the former has an edge on flavor. This bread is assembled in mere minutes, but if you're even more pressed for time than *we* are, you can always take the acceptably easy way out and serve a good storebought bread—preferably one with substance. Recently a local bakery started offering a rye-dillweed bread which certainly would work nicely here.

Our final blaze of color in the main course is the salad, with its dashes of green, orange, red, and black. In addition to being something of a painter's palette, the salad combines a variety of textures ranging from the very crisp onion rings to the creamy smoothness of cheese. As long as fresh green beans are available, this salad could be served at any time of the year when novelty is wanted. We like it best in summer, however, when green beans are so fresh as to need no more than a couple of minutes of cooking time.

Not to be outdone by preceding courses, the dessert for the vegetarian dinner is an ambrosial creation of whatever fruits are on hand, mixed with a delectable and deliciously cold custard sauce which you can pour from a pitcher. What we wanted to serve here was a fruit dessert that was flexible enough to accommodate those lucky people who from time to time have access to fresh raspberries, blackberries, or boysenberries. People who never see these berry delicacies can use blueberries with no lessening of effect. The main thing to keep in mind with the dessert is that you need a total of about 4 cups of fruit. Within that total, you can use practically any combination of fruit, as long as the fruits blend with each other in taste and color and with the custard sauce.

Because of the delicate interplay of flavors in the minestrone casserole, you'll want a wine that is light and easy to drink—something like a young Beaujolais served slightly chilled (the best Beaujolais is Beaujolais Villages) or a cool, crisp Chablis or Blanc de Blancs. Most simple table wines should serve you well with this menu.

Melon Soup

6 servings

1	*medium cantaloupe*
1	*medium honeydew*
½	*cup fresh lemon juice*
½	*cup fresh orange juice*
6	*tablespoons vodka*

Cut open the melons and remove the seeds. Cut out all the edible flesh in 1- to 2-inch chunks and place in a food processor fitted with the steel blade; process the melons until you have a smooth purée. Add the lemon juice, orange juice, and vodka to the purée, and process briefly to blend; taste to correct the flavor. Refrigerate the soup until well chilled, about 4 hours. *At this point, the soup can be stored in the refrigerator, covered, for 2 to 3 days.*

When ready to serve, stir the soup and pour into bowls or cups.

Minestrone Casserole

6 to 8 servings

2	*large tomatoes, peeled and sliced*
1	*large onion, thinly sliced*
1	*medium to large zucchini, cut into ½-inch slices*
1	*medium to large yellow squash, cut into ½-inch slices*
½	*head Romaine lettuce, shredded*
1	*10-ounce package frozen peas, thawed*

In a deep 4-quart casserole that can be put on top of the stove, make a layer of the tomatoes, onion, zucchini, yellow squash, lettuce, and peas, generously salting each layer and adding some pepper and a tiny pinch of garlic powder to every other layer. Sprinkle the rice over the peas and pour the oil over all, taking care not to disturb the layers of vegetables. Cover and cook over low heat for 10 minutes, or until the tomatoes have released their juice (you will be able to hear this). Stir the vegetables gently to mix them up, then cover the casserole and continue cooking over low heat for another 10 minutes. Remove the casserole from the heat and allow to cool. Taste to correct the seasoning; you will probably need to add more salt. *At this point, the minestrone can be held for 2 to 3 hours.*

When ready to cook, preheat the oven to 400 degrees.

Spoon ¼ to ½ cup of the vegetable liquid from the minestrone and discard. Gently stir in the kidney beans. Pour the minestrone into a greased 9 x 13 x 2-inch shallow baking dish.*

In a medium mixing bowl, beat the eggs well and beat in the cream; stir in the Gruyère cheese and nutmeg. Pour the egg mixture over the minestrone, using a fork or spoon to gently let the mixture seep down into the minestrone. Bake 10 minutes at 400 degrees, then lower the heat to 350 degrees and bake another 20 minutes, or until the minestrone is set and a toothpick inserted in the center comes out clean. Let the minestrone stand for 10 minutes before cutting into squares and serving. Sprinkle each serving with the Parmesan cheese.

* You can also use two 10-inch ceramic quiche dishes with a 1¼-inch depth.

Salt and freshly ground black pepper to taste

Garlic powder to taste

¼ cup long-grain white rice

¼ cup vegetable oil OR a combination of vegetable and olive oil

1 16-ounce can dark red kidney beans, drained

6 eggs

1 cup light cream OR half-and-half cream

1 cup Gruyère cheese OR Swiss cheese, grated

½ teaspoon nutmeg

½ cup Parmesan cheese, grated

Beer and Dill Bread

Makes 1 loaf

Preheat the oven to 375 degrees.

In a large mixing bowl, sift together the flour, baking powder, sugar, salt, and dillweed.

In a small mixing bowl, combine the beer, egg, and vegetable oil. Pour this mixture into the dry ingredients and stir until you have a smooth batter.

Grease a 9 x 5 x 3-inch loaf pan and dust with flour; turn the pan upside down and tap to remove any excess flour. Pour the batter into the loaf pan and smooth it into the corners. Wet the back of a metal spoon and smooth over the top of the batter to even it.

3 cups flour

4 teaspoons baking powder

2 tablespoons sugar

1½ teaspoons salt

1 tablespoon dillweed

1 12-ounce can light beer, at room temperature

1 egg, well beaten

2	tablespoons vegetable oil
3	tablespoons butter, melted

Pour 2 tablespoons of the melted butter over the top of the batter. Bake the bread for 70 minutes or until a straw or knife inserted in the center comes out clean.

Remove the bread from the oven to a cooling rack and brush the top with the remaining 1 tablespoon of melted butter; let cool completely. *At this point, the bread can be held for several hours; or it can be refrigerated, well-wrapped in plastic wrap or foil, for 1 week; or it can be frozen.*

The bread can be served at room temperature or it can be warmed in a 350-degree oven for 20 to 30 minutes, wrapped in foil. Slice thickly and serve with or without butter.

Green Bean, Cheese, and Olive Salad

6 servings

1½	pounds fresh green beans
12	to 14 pitted black olives, thinly sliced
1	small red onion, thinly sliced
⅔	cup Longhorn (Colby) cheese, grated
6	lettuce leaves

Dressing

¼	teaspoon dry mustard
¼	teaspoon paprika
	Pinch of sugar
½	teaspoon salt

Break off the stem end of the beans and snap them into approximately 2-inch lengths. In a large kettle, bring 4 to 6 quarts of salted water to a boil and plunge in the beans. Cover until the water returns to a boil, uncover, and cook for no more than 3 to 5 minutes, until barely tender. Drain the beans in a colander and run under cold water to stop the cooking. Pat the beans dry on paper towels. In a large mixing bowl, combine the beans with the olives and onion rings.

In a medium mixing bowl, prepare the dressing by combining the mustard, paprika, sugar, salt, pepper, garlic, and vinegar; whisk in the oil until thoroughly blended. Pour the dressing over the beans and toss to coat everything. Let the salad stand 1 hour, then refrigerate until chilled, stirring occasionally. *At this point, the salad can be stored in the refrigerator, covered, for 1 day.*

When ready to serve, add the cheese to the salad and toss again. Place the lettuce leaves on salad plates and spoon the salad onto the lettuce. Serve immediately.

⅛ teaspoon freshly ground black pepper

1 small clove garlic, finely chopped

¼ cup red wine vinegar

¾ cup vegetable oil OR a combination of vegetable and olive oil

Summer Fruits in Soft Custard

6 servings

Pick over the berries for any stems or bruised fruit, then wash them and drain well. In a large bowl, place the berries, peaches, and plums and sprinkle with some sugar to taste; don't overdo the sugar because the custard is sweet and you want the various fruit flavors to stand out. *At this point, the fruit can be stored in the refrigerator, covered, for 1 day.*

In the top of a double boiler, beat the egg yolks until smooth; add the sugar, flour, and salt, and continue beating until smooth. Slowly add the milk and cream to the egg mixture and beat until smooth. In the bottom of the double boiler, bring an inch of water to a boil, lower the heat to simmer and place the top part of the double boiler over the heat. Cook the custard mixture over the water, stirring constantly, until the mixture thickens to coat the back of your spoon; this will take about 15 minutes.

Off the heat, place the pan containing the custard in a pan of cold water and continue stirring for a couple of minutes; remove and let cool. When the custard has cooled enough to refrigerate, stir in the vanilla extract. *At this point, the custard sauce can be stored in the refrigerator, covered, for 3 to 4 days.*

1½ to 2 *cups fresh berries (blackberries, boysenberries, or blueberries)*

3 *medium to large peaches, peeled and sliced*

2 *plums, sliced*

Sugar to taste

1 *banana, peeled and sliced*

Custard Sauce

4 *egg yolks*

⅓ *cup sugar*

1 *tablespoon flour*

Pinch of salt

1½ *cups milk*

½ *cup heavy cream*

1½ *teaspoons vanilla extract*

When ready to serve, add the banana to the fruit, then spoon the fruit into individual dessert dishes and pour the custard sauce over each serving. Pass any extra sauce in a small pitcher.

Black Bean Soup
Stuffed Cabbage Rolls with Tomato–Sour Cream Topping
Winter Salad of Beets, Mushrooms, and Green Beans
Apples with Cheese and Walnuts

We are not vegetarians, so we regarded the creation of a winter-time vegetarian dinner menu as being a considerable challenge. We wanted a dinner that was appetizing without being full of peculiar food combinations and hearty without relying on starch. As always, our goal also was to set food on the table that is pleasing to the eye.

We met with a lot of frustration but we shared a lot of laughs. For a long time, for example, we were determined to feature beets in the entrée; we tested so many beet concoctions that our fingertips seemed permanently stained red. Eventually, we relegated the beets to a salad for the dinner that highlights vegetables which are available in the dead of winter: beets, mushrooms, green beans, and some celery. This wise decision freed us to turn our attention for the entrée to another dependable vegetable staple in winter—the lowly cabbage.

We love stuffed cabbage rolls, but had never thought of doing anything with them here because we assumed they were difficult to make, and of course we couldn't imagine any filling for them that didn't contain meat. Well, we soon learned that while cabbage rolls are time-consuming—taking about three hours to assemble—they are *not* hard to make. For the fillings, we just started throwing together vegetarian things we're especially fond of, like brown rice, sunflower seeds, and nuts, and ended up with an absolutely unbeatable stuffing that is as delectable as anything made with beef or pork; furthermore, the stuffing is a sensation treat for the tongue in terms of textures.

The cabbage roll recipe calls for one large green cabbage, which is enough as long as the cabbage is in good shape. However, we have had the experience of buying cabbages that look fine on the outside, but when we peeled away the leaves we discovered brown leaves inside. Therefore we encourage you to buy two cabbages just to be on the safe side; besides, they're cheap. It is important to have perfect cabbage leaves for the rolls, and leaves that are fairly uniform in size. You can always use up leftover cabbage later in a soup or braise it as a side vegetable to some meat.

These cabbage rolls improve slightly in flavor when they are made a day in advance and stored in the refrigerator. And because they take three hours to prepare, you might want to make them the day before your dinner party. On the other hand, since everything else in the menu is so easy and quick to make, you really can do the cabbage rolls the same day of the party. The choice is yours.

The black bean soup recipe produces a scant cup of soup per person but it is quite filling, so we think the modest portion is plenty. However, you should serve it in cups instead of bowls.

We suggest that the most effective way to present the main course is to arrange the plates in the kitchen, placing two cabbage rolls on each plate with the sauce and sour cream topping, and the salad in its lettuce leaf cup alongside. However, you might want to offer the salad as a separate course between the main course and dessert; thus, you could drop the first course of black bean soup and add to the dinner plate some spears of fresh or frozen broccoli tossed in lemon butter. This may be the only choice for people who have trouble locating cans of black bean soup, though we've never had a problem finding them.

The dessert of apples with cheese and walnuts is a real honey— a snap to make, very pretty on the plate, and a delightful marriage of sweet-sour tastes and crisp-creamy textures. There really couldn't be a more fitting conclusion to this vegetarian dinner.

The wine to accompany what is essentially an earthy dish should be a sturdy, no-nonsense red such as a Zinfandel, Burgundy, or Chianti.

Black Bean Soup

6 servings

In a large saucepan, place the contents of the soup cans and slowly stir in 2 cups cold water until completely blended; make sure you get rid of the lumps. Heat the soup over medium heat just to boiling; lower the heat and simmer for 10 to 15 minutes until piping hot, stirring occasionally. Stir in the ½ cup of sherry. *At this point, the soup can be held off the heat for 2 to 3 hours.*

Shortly before serving, reheat the soup over low-medium heat until piping hot, stirring occasionally; stir in the additional 2 tablespoons of sherry. Pour the soup into warm cups, float a slice of lemon on top, and garnish with a small sprinkling of parsley. Serve immediately.

2	*11-ounce cans black bean soup, undiluted*
½	*cup dry sherry plus 2 tablespoons*
6	*thin slices lemon*
2	*tablespoons parsley, finely chopped*

Stuffed Cabbage Rolls with Tomato–Sour Cream Topping

6 to 8 servings

In a medium saucepan, cook the brown rice according to the package directions. Remove from the heat and reserve.

Remove any discolored outer leaves from the cabbage (see the introduction to this menu for a recommendation about buying two cabbages as a precaution). In a large kettle, bring to a boil 6 to 8 quarts of water, add the cabbage and cook, covered, for 10 minutes. Remove the cabbage, and when cool enough to handle, carefully peel away leaves until you have approximately 16 to 18 leaves (the number of stuffed rolls will depend on the size of

1	*cup brown rice*
1	*large green cabbage*
	Salt and freshly ground black pepper to taste
1	*teaspoon ground cumin*
8	*tablespoons (1 stick) butter*
2	*medium onions, finely chopped*

2   cloves garlic, finely
    chopped

½   cup sunflower seeds,
    toasted

½   cup walnuts, finely
    chopped

2   tablespoons soy sauce

½   teaspoon thyme

½   teaspoon marjoram

2   small tart apples

⅓   cup raisins

1   egg, lightly beaten

1   8-ounce can tomato
    sauce

½   cup dry white wine

1   8-ounce container sour
    cream OR plain yogurt

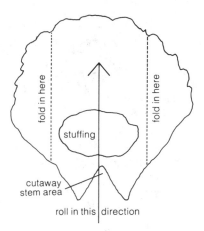

your cabbage leaves). Cut away in a V-for-mation the tough stem base from the bottom of each leaf (see diagram). Season each leaf with salt, pepper, and a pinch of cumin.

Preheat the oven to 350 degrees.

In a large skillet, melt 4 tablespoons of the butter over low-medium heat and sauté the onion, garlic, sunflower seeds, and walnuts until the onion is tender. Off the heat, stir in the soy sauce, thyme, marjoram, salt, and pepper; let cool. Peel, core, and cut the apples into a ½-inch dice. Stir the apples into the skillet along with the raisins, egg, and the cooked rice; season again with salt and pepper.

Place ¼ cup of the stuffing near the thicker base of each cabbage leaf. Then fold the sides of the leaf inward and roll the leaf up tightly toward the thin outer edge (see diagram). Place each cabbage roll, seam side down, in a greased, shallow baking dish measuring approximately 9 x 13 x 2 inches. Spoon the tomato sauce over the cabbage rolls to cover. Add the wine to the bottom of the dish by carefully pouring it down the dish's sides.

In a small saucepan, melt the remaining 4 tablespoons of butter and drizzle over the cabbage rolls. Cover the dish with foil and bake for 30 to 45 minutes, until bubbling and cooked through. Remove from the oven.

At this point, the dish can be held for several hours, loosely covered; or it can be stored in the refrigerator, covered, for 1 day. If you make the dish the day of the party and hold it, reheat it in a 350-degree oven for 20 to 30 minutes and serve. If you make the dish a day in advance, let it cool completely before storing in the refrigerator. Then let the cabbage rolls come to room temperature for 1 hour before reheating for about 30 minutes.

When the cabbage rolls are hot and ready to serve, spoon over the tomato sauce and serve each portion of 2 cabbage rolls with a generous dollop of sour cream.

Winter Salad of Beets, Mushrooms, and Green Beans

6 servings

Break off the stem end of the beans and snap them into approximately 2-inch lengths. In a large kettle, bring to a boil 4 to 6 quarts salted water and plunge in the beans. Cover until the water returns to the boil, uncover, and cook for 5 to 7 minutes, until just tender. Drain the beans in a colander and run under cold water to stop the cooking. Pat the beans dry on paper towels.

Wash the celery, trim the ends, and cut into a ½-inch dice. Place the celery, mushrooms, and beans in a large bowl.

In a medium mixing bowl, make the dressing by combining the scallions, capers, parsley, mustard, salt, pepper, and vinegar; whisk in the oil until everything is thoroughly blended. Pour the dressing over the vegetables and toss gently to coat everything. Let the salad stand 1 hour, then refrigerate until chilled, stirring occasionally. *At this point, the salad can be stored in the refrigerator, covered, for 1 day; stir occasionally.*

Shortly before serving, add the beets to the salad and give it another good stir. Place a lettuce leaf on each salad plate and spoon individual portions of the salad onto the leaves.

1   *pound fresh green beans*

2   *celery stalks*

¾   *pound mushrooms, thinly sliced*

1   *8-ounce can julienne of beets, drained*

6   *lettuce leaves*

Dressing

2   *tablespoons scallions (white part only)* OR *shallots, finely chopped*

2   *tablespoons capers, drained*

3   *tablespoons fresh parsley, finely chopped*

1   *tablespoon Dijon mustard*

   Salt and freshly ground black pepper to taste

¼   *cup red wine vinegar*

⅔   *cup vegetable oil* OR *a combination of vegetable and olive oil*

Apples with Cheese and Walnuts

6 servings

---

4 *medium to large red Delicious apples*

Juice of ½ lemon

2 *ounces cream cheese, softened to room temperature*

3 *ounces Camembert cheese* OR *Brie cheese, softened to room temperature*

11 *teaspoons full-bodied sherry* OR *tawny port*

¼ *cup walnuts, finely chopped*

6 *tablespoons light brown sugar, packed*

Wash the apples and, using an apple corer, core them, making sure you have removed all the seeds and the skin of the seed cavities; you should have a hole about 1 inch in diameter. Brush the insides of the apples with the lemon juice to prevent the flesh from turning brown (the easiest way to do this is with your finger).

In a small mixing bowl, cream together the cheeses and 2 teaspoons of the sherry until completely blended and smooth. Stir in the walnuts until blended. Stuff the apples with the cheese mixture, using a small spoon like a demitasse or measuring spoon. With a damp paper towel, wipe off any of the cheese that gets smeared on the apples. Wrap each apple in plastic wrap and refrigerate for 4 to 6 hours. *At this point, the apples can be stored in the refrigerator for 1 day.*

When ready to serve, cut each apple into 6 wedges, for a total of 24 wedges. Place 4 wedges on their side on each individual dessert plate. In a small mixing bowl, combine the brown sugar with the remaining 9 teaspoons (3 tablespoons) of sherry to form a syrup; drizzle this over each portion of apples and cheese. Serve immediately with a knife and small fork for cutting.

5

Menus for Brunches, Cocktail Buffets, & the Holidays

White Wine Spritzers OR *Daiquiris*
Pipérade Omelet
Open–Faced Crab Meat
Sandwiches with Avocado
Zucchini–Carrot Kugel
Melon and Pineapple
Platter with Green Grapes

A brunch in the summer can be the focus of many social occasions, such as getting the next-door neighbors together; entertaining old friends who are just passing through on their way to some happy vacation ground; having good friends over in the heat of the day for a swim or a croquet tournament; producing a royal send-off for weekend guests who have to return to the steam and grime of the city. Whatever the reason, we think a summer brunch is a lovely, lighthearted, and fun affair that hovers at noon in the sun-dappled shade somewhere between breakfast and supper, a pleasure stop on a fabulous journey or a preface to an afternoon of rest or sport. Brunch is a special time for those hazy, lazy days when you don't want to make a production out of the day's first or last meals, relying instead on something creative for dining at midday.

We assume that because the sun comes up so early in summer, your guests will have had some breakfast at home, and therefore won't arrive at the brunch feeling ravenous. So we ignore appetizers, and we stay away from dishes that smack of cereals, coffee cakes, and breakfast meats. Instead, we offer some rather elegant but easy fare that suggests lunch but isn't heavy, rich, or formal. Because people generally don't gorge themselves in summer weather, we have kept the food light and full of the fresh ingredients indigenous to the season. Imagine a dining table or patio picnic table set with a huge bouquet of mixed flowers surrounded by the colorful pipérade omelet full of tomatoes and green peppers, the French bread sandwich rounds of broiled crab meat with the surprise of cool avocado, generous squares of the pretty zucchini-carrot kugel, and a basket heaped with wedges of honey-dew, pineapple, and clusters of seedless green grapes. The appearance of such delicious food will be upstaged only by some of its novelty.

Just as the solid food is light, so are the libations. You can serve one or both of these recipes, depending on how fond your guests are of drinking. The daiquiris can be made in advance and kept refrigerated in a pitcher. Because of the club soda, the spritzers have to be mixed with each drink. For a drink to go with the brunch, you can serve either pitchers of iced tea (perhaps one or two of the newer herbal, spice, or fruit teas would be appropriate) or iced coffee. If it's not too hot, you might want to serve hot coffee.

One problem with brunches is the brief amount of time you have to fix the food on the day of the party. You barely have the kids' cornflakes flushed down the garbage disposal and the Sunday papers picked up before the guests are ringing the doorbell. Well, as far as our party menu goes, every dish can be at least partly assembled the day before, and the zucchini-carrot kugel can be made completely a day in advance.

For the crab meat sandwiches, toast the French bread and mix up the crab meat spread and the cream cheese topping the night before. At the same time, wash or cut up all the fruit. Ready the onions, peppers, and tomatoes for the pipérade omelet and store in the refrigerator; in fact, this is a good idea for the tomatoes because you can pour off any accumulated juice before adding them to the omelet.

A *pipérade* is a French egg dish which combines tomatoes, peppers, onions, and ham; actually, it tastes a lot like our Western omelet except there are more vegetables in a pipérade. We have elaborated on the classic pipérade for our own variation by substituting cheese for the ham and adding some tomato paste and cream. Fortunately, this approach to the omelet does not require the tricky routine for cooking that the traditional omelet does (who needs it when making omelets for 10 people?). What we do is simply combine the ingredients in a large skillet and cook until the eggs are practically set; then we run the omelet under the broiler to melt the Parmesan cheese and impart a gorgeous tomato-red glaze to the top. By using a skillet, you can cut the omelet in wedges, a shape which fits pleasingly on a plate with the circle-shaped sandwich and the squarish kugel.

The secret to the success of the crab meat sandwiches is a ripe avocado and a good quality of Italian or Portuguese bread. The bread's texture should be firm, not doughy like so many American breads; of course the toasting process will help to harden the bread. If you are unable to purchase Italian or Portuguese bread, consider using English muffins as a substitute (one whole muffin or two halves per person). If your store almost never stocks avocadoes when they are ripe, be sure to buy your avocado several days in advance to give it time to ripen in your kitchen. An unripe avocado takes about 4 to 5 days to ripen. We appreciate that many people will balk at the price of two cans of crab meat. However, when you consider that most other ingredients in the menu are dirt cheap because they are so plentiful, you might feel more justified in making one extravagant purchase for a party.

The zucchini-carrot kugel is our one and only manufactured sweet for the sweet tooth crowd, yet its freshness, honesty, and goodness will win over fanatic nutritionists and calorie counters as well as lovers of anything with sugar on it. In addition to being delicious, the kugel is also versatile, just as delectable when served hot, cold, or at room temperature. You can decide on how to serve the kugel when you see what the weather is like the day of the brunch.

You don't have to meticulously follow our recipe for the fruit platter. Our visual goal is for the beautiful pale green colors of the honeydew and the grapes to be predominant. However, you can certainly substitute cantaloupe for the honeydew; or you can use a honeydew and a cantaloupe and skip the pineapple. What you want to end up with on the platter is at least three pieces of fruit per person.

White Wine Spritzers

Makes 1 drink

½ *cup dry white wine* OR
    dry rosé wine

¼ *cup club soda*

In a 10-ounce wineglass, place 3 or 4 icecubes and pour the wine over them. Add the soda and stir. Serve immediately.

Daiquiris

6 to 8 servings

1 *6-ounce can frozen
    lemonade, slightly
    thawed*

1½ *cups light rum*

In the container of an electric blender, put 3 or 4 icecubes, the lemonade, and the rum. Process until well blended and the ice is pulverized.

Fill 6 to 8 small old-fashioned glasses, wineglasses, or champagne glasses about three-fourths full of ice (shaved ice is preferred) and pour the daiquiri into them. Serve immediately.

Pipérade Omelet

8 to 10 servings

2 *tablespoons butter*

1 *tablespoon vegetable oil*
    OR *olive oil*

2 *medium onions, thinly
    sliced*

2 *medium green peppers,
    thinly sliced*

Preheat the oven to BROIL.

In a 12-inch skillet, melt the butter and oil over low-medium heat and sauté the onions and peppers until tender. Add the tomatoes, oregano, basil, hot pepper sauce, salt, and pepper, and simmer for 5 minutes, stirring occasionally. Remove from the heat and reserve.

In a large mixing bowl, beat the eggs well, then beat in the cream and tomato paste until the tomato paste is completely blended. Stir in the Swiss cheese and parsley. Pour the egg mixture into the skillet with the vegetables and stir until well blended. Return the skillet to the stove and cook the contents over very low heat until the eggs start to set (do not stir); at this point, loosen the eggs around the edge with a spatula. When the eggs are nearly set, sprinkle the Parmesan cheese over the top and place the omelet in the oven 6 inches from the broiler heat, until the cheese is puffed up, golden, and bubbly and the eggs are completely set; this will take about 2 to 3 minutes, so be sure to watch the omelet carefully while it's in the oven.

The omelet can be served either hot or cold. If serving it hot, you can either serve immediately or you can let the omelet stand at room temperature for 2 hours, then reheat it, covered with foil, in a 350-degree oven for 15 to 20 minutes.

If you make the omelet a day in advance, let it cool completely after taking it out of the oven. *At this point, the omelet can be stored in the refrigerator, covered, for 1 day.* To serve cold, let it come to room temperature for 20 to 30 minutes before serving; this takes off some of the chill. To serve hot, let it come to room temperature for 30 to 45 minutes before proceeding to reheat as directed above.

Cut the omelet into pie-shaped wedges and serve out of the skillet or on a platter.

2   *medium, ripe tomatoes, peeled, seeded, and coarsely chopped*

½   *teaspoon dried oregano*

1   *teaspoon fresh basil, finely chopped* OR ¼ *teaspoon dried basil*

Dash hot pepper sauce

Salt and freshly ground black pepper to taste

12   *eggs*

¼   *cup heavy cream*

2   *tablespoons tomato paste*

½   *cup Swiss, Gruyère* OR *sharp Cheddar cheese, grated*

2   *tablespoons fresh parsley, finely chopped*

¼   *cup Parmesan cheese* OR *Romano cheese, grated*

Open–Faced Crab Meat Sandwiches with Avocado

8 to 12 servings

In a medium mixing bowl, combine the crab meat, mayonnaise, sour cream, salt, and pepper. In another mixing bowl, combine the cream cheese, egg yolks, onion, catsup, Wor-

2   *7½-ounce cans crab meat, drained*

⅓   *cup mayonnaise*

2 tablespoons sour cream

Salt and freshly ground black pepper to taste

2 3-ounce packages cream cheese, softened to room temperature

2 egg yolks, lightly beaten

1 teaspoon onion, grated

2 tablespoons catsup

1 teaspoon Worcestershire sauce

1/2 teaspoon Dijon mustard

8 to 12 slices Italian bread OR Portuguese bread, about 1-inch thick

Butter to taste

1 ripe avocado

cestershire sauce, and mustard. *At this point, both mixtures can be stored in the refrigerator, covered, for 1 to 2 days.* Let them come to room temperature for 30 to 45 minutes before cooking.

When ready to cook, preheat the oven to BROIL.

Lightly toast both sides of the bread and spread one side thinly with butter; let cool slightly. Spread the buttered side of each bread slice with 2 tablespoons of the crab meat mixture and spread over this 1 tablespoon of the cream cheese mixture. Place the bread slices on an ungreased cookie sheet and broil 6 inches from the heat until the tops are puffed up, golden brown, and bubbly; this takes about 3 to 5 minutes. Remove from the heat.

While the sandwiches are cooking, peel the avocado and cut into 10 or 12 slices. Arrange 1 slice over the top of each sandwich and serve immediately.

Zucchini–Carrot Kugel

8 to 10 servings

1 pound carrots

1 pound zucchini

1/2 cup raisins

4 eggs

1 cup ricotta cheese OR small, dry curd cottage cheese

1/4 cup sour cream

2 tablespoons granulated sugar

Preheat the oven to 350 degrees.

Trim the ends of the carrots and scrape them. Wash the zucchini and trim away the ends, but do not peel the skin. In a food processor fitted with the shredding disk, or with a hand grater, grate the carrots and the zucchini. Place the zucchini in a sieve or colander and let stand for 15 to 20 minutes, then use your fingers to squeeze as much moisture as you can out of the zucchini. Dry it even further on paper towels; it is important to rid the zucchini of moisture to prevent the kugel's having a runny consistency. Place the zucchini, carrots, and raisins in a large mixing bowl.

In a medium mixing bowl, beat the eggs lightly, then beat in the ricotta cheese, sour cream, granulated sugar, and cinnamon until thoroughly blended. Pour the mixture into the bowl with the zucchini and carrots, and stir everything gently until completely blended. Spoon the kugel mixture into a greased, shallow baking dish measuring approximately 7 x 11 x 2 inches and smooth over the top.

In a small saucepan, melt the butter over low heat. In a small mixing bowl, combine the brown sugar and walnuts, and sprinkle over the top of the kugel; press to pat down. Drizzle the melted butter evenly over the top of the dish and bake for 45 to 60 minutes, until a toothpick inserted in the center comes out clean. Remove from the oven and let cool on a rack. *At this point, the kugel can be held for several hours; or it can be stored in the refrigerator, covered, for 1 to 2 days.*

The kugel can be served cold, warm, or at room temperature. If you serve the kugel at room temperature after it has been refrigerated, let it come to room temperature for 1 hour before serving. If you serve it warm, let it come to room temperature, then warm it in a 350-degree oven for 15 to 20 minutes. When ready to serve, cut the kugel into squares and put on a small platter.

1   *teaspoon cinnamon*

¼   *cup brown sugar*

¼   *cup walnuts, finely chopped*

2   *tablespoons butter*

Melon and Pineapple Platter with Green Grapes

8 to 10 servings

1	*large honeydew melon*
1	*small fresh pineapple*
1½	*pounds green grapes*
	Sprigs of fresh mint (optional)

Cut the honeydew in half lengthwise and remove the seeds. Cut each half into 5 pieces and cut away enough of the rind so the pieces can be eaten with the fingers.

Cut away the pineapple's exterior. Cut the pineapple lengthwise into halves or into quarters and remove the white core with a very sharp knife. Cut the edible flesh into pieces that are small enough to pick up with the fingers.

Wash the grapes and break into small bunches of 6 to 8 grapes each; you should have 10 bunches.

Refrigerate the fruit. *At this point, the fruit can be stored in the refrigerator, covered, for 1 day.*

When ready to serve, arrange the fruit decoratively on a large platter and garnish with the optional mint.

Bloody Marys AND
Sherried Orange Juice
    Farmer's Eggs (Eggs with Bacon,
  Potatoes, Cheese, and Nuts) OR
     Sailor's Eggs (Eggs with
    Crab Meat, Shrimp, and Mushrooms)
     Sausage–Oyster Patties
      Lemon Bread OR
      Poppy Seed Bread
           Grapefruit Steeped in Port

When the weather outside is frightful and dark descends at about four o'clock in the afternoon, a brunch can be a social affair that seems to take care of the whole day and leaves people feeling glad they got together. If there is a blanket of fresh snow on the ground, tell the people you invite to bring equipment so they can go cross-country skiing or ice skating after the brunch. Or if it is one of those bitter cold, steel-gray days, you can encourage everyone to linger to watch a football game or play Scrabble. Whatever "happening" evolves in connection with the brunch, your guests will appreciate food that warms them up and sticks to their ribs. The brunch menu will set them up for an afternoon of physical or mental stimulation and challenge.

While you can't predict ahead of time which of your drink choices a guest is going to request, we suggest you prepare the full recipe of Bloody Marys. That way you won't have to bother with making individual drinks except to add the vodka and a stalk of celery; and any vegetable juice mixture left over will keep for one or two weeks in the refrigerator. A pitcher of plain orange juice should be ready for mixing drinks with too—some people may even want to drink the orange juice plain. You can also offer people a glass of plain, dry sherry, always a soothing noontime libation.

The hassle with brunch is the minimal amount of time you have to cook between the ringing of the alarm clock and the appearance of the first guests at your door. This is why we have created, for the brunch's main course, two splendid egg dishes which can be made one day in advance and refrigerated. In addition, both breads are made ahead of time, and so are the sausage-oyster patties and the grapefruit dessert. With the entire brunch out of the way the day *before* the party, you can go to bed and sleep without a care in the world.

You will notice that the menu presents choices for the entrée and the bread. In the case of the entrée, the farmer's eggs feature meat and potatoes, and the sailor's eggs contain seafood; the decision can be based on personal preference or on the time of day when the brunch takes place (for a mid- to late-morning affair, the farmer's eggs might seem more appropriate; for a brunch that starts around noon, you could consider the sailor's eggs a better choice). Neither bread is overly sweet and both combine equally well with either of the two entrées; therefore take your pick of the breads, or you may want to serve both. We should also point out that you could increase the number of guests if you want to make both egg dishes and both breads. This is an extremely flexible menu.

The combination of pork sausage and oysters is an old one dating back more than a hundred years, when oysters were plentiful and many families raised their own pigs. We think you'll be delighted with the flavors of land and sea coming together in these patties; it's an unusual taste. Furthermore, they are incredibly easy to assemble and not at all messy to cook, since they bake in the oven. By the way, you can cook the patties the day before the brunch, if you want (our recipe directs you to just assemble them the day before); let them cool completely and refrigerate. Then, on the day of the brunch, preheat the oven to 375 degrees and warm up the patties, covered, for 15 to 20 minutes.

The presentation of the brunch food on your dining room table should get everyone's adrenaline pumping. The farmer's eggs look irresistible with their topping of shiny, sautéed walnuts; the sailor's eggs paint a regal picture of a pair of substantial quiches; the rich brown sausage-oyster patties against green parsley sprigs smell spicy and earthy in the same breath; and the breads—should you offer both—are a fetching contrast of pale yellow and speckled black on white.

The grapefruit in port wine is a deliberately simple sweet to offer after so much food; more importantly, it's a refreshing palate cleanser. You will need to serve the fruit in small cups or bowls so as to be able to spoon the juice over each portion. Try to use pink grapefruit for the color.

The best beverage with this brunch is plenty of strong, hot coffee.

Bloody Marys

In a large pitcher, place 4 or 6 icecubes and pour in the contents of one of the cans of vegetable juice. Stir in the horseradish, Worcestershire sauce, hot pepper sauce, salt, pepper, and the optional chili peppers. Press the chili peppers against the side of the pitcher to squeeze some of their flavor into the mixture. Add the contents of the other can of vegetable juice, stir, and let stand for 1 hour. *At this point, the Bloody Mary mix can be stored in the refrigerator, covered, for 2 to 3 days.*

When ready to serve, add icecubes to each cocktail glass; the glasses should hold about 12 ounces of liquid. Pour in the desired amount of vodka (we use 1½ ounces). Fill the rest of the glass with the vegetable juice mixture, give it a good stir, and garnish the drink with a stalk of celery.

2 *24-ounce cans vegetable juice*

4 *teaspoons horseradish*

1 *teaspoon Worcestershire sauce*

¼ *teaspoon hot pepper sauce*

Salt and freshly ground black pepper to taste

2 *to 3 green chili peppers (optional)*

10 *to 12 celery stalks, washed and trimmed*

Vodka to taste

Sherried Orange Juice

In a 10-ounce wineglass, place 4 icecubes and pour the sherry over them. Add the orange juice (be sure to use fresh or frozen—nothing powdered or canned), and stir thoroughly. Serve immediately.

1½ *ounces dry sherry*

About ½ cup orange juice

Farmer's Eggs (Eggs with Bacon, Potatoes, Cheese, and Nuts)

8 to 10 servings

1   *large red (new) potato, about ¾ pound*

8   *slices bacon*

½   *cup walnuts, coarsely chopped*

1   *large onion, finely chopped*

     Salt and freshly ground black pepper to taste

12   *to 14 eggs*

½   *pound (2 sticks) butter*

1   *cup sour cream*

12   *ounces Swiss cheese* OR *Gruyère cheese, grated*

½   *cup fresh parsley, finely chopped*

Peel the potato, cut into a ¼-inch dice, and put in a bowl of cold water to keep from turning brown.

In a large skillet, fry the bacon over medium heat until crisp. Drain well on paper towels until cool, then crumble into bits and reserve. Pour out all but 2 tablespoons of the bacon drippings, add the walnuts to the skillet and sauté over low-medium heat until golden. Remove with a slotted spoon and reserve until cool.

Drain the potato cubes and dry thoroughly on paper towels. Add the potato and onion to the skillet and sauté in the bacon drippings until golden and tender, about 10 to 15 minutes. Remove with a slotted spoon and season with salt and pepper; reserve and let cool.

In a medium saucepan, melt the butter over low heat.

In a large mixing bowl, beat the eggs well and stir in the sour cream, cheese, bacon, potato, onion, and additional salt and pepper to taste. Rapidly stir in the melted butter. Pour the egg mixture into a greased, shallow baking dish measuring approximately 9 x 13 x 2 inches. *At this point, the eggs can be stored in the refrigerator, covered, for 1 day.* Let the dish come to room temperature for 30 to 45 minutes before cooking.

Preheat the oven to 325 degrees.

Bake the eggs for 50 minutes, or until a toothpick inserted in the center comes out clean. For ease of serving, let the eggs stand 10 minutes before cutting into squares. Sprinkle the walnuts and parsley over the top of the dish.

Sailor's Eggs (Eggs with Crab Meat, Shrimp, and Mushrooms)

8 to 10 servings

Preheat the oven to 350 degrees.

In a large skillet, melt 4 tablespoons of the butter over low-medium heat and sauté the onions and mushrooms until most of the mushroom juice has evaporated. Off the heat, add the remaining 2 tablespoons of butter; when melted, stir in the crab meat and shrimp and toss gently until the shellfish are coated with butter. Let the mixture cool completely.

In a large mixing bowl, beat the eggs well and add the sour cream, sherry, nutmeg, salt, and pepper; stir vigorously until well mixed. Pour the egg mixture into the skillet and stir to combine everything. Divide the contents of the skillet evenly between 2 greased 9-inch pie plates. Sprinkle a little paprika over each pie.

Bake the eggs for 45 to 60 minutes, or until a toothpick inserted in the center comes out clean. Let the pies stand for 10 minutes, then cut into wedges and serve immediately.

If you want to make sailor's eggs the day before your party, let the dish cool completely after you take it out of the oven. *At this point, the eggs can be stored in the refrigerator, covered, for 1 day.* Let the eggs come to room temperature for 30 to 45 minutes before reheating in a 350-degree oven for 20 to 30 minutes, until warmed through.

6   *tablespoons butter*

1   *medium onion, thinly sliced*

12 *ounces mushrooms, thinly sliced*

2   *6-ounce cans crab meat, drained*

1   *4½-ounce can tiny shrimp, drained*

8   *eggs*

1   *cup sour cream*

4   *tablespoons dry sherry*

⅛ *teaspoon nutmeg*

   Salt and freshly ground black pepper to taste

   Paprika

Sausage–Oyster Patties

8 to 10 servings

1   *8-ounce can oysters*

¼   *cup dry sherry*

1   *pound bulk pork sausage*

1   *teaspoon Dijon mustard*

1   *teaspoon horseradish*

2   *tablespoons fresh parsley, finely chopped*

1   *egg, lightly beaten*

Paprika to taste

Parsley sprigs for garnish

In a small saucepan, combine the oysters, their juice, and the sherry. Bring to a gentle boil over medium heat, reduce the heat and simmer until the edges of the oysters begin to curl slightly, about 10 minutes. Drain and let cool, then chop the oysters coarsely.

In a medium mixing bowl, combine the sausage, mustard, horseradish, parsley, egg, and oysters and, using your fingers, mix the ingredients together until everything is blended. Divide the sausage mixture into 10 portions and flatten each portion with the palm of your hand to about the size of a standard hamburger patty. Lightly dust the sausage-oyster patties with paprika. *At this point, the patties can be stored in the refrigerator, covered in plastic wrap, for 1 day; or they can be frozen.*

When ready to cook, preheat the oven to 375 degrees.

Place the patties on an ungreased cookie sheet and bake for 20 minutes. Turn the patties over and bake another 10 to 15 minutes. Serve immediately on a warm platter, garnished with the parsley sprigs.

Lemon Bread

Makes 1 loaf

8   *tablespoons (1 stick) butter, softened to room temperature*

1   *cup granulated sugar*

2   *eggs, well beaten*

Preheat the oven to 350 degrees.

In a large mixing bowl, cream together 6 tablespoons of the butter and the granulated sugar. Add the eggs and stir until smooth, then add the milk and stir until completely blended and smooth. Add the lemon rind.

In a medium mixing bowl, sift together the flour, baking powder, and salt. Add the dry ingredients to the liquid mixture and stir until the dough is smooth. Stir in the sesame seeds.

Grease a 9 x 5 x 3-inch loaf pan and dust with flour; turn the pan upside down and tap to remove any excess flour. Pour the bread dough into the pan and smooth it into the corners. Wet the back of a metal spoon and smooth over the top of the dough to even it. Bake for 1 hour, or until a straw or knife inserted in the center comes out clean.

Just before the bread is done, melt the remaining 2 tablespoons of butter and add the lemon juice. The minute the bread is removed from the oven, drizzle the lemon-butter mixture over the top, especially into any cracks that formed during the baking. When the bread has cooled a little, sprinkle the confectioners' sugar over the top; let cool completely on a rack. *At this point, the bread can be held for several hours; or it can be refrigerated, well-wrapped in plastic wrap or foil, for 1 week; or it can be frozen.*

The lemon bread can be served at room temperature, or it can be warmed in a 350-degree oven for 20 to 30 minutes, wrapped in foil. Slice thickly and serve with or without butter.

½   cup whole milk

    Grated rind and juice of 1 lemon, separate

1½   *cups flour*

2   *teaspoons baking powder*

¼   *teaspoon salt*

½   *cup sesame seeds, toasted*

2   *tablespoons confectioners' sugar*

Poppy Seed Bread

Makes 1 loaf

Preheat the oven to 350 degrees.

In a large mixing bowl, cream together the butter and sugar. Add the eggs and stir until smooth; add the buttermilk and continue stirring until completely blended and smooth.

In a medium mixing bowl, sift together the flour, baking powder, and nutmeg; stir in the

6   *tablespoons butter, softened to room temperature*

1   *cup sugar*

2   *eggs, well beaten*

1   *cup buttermilk*

1¾   *cups flour*

3   *teaspoons baking
    powder*

¼   *teaspoon nutmeg*

1   *2¼-ounce package
    poppy seeds* OR *½ cup
    poppy seeds*

poppy seeds. Add the dry ingredients to the liquid mixture and stir until the dough is smooth.

Grease a 9 x 5 x 3-inch loaf pan and dust with flour; turn the pan upside down and tap to remove any excess flour. Pour the bread dough into the pan and smooth it into the corners. Wet the back of a metal spoon and smooth over the top of the dough to even it. Bake for 50 to 60 minutes, or until a straw or knife inserted in the center comes out clean. Let cool completely on a rack. *At this point, the bread can be held for several hours; or it can be refrigerated, well-wrapped in plastic wrap or foil, for 1 week; or it can be frozen.*

The bread can be served at room temperature, or it can be warmed in a 350-degree oven for 20 to 30 minutes, wrapped in foil. Slice thickly and serve with or without butter.

Grapefruit Steeped in Port

8 to 10 servings

3   *medium white* OR *pink
    grapefruit*

5   *teaspoons brown sugar,
    packed*

⅓   *cup tawny port*

Cut the grapefruit in half and cut out the grapefruit segments with a serrated grapefruit knife; place in a bowl along with the juice. Sprinkle the brown sugar over the fruit and pour the port over it; stir to blend. Chill overnight. *At this point, the grapefruit can be stored in the refrigerator, covered, for 1 to 2 days.* Let it come to room temperature for 30 to 45 minutes before serving. Serve in small bowls or cups with some of the juice.

Marinated London
Broil with Olive Garnish

    Chicken Breasts in Tuna Sauce

       Egg Salad–Blue Cheese
      Mold with Cherry Tomatoes

         Carrots and Basil in
         Sweet–Sour Dressing

           Green Bean Salad
           with Yogurt Dressing

               Hot Rolls

                 Fruit Bowl

At first glance, cocktail buffet menus appear overwhelming in terms of grocery shopping and food preparation. You think of having one free day during the week to cook, if you're lucky, which means you can probably manage a small dinner party; but an elegant spread for 14 to 16 people seems too much to cope with. We sympathize wholeheartedly with this response, having long ago given up on throwing big cocktail parties where we worked like athletes in training and felt empty when it was all over. However, we also appreciate the practicality of inviting more than a dozen guests for a social occasion, especially when you owe a number of people or it has been several months since you last entertained anyone besides in-laws or a troop of cub scouts.

The approach we have taken with both cocktail buffet menus in this book is to make the event as much like our dinner parties as possible, except that people won't be sitting around the dinner table. In other words, we have remained true to our policy of being able to cope on the day of the party because much of the menu has been prepared in advance, leaving ample time to attend to last-minute details without going crazy in the process. It's especially easy to be on top of things with the summertime cocktail buffet because each and every dish can be made at least one day before the party—some even have to be put together earlier than that—and they are all served either cold or at room temperature;

thus, there's no cooking, no juggling for space in the oven, and no heating up the kitchen while the party's going on. In fact, there's so little for you to do during the party that you should have a wonderful time.

The work on the cocktail buffet begins about a week earlier with some of the grocery shopping. This is especially important for the fruit for the dessert course, which might need to ripen. You can marinate the beef for several days, and the egg salad mold will also keep nicely for 2 or 3 days. Already you have three dishes out of the way. Finally, we recommend that you decide on party hors d'oeuvres and try to prepare these as soon as possible. Since there is no cheese in the menu, you might select a favorite cheese ball from the appetizer chapter, make it the weekend before, and refrigerate it (our cheese balls can also be frozen up to a month ahead of a party). Other make-ahead appetizers that go well with the cocktail buffet menu are a dip for raw vegetables (our dips keep several days); the smoked oyster spread or the ham roll-ups; and either the cheese sticks or cheese drops, both of which can come out of the freezer.

Toward the end of the week, you can cook your beans and carrots for the two salads, mix them with their respective dressings, and refrigerate, giving them a stir every once in a while. If you use fresh basil with the carrots, don't add it to the salad until the day of the party, because the longer basil sits in a dressing, the darker it gets. You can also make the tuna sauce for the chicken, and if you want, you can sauté the chicken breasts and broil the meat the night before the party and store them in the refrigerator, well wrapped. Chop up the olives for garnishing the London broil and get a good night's sleep.

Thus, when the day of the party dawns, you have nothing more complicated or taxing to accomplish than slicing the London broil, making the dessert, which consists of washing fresh fruit and piling it into a decorative bowl, and fixing the raw vegetables for a dip, if that is what you're serving with drinks. As you can see, a hard week at the office or at home need not deter you from experiencing pleasure over the forthcoming festivities. There's plenty of time to get your act together or to do some other food preparation that you might not have got done earlier.

About 30 minutes before you want people to start eating, warm up the dinner rolls in the oven and butter them. The rolls can be anything from a local bakery or supermarket that you've enjoyed in the past, such as French rolls or Parker House rolls. Try to stick to small rolls because plates are going to be brimming, and besides, there is so much food that people won't need to fill up on bread.

The table centerpiece is the bowl of fresh fruit, the rest of the decoration is the several platters of food with contrasting colors. Whether you serve the buffet indoors or out, you really don't need anything else to brighten up or call attention to the display, except for some candles for extra light. If you want flowers on the table, you can put them in two matching vases on either side of the fruit bowl, but this isn't necessary.

The best wine for the buffet is a red, but people do love white wine in the summertime. Since you are serving a number of people, we recommend that you offer a choice of a well-chilled white that is ordinary but dry, and a cooled-off red that is also ordinary, dry, and on the light side, such as a Gamay Beaujolais or a Ruby Cabernet. Fill half the glasses with white, half with red, and place them on the buffet table to be picked up last. Pour any remaining wine into decanters for refills.

Marinated London Broil with Olive Garnish

14 to 16 servings

3 to 4 *pounds London broil (sirloin tip)* OR *top round steak, about 1½ inches thick*

2 *tablespoons brown sugar*

½ *teaspoon ground ginger*

½ *teaspoon dry mustard*

1 *clove garlic, mashed*

½ *cup soy sauce*

⅓ *cup dry red wine*

1 *5½-ounce jar pimiento-stuffed green olives, finely chopped*

Carefully trim the meat of all fat.

In a medium mixing bowl, combine the brown sugar, ginger, mustard, and garlic; stir in the soy sauce and wine. Place the meat in a shallow dish large enough to hold it and pour the marinade over it. Refrigerate for at least 6 hours, turning frequently. *At this point, the meat can be stored in the refrigerator, covered, for 2 to 3 days; turn occasionally.* Let the meat come to room temperature for 1 hour before cooking.

Preheat the oven to BROIL.

Place the meat on the broiler pan and broil 6 inches from the heat for about 5 to 7 minutes on each side; the length of broiling time depends on desired degree of doneness. Remove from the oven and allow to cool; then chill in the refrigerator for a minimum of 5 hours. *At this point, the meat can be stored in the refrigerator, covered, for 1 day.*

Shortly before serving, place the meat on a cutting board and slice with a very sharp knife into ⅛-inch-thick slices; hold the knife at a 45-degree angle to the meat and cutting board, and slice against the meat's grain. Arrange the meat on a serving platter and sprinkle the chopped olives over it.

Chicken Breasts in Tuna Sauce

14 to 16 servings

Cut each chicken breast in half, trim away any fat and membrane, and flatten with a meat pounder or the heel of your hand; dry with paper towels. Sprinkle with the lemon juice, salt, and pepper.

In a large skillet, melt 2 tablespoons of the butter and 2 tablespoons of the oil over medium heat and sauté half the chicken until golden brown and cooked through, about 10 to 15 minutes; you may have to lower the heat to prevent burning. Remove the chicken and reserve. Melt the remaining butter and oil and sauté the rest of the chicken in the same way. Let the chicken cool, then refrigerate 4 to 5 hours, until well chilled. *At this point, the chicken can be stored in the refrigerator, covered, for 1 to 2 days.*

To prepare the sauce: In a medium mixing bowl, break up the tuna into flakes. Stir in the mayonnaise, capers, 4 tablespoons of the parsley, tarragon, and lemon juice. Whisk in the olive oil until the mixture has the consistency of thick cream. *At this point, the tuna sauce can be stored in the refrigerator, covered, for 1 to 2 days.* If the sauce becomes too thick in the refrigerator, thin it with a little oil.

Shortly before serving, arrange the chicken breasts on a platter and spoon over the tuna sauce. Garnish with the remaining 2 tablespoons of parsley.

8 *small to medium whole, boneless, skinless chicken breasts*

Juice of 1 lemon

Salt and freshly ground black pepper to taste

4 *tablespoons butter*

4 *tablespoons vegetable oil*

Sauce

1 *9-ounce can tunafish in oil, drained*

1 *cup mayonnaise*

¼ *cup capers*

6 *tablespoons fresh parsley, finely chopped*

2 *tablespoons fresh tarragon, finely chopped* OR *2 teaspoons dried tarragon*

¼ *cup lemon juice*

6 *tablespoons olive oil*

Egg Salad–Blue Cheese Mold with Cherry Tomatoes

14 to 16 servings

12 *hard-boiled eggs, finely chopped*

1 *large green pepper, finely chopped*

½ *cup fresh parsley, finely chopped*

1 *tablespoon onion, grated*

4 *ounces blue cheese* OR *Roquefort cheese, crumbled*

1½ *cups mayonnaise*

½ *cup sour cream*

1 *teaspoon Dijon mustard*

½ *teaspoon Worcestershire sauce*

½ *teaspoon paprika*

2 *packages unflavored gelatin*

1 *teaspoon salt*

1 *pint cherry tomatoes* OR *2 medium-large tomatoes*

In a large mixing bowl, combine the eggs, green pepper, parsley, onion, blue cheese, mayonnaise, sour cream, mustard, Worcestershire sauce, and paprika; stir the ingredients very gently to blend.

In a medium mixing bowl, soften the gelatin in ½ cup cold water for about 10 minutes. Add 1 cup boiling water and the salt, and stir to blend. Stir the gelatin into the egg mixture; the result will be quite liquid. Pour into a 6-cup no-stick ring or regular mold, or into a greased mold. Chill until set, about 4 to 6 hours. *At this point, the egg salad-blue cheese mold can be stored in the refrigerator, covered, for 2 to 3 days.*

Shortly before serving, unmold the salad onto a serving plate; this is best accomplished by quickly dipping the mold into a pan of hot water. If you used a ring mold, fill the center of the dish with the cherry tomatoes; with a regular mold, peel the tomatoes, cut into wedges, and place them around the dish. Serve immediately.

Carrots and Basil in Sweet–Sour Dressing

14 to 16 servings

Trim the ends of the carrots, scrape them, and cut each carrot in half.

In a large saucepan, place the carrots, garlic cloves, and salt, and cover with cold water. Bring the water to a boil, lower the heat and cook, covered, 10 minutes, until the carrots are barely tender. Drain the carrots in a colander and run cold water over them; discard the garlic. Cut the carrots into a ½-inch dice and put in a medium bowl.

In a food processor fitted with the steel blade, or with a very sharp knife, chop the basil leaves to a fine mince and add to the carrots.

In a medium mixing bowl, make the dressing by combining the sugar, salt, and mustard; then stir in the Worcestershire sauce, tomato paste, and vinegar until blended. Whisk in the oil until thoroughly blended. Pour the dressing over the carrots and toss gently to coat everything. *At this point, the carrots can be held for several hours, or they can be stored in the refrigerator, covered, for 1 to 2 days;* stir occasionally.

When ready to serve, spoon into a decorative bowl.

2½	to 3 *pounds carrots*
2	*cloves garlic, peeled but left whole*
	Salt to taste
1	*cup fresh basil leaves, loosely packed*

Dressing

¼	*cup sugar*
1	*teaspoon salt*
½	*teaspoon dry mustard*
1	*teaspoon Worcestershire sauce*
3	*tablespoons tomato paste*
¼	*cup cider vinegar*
½	*cup vegetable oil* OR *a combination of vegetable and olive oil*

Green Bean Salad with Yogurt Dressing

14 to 16 servings

3   to 3½ *pounds fresh green beans*

2   *small cloves garlic, mashed*

1½   *teaspoons ground cumin*

Salt and freshly ground black pepper to taste

2   *teaspoons Dijon mustard*

3   *tablespoons plain yogurt*

3   *tablespoons red wine vinegar*

¾   *cup vegetable oil* OR *a combination of vegetable and olive oil*

Break off the stem end of the beans and snap them into approximately 2-inch lengths. In a large kettle, bring to a boil 8 to 10 quarts salted water and plunge in the beans. Cover until the water returns to the boil, uncover, and cook for no more than 3 to 5 minutes, until barely tender. Drain the beans in a colander and run cold water over them until cool.

In a medium mixing bowl, combine the garlic, cumin, salt, pepper, mustard, and yogurt, then stir in the vinegar; whisk in the oil until it is thoroughly blended.

If the beans are not completely dry, pat them with paper towels. Place the beans in a large shallow dish and pour the dressing over them, turning them until they are well coated. *At this point, the beans can be held for several hours, or they can be stored in the refrigerator, covered, for 1 to 2 days; turn occasionally.* Let the beans come to room temperature for 45 to 60 minutes before serving.

Turn into a decorative bowl for serving.

Antipasto Platter
    Cheese–Filled Crêpes in
Marinara Sauce
        Chicken and Sausage Crêpes in
    a Creamy Cheese Sauce
            Broccoli, Cauliflower, and
        Red Pepper Salad
                Buttered Italian Bread
                    Frozen Rum–Raisin Cream

When we were little girls living our sheltered existences, we thought all Italian food came out of tin cans and was invariably colored orange-red. How far from the truth this was didn't dawn on us until years later, when we traveled in Europe and settled in New York's Greenwich Village; there we became regulars at the numerous neighborhood restaurants that serve fresh and extensive Italian cuisine. One of us lived in a four-story walk-up apartment that overlooked the garden of Emilio's restaurant, from which the aromas of tomato, Parmesan cheese, and oregano wafted to the stars. It didn't take long before we were passing right over a menu's honest spaghetti offerings in favor of those twin epicurean delights, cannelloni and manicotti. So it is to the memory of our halcyon youth and the many friendly mom-and-pop restaurants in the Village which sustained us (Joe's, Mary's, Rocco's, and Monte's, to name a few) that we dedicate our all-seasons cocktail buffet menu.

Because this is such an all-purpose, satisfying menu sure to please just about everybody, we think you will rely on it many times when you want to serve a crowd something more classy and unusual than a casserole or a stew. The food is both light and filling enough to be acceptable at any time of the year, with the possible exceptions of July and August, when you might want to feature more fresh produce. There *is* work to be done on the day of the party, so when we direct you to have finished putting together certain dishes or parts of dishes beforehand, be sure you've done it!

The very first dish to get out of the way is the dessert, which can—and should—be made several days or even a couple of weeks in advance. This recipe can be put together very quickly. All you have to remember to have on hand are muffin-tin liners and a pint of dark rum. When these delicious little creams are un-molded from the paper liners and put on dessert plates, they look a little boring because they're relatively colorless; this is why we recommend garnishing them with gratings or curls of chocolate. You could also top each dessert with half a candied cherry, the typical decorative touch you see on frozen biscuit tortoni in Italian restaurants. Personally, we like the chocolate better. Just this year we have become aware of a kitchen item called a chocolate mill. Retailing for around fifteen dollars, this hand-operated gadget produces sumptuous curls of hard chocolate, a much more enticing garnish than the usual grated chocolate.

The main attractions of the cocktail buffet menu are, as promised, two dishes which are very much like cannelloni and manicotti, except that the traditional Italian fillings are wrapped in crêpes instead of pasta shapes. We do this for two reasons: A crêpe is infinitely lighter and less fattening than either the cannelloni or manicotti pasta dough; and while anyone can make a crêpe, not everyone has the means to make pasta, nor can the storebought cannelloni or manicotti always be found. We hope to be forgiven by Italian cooks for giving their marvelous creations a Gallic touch.

The crêpes *sans* fillings can be made a couple of days before the party, though if you have time to make them the night before, they will be tastier. There are several electric crêpe makers on the market, but we feel we have more control over the finished product when we use a 7-inch or 8-inch skillet with rounded sides and a no-stick surface; this latter feature is essential.

The fillings for the crêpes can be made ahead of time, too; in fact, you might consider putting together the fillings *before* the crêpes, then cooking the crêpes the morning of the party so they'll be really fresh. The fillings are a snap to make and keep well in the refrigerator. The marinara sauce which covers the cheese-filled crêpes can also be made a day or two before the party and refrigerated. Thus, the only sauce you have to worry about on the day of the party is the cream sauce for the chicken and sausage crêpes.

The final assembly of the crêpes should be undertaken 4 or 5 hours before the party is scheduled to start. If you are short of room in the refrigerator for two big pans of crêpes, you can put them outside if the temperature is 40 degrees or lower; or you can store them in a neighbor's refrigerator (we realize that refrigerator space is sometimes a problem, and encourage people to rely on their neighbors when in a bind).

If you have only one oven, you could have a problem juggling the baking of the two crêpe recipes and the heating up of the bread unless you think things through ahead of time. Your best bet is to warm up the bread, sliced and wrapped in foil, *before* you put the crêpes in the oven. Keep the bread wrapped in the foil, and while the crêpes are cooking, place the bread on an electric hot tray.

When the crêpes are being served buffet-style—as they would be for this particular dinner party—you might want to personally lift out the crêpes from their baking dishes for your guests as they pass by with their plates. Crêpes can be tricky to extract if one is also holding a plate and silverware; in addition, you can make sure that each guest gets one of each kind.

There is preliminary work that can be accomplished for the antipasto platter and the salad. The pickled pineapple has to be prepared well in advance, and the ham roll-ups can be assembled two or three days before the party. If you intend to serve raw vegetables on the antipasto plate, these can be readied and refrigerated either the night before or early in the morning. The worst of the salad making can be taken care of a day in advance— namely, the peeling of the broccoli stalks and the quick cooking of both broccoli and cauliflower.

We want you to have fun with the antipasto platter. You don't have to follow our recommendations to the letter. Browse through your supermarket or delicatessen for items that are Italian. There are many foods out of cans and jars which we have not included in the recipe. What you want to achieve with the platter is a balance of color, taste, and texture, plus the look and feel of an antipasto. If you are concerned that the antipasto platter might not provide enough hors-d'oeuvre food, you can put out a separate plate of cheese with crackers (an Italian Fontina cheese, for example) and a bowl of nuts.

As with our summer cocktail buffet, we think this is one menu that goes well with either white or red wine because one crêpe calls for white, the other for red—but neither cries out strongly for one or the other wine. Fill half the wineglasses with a cold dry white which could be a little bit fruity, and half the glasses with a hearty red.

Antipasto Platter

14 to 16 servings

This appetizer can be decreased or increased, depending on the number of people you have invited for dinner.

2   *5-ounce cans eggplant appetizer (caponata)*

     Small crackers

8 to 9 *Romaine lettuce leaves*

1   *recipe pickled pineapple (page 234)*

1½   *recipes ham roll-ups (page 236)*

1   *6-ounce jar marinated artichoke hearts*

1   *6-ounce jar marinated Brussels sprouts*

1   *3½-ounce tin smoked clams* OR *smoked oysters*

1   *pound Provolone cheese, cut into bite-size cubes*

     Cherry tomatoes

     Black olives

     Celery sticks

     Carrot sticks

     Radishes

On a large round platter, place a small shallow bowl filled with the eggplant appetizer, arrange crackers around it and supply a small knife for spreading (if you cannot locate any eggplant appetizer in your grocery store, omit the crackers and fill the bowl with a substitute such as olives). Around the crackers arrange the lettuce leaves, and on each leaf, place the rest of the ingredients in an attractive order (see diagram).

Serve as soon as guests are settled with their drinks, and provide plenty of toothpicks.

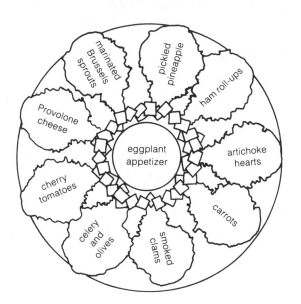

Cheese–Filled Crêpes in Marinara Sauce

14 to 16 servings

In a large mixing bowl, make the filling by combining the ricotta, mozzarella, and Parmesan cheeses, the eggs, parsley, salt, and pepper; stir until thoroughly blended. *At this point, the filling can be stored in the refrigerator, covered, for 1 to 2 days.*

In a large skillet, make the marinara sauce by heating the oil over low-medium heat and sautéing the onion and garlic until tender. Add the tomatoes, tomato paste, parsley, sugar, oregano, basil, salt, and pepper, and simmer over low heat 20 to 30 minutes, stirring occasionally. Remove from the heat and let cool. *At this point, the sauce can be held for several hours, or it can be stored in the refrigerator, covered, for 3 to 4 days.* Let it come to room temperature for 1 hour before using.

When ready to assemble the crêpes, place a crêpe on your work surface and spoon about 3 tablespoons of the cheese filling onto it near the "handle" edge. Spread the filling out to either side, then proceed to roll the crêpe around the filling until it is completely rolled up. Place the crêpe seam side down on a greased, shallow baking dish measuring approximately 12 x 18 x 2 inches. Repeat the procedure for each crêpe, nestling the crêpes close together in the baking dish. *At this point, the crêpes can be stored in the refrigerator, covered, for 1 day.* Let them come to room temperature for 1 hour before cooking.

Preheat the oven to 375 degrees.

Spread the marinara sauce over the crêpes to cover them completely. If any areas look dry or bare, cover with some of the optional tomato sauce. It is important that the crêpes have plenty of sauce on them to prevent any

20 to 25 *crêpes (page 203)*

1   *8-ounce can tomato sauce (optional)*

¼   *cup Parmesan cheese* OR *Romano cheese, grated*

Filling

2   *pounds ricotta cheese* OR *small, dry curd cottage cheese*

1   *pound mozzarella cheese, grated*

⅓   *cup Parmesan cheese* OR *Romano cheese, grated*

2   *eggs, lightly beaten*

¼   *cup fresh parsley, finely chopped*

     Salt and freshly ground black pepper to taste

Sauce

¼   *cup olive oil* OR *a combination of olive and vegetable oil*

1   *large onion, finely chopped*

2   *cloves garlic, finely chopped*

3   16-*ounce cans Italian
    plum tomatoes, drained
    and coarsely chopped*

1   6-*ounce can tomato
    paste*

¼   *cup fresh parsley, finely
    chopped*

1   *teaspoon sugar*

½   *teaspoon oregano*

¼   *teaspoon basil*

    *Salt and freshly ground
    black pepper to taste*

drying out during the baking. Sprinkle the ¼ cup Parmesan cheese over the sauce.

Bake the crêpes, covered, for 20 to 25 minutes, until the sauce is bubbling and the crêpes are heated through. Serve immediately.

Chicken and Sausage Crêpes in a Creamy Cheese Sauce

14 to 16 servings

20 to 25 *crêpes (page
    203)*

¼   *cup fresh parsley,
    finely chopped*

Filling

1   10-*ounce package fro-
    zen chopped spinach*

1½ *pounds sweet Italian
    sausage* OR *a combi-
    nation of sweet Italian
    sausage and hot Ital-
    ian sausage*

3   *cups cooked chicken,
    diced*

To make the filling: In a medium saucepan, cook the spinach in 1 cup boiling, salted water until the spinach is thawed, breaking it up with a fork as it cooks to hasten the process. Drain the spinach in a sieve or colander and run cold water over it. Using your hands, squeeze out all the moisture from the spinach and place in a large mixing bowl.

Remove the casings from the sausage. In a medium skillet, place the sausage and heat the skillet over medium heat; cook the sausage, breaking it up into small pieces, until it is completely cooked through and done, about 15 minutes; let cool slightly. Using a slotted spoon, remove the sausage from the skillet and place in the mixing bowl with the spinach. Add the chicken, cheese, oregano, salt, pepper, and eggs to the bowl and stir to combine all ingredients.

To assemble the crêpes, place a crêpe on your work surface and spoon about 3 tablespoons of the filling onto the crêpe near the "handle" edge. Spread the filling out to either side, then roll the crêpe around the filling until it is completely rolled up. Place the crêpe, seam side down, on a greased, shallow baking dish measuring approximately 12 x 18 x 2 inches. Repeat the procedure for each crêpe, nestling the crêpes close together in the baking dish. *At this point, the crêpes can be stored in the refrigerator, covered, for 4 to 5 hours. Let them come to room temperature for 1 hour before cooking.*

While you are bringing the crêpes to room temperature, make the cream sauce. In a medium saucepan, melt the butter over low heat and stir in the flour until smooth. Slowly pour in the cream and cook over low heat, stirring constantly, until the sauce is thickened. Season to taste with salt and pepper, and stir in the cheese until it is completely melted. Spread the cream sauce over the crêpes to cover them completely.

Preheat the oven to 375 degrees.

Bake the crêpes, covered, for 20 to 25 minutes. Remove from the oven and turn the oven heat to BROIL. Return the crêpes to the oven and broil 6 inches from the heat, uncovered, until golden brown and bubbly. Sprinkle the crêpes with the parsley and serve immediately.

½   cup Parmesan cheese OR Romano cheese, grated

½   teaspoon oregano

    Salt and freshly ground black pepper to taste

2   eggs, lightly beaten

Sauce

3   tablespoons butter

3   tablespoons flour

2   cups light cream OR half-and-half cream

    Salt and freshly ground white pepper to taste

½   cup Parmesan cheese OR Romano cheese, grated

Crêpes

Makes 40 to 50 crêpes

Let the eggs come to room temperature for 30 to 45 minutes, then break into a large mixing bowl and beat lightly. Add the flour and salt and, using a wire whisk, beat until smooth. Slowly pour in the water and continue beating

10   eggs

2½   cups flour

½   teaspoon salt

2½   cups water

until just smooth; do not overmix. Let the crêpe batter stand for 30 to 60 minutes.

Heat a 7- or 8-inch skillet with a no-stick surface and sloping sides over medium heat; when hot, pour in a scant 3 tablespoons of batter (this is done more efficiently if you use a ladle that holds 3 tablespoons of liquid). Quickly swirl the batter in the skillet until the bottom is covered, then pour out any excess batter to create a "handle" of sorts against the side of the skillet (the excess batter gets poured back into the rest of the batter in the bowl). Cook the crêpe until the top is no longer shiny and the crêpe begins to pull away from the edges of the skillet; this takes just a few seconds. Pull up the handle of the crêpe and lift it right out of the pan; to avoid burning your fingers, you may need to use a small spatula to pull the handle away from the skillet before picking up the crêpe. Place the crêpe on a large sheet of waxed paper with the glazed side up (this is the side that faces you as you cook it).

Repeat the procedure for the rest of the crêpes. When you have filled up your sheet of waxed paper with a single layer of crêpes, tear off another sheet, put this on top of the crêpes, and fill it as you go on cooking. Continue layering the crêpes in this fashion. Let the crêpes cool until ready to use. *At this point, the crêpes can be held for several hours; or they can be refrigerated for 1 day; or they can be frozen.* Let them thaw and come to room temperature before assembling with the respective fillings.

Broccoli, Cauliflower, and Red Pepper Salad

14 to 16 servings

In a medium mixing bowl, make the dressing by combining the salt, mustard, paprika, basil, black pepper, sugar, and garlic; stir in the vinegar. Whisk in the oil until thoroughly blended.

Cut off an inch from the ends of the broccoli stalks and separate the stalks from the flowerettes. Cut the flowerettes into bite-size pieces. Scrape the tough outer skin from the stalks and cut into bite-size pieces.

Cut away the green leaves from the cauliflower head and cut the flowerettes into bite-size pieces.

In a large kettle, bring 8 to 10 quarts salted water to a boil, plunge in the broccoli and cauliflower pieces and, when the water returns to the boil, drain immediately into a colander. Run cold water over the vegetables, then dry thoroughly on paper towels. Place in a large bowl.

Clean the mushrooms, trim away the bottom of the stems and cut into halves or quarters, depending on size. Add to the broccoli and cauliflower. Whisk the dressing again, then pour it over the vegetables and toss gently to coat everything; let the vegetables stand 1 hour before refrigerating. *At this point, the vegetables can be stored in the refrigerator, covered, for several hours or overnight.*

Shortly before serving, place the broccoli, cauliflower, and mushrooms in a large salad bowl, add the roasted peppers, and toss everything well. Taste to correct seasoning, adding more salt or a sprinkling of vinegar if necessary. Serve immediately.

Dressing

1	teaspoon salt
1	teaspoon dry mustard
½	teaspoon paprika
½	teaspoon basil
¼	teaspoon freshly ground black pepper
	Generous pinch sugar
1	clove garlic, mashed
½	cup red wine vinegar
1½	cups vegetable oil AND olive oil, combined
2	bunches fresh broccoli
1	head cauliflower
1½	pounds fresh mushrooms
1	7-ounce can roasted peppers, drained and chopped OR 2 4-ounce jars pimiento, drained and chopped

(Note: If you prefer the look of white mushrooms in the salad, add them before serving along with the roasted peppers. They can be sliced 2 to 3 hours earlier and kept tightly covered in the refrigerator.)

Frozen Rum–Raisin Cream

Makes 16 frozen creams

2	*8-ounce packages cream cheese, softened to room temperature*
2	*scant cups confectioners' sugar*
2	*cups heavy cream*
1	*cup dark rum*
1	*teaspoon vanilla extract*
¾	*cup seedless raisins, chopped*
¾	*cup pecans* OR *walnuts, finely chopped*
	Grated chocolate for garnish

In a food processor fitted with the steel blade, process the cream cheese, sugar, cream, rum, and vanilla extract until smooth; this may have to be done in 2 batches (you can also cream together everything by hand). Pour into a large mixing bowl and stir in the raisins and nuts.

Place 16 paper liners in 2 standard tins for cupcakes or muffins (you will be using only part of 1 tin). Spoon the rum-raisin cream mixture into the liners so the mixture is evenly distributed; your liners should be nearly full. Freeze the rum-raisin creams for 12 hours or more. *At this point, the dessert can be stored in the freezer for 1 to 2 months.*

When ready to serve, remove the rum-raisin creams from the paper liners and invert on individual dessert plates. Sprinkle a little grated chocolate over each cream and serve immediately.

Roast Turkey with Giblet Gravy
  Herbed Corn–Bread Stuffing OR
Sausage–Wild Rice Stuffing
    Squash and Corn Custard
    OR *Carrot–Sweet Potato Purée*
      Green Beans with Water Chestnuts
      OR *Braised Brussels Sprouts*
        Cranberry Sauce
          Pumpkin Cream Pie
            OR *Frozen Mincemeat Pie*

For people who work full- or part-time, the Thanksgiving and Christmas holidays loom as a chore, a responsibility, perhaps even a burden to be endured. This is especially true if one has somehow gotten roped into hosting the main event of either holiday—the family dinner. We think it's a shame that just because so many more people—especially female people—are working now than in our mothers' and grandmothers' generations, we cannot manage to derive as much pleasure and enjoyment as our forebears out of preparing an impressive feast for those we love.

Of course no one can dispute that our mothers and grandmothers had days on end which they chose to devote to cooking and baking and candlestick making. The end result of such lavish preparation was a groaning board of dozens of mouthwatering, made-from-scratch dishes—enough food for the Russian army or at least for a large family extending to second cousins and great-aunts.

When we first conceived of this book, we determined that one of our projects would be to put some merriment back into making a dinner for the holidays. And we believe we have succeeded. In fact, we have succeeded several times under the most realistic of circumstances, for during the writing of the book, two Thanksgivings and two Christmases have come and gone, and we have served our perfect holiday dinner for each occasion.

The main thing to keep in mind when contemplating the prospect of a holiday dinner is that you will have very little time. As far as Thanksgiving goes, most people have to work until five o'clock the afternoon before; and at Christmas, people are up to their mistletoe in all kinds of time-consuming activities like tree decorating, package wrapping, Christmas card writing, and cookie baking. Therefore you want a dinner menu that will be extremely easy to put together—though of course, you want it to be beautiful and delicious too.

You can control the ease of your dinner preparations by limiting the number of people you include in the party and by sticking to a few simple but filling recipes such as the ones in our holiday menu. We thought for a long while about the number of people our perfect holiday dinner would serve and finally decided that 8 to 10 diners makes the most sense. Eight to 10 would seem to suit quite a few combinations of extended family members and friends. It is also a number that can be comfortably seated around the dinner table. For people who want or need to invite a bigger crowd, the recipes in the menu are easily doubled and the whole menu can be served buffet-style.

We have set up our holiday menu to give you a choice of turkey stuffings, green vegetables, yellow vegetables, and pies. In other words, you can choose whether you want to stuff your bird with seasoned corn bread or with sausage and rice, whether to feature squash and corn in one of the vegetable dishes or carrots and sweet potatoes, whether to serve green beans or Brussels sprouts, and so forth. Don't imagine that you're supposed to serve both choices of green and yellow vegetables, because you're not! We offer choices so that families can pick their favorite, most traditional foods for this season of the year. Only when it comes to the pies might you want to make both the pumpkin and the mincemeat—especially if you are having 10 for dinner, because it's hard to cut 10 wedges out of a single pie.

If you plan your dinner so the table is adorned with the turkey, a green vegetable, a yellow vegetable, a dish of cranberry sauce and, if you want, a relish dish of celery sticks and black olives, you will have a visually appealing spread and one that fills everyone to capacity. Best of all, your time in the kitchen on the day of the dinner will not have exceeded 3 hours.

Our rather unusual method of cooking the turkey is to place the trussed bird in an adjustable, V-shaped rack in the pan over a little water in which float some pot vegetables and the giblets. Thus, instead of truly roasting, which is the way most recipes would have you cook a turkey, our bird is more or less steamed. This method produces the most fantastically moist and flavorful turkey we have ever tasted, and this is true whether the turkey is an expensive, fresh-killed bird or the cheapest frozen bargain at the meat counter. Furthermore, because the bird is rubbed with paprika and remains uncovered for most of the cooking, the skin emerges a glorious reddish-golden color. The water beneath the turkey gets permeated with the flavors of the vegetables, the giblets, and whatever drippings fall from the turkey into the water; this creates a base for a good turkey gravy which can be made right in the pan. Our turkey recipe is extremely efficient and incredibly easy to execute.

Not everyone lives where they can obtain a fresh turkey, but for those who do, we recommend that you try one. The advantages to the fresh birds are: More dark meat than you find in frozen birds; you don't have to worry about the thawing time; and the fresh turkeys often have a flavor edge over frozen. A general rule of thumb for how much turkey to buy is 1 pound per person being served, but we have found this to provide very skimpy servings. Therefore, for 8 to 10 people, we suggest you buy a 14- to 16-pound turkey. However, even with the additional poundage, you may not have many leftovers—perhaps no more than enough to make a turkey soup. It's important to figure out ahead of time if you want to get a lot of turkey sandwiches or turkey casseroles out of the bird; and if you do, then buy something bigger than we recommend.

One word of advice to the turkey carver: Unless your turkey platter is absolutely immense, you will need a second warm platter beside you on which to place the carved meat.

More so than in other menus in this book, there is a certain reliance on canned or packaged goods in the holiday menu, but only where we have tested the products and decided there was no loss in flavor or nutritional value. For example, we openly advocate the purchase of a canned cranberry sauce instead of going to the tedious trouble of making your own. The best-known brand of cranberry products puts out an admirable cranberry sauce. For the corn-bread stuffing, we direct you to use as your base a package of herb-seasoned stuffing and a package of corn-bread stuffing. Again, this not only saves you the time and involvement of making corn bread and drying bread cubes, it gives you a stuffing that is extremely tasty and has an excellent texture. Just be sure you buy a reputable brand of packaged stuffing.

Finally, our pumpkin pie is in a frozen pie crust from the supermarket and features canned pumpkin; our mincemeat pie is in a graham cracker crust made with a box of crumbs you can buy, and the mincemeat is out of a jar. We would not really discourage you from making your own pie crust for the pumpkin pie, but if you are pressed for time and your local grocery store offers a good frozen product (ours offers two or three brands of good frozen pie crust), we say, "Go ahead and use it." Furthermore, we think it's obvious that canned pumpkin is preferable to cutting up and cooking your own for just 1½ cups of pumpkin; and the canned version is just as good. Time is saved when you use the ready-made graham cracker crumbs instead of rolling out your own; the boxed crumbs are finely ground and make a nice, dense crust for the ice cream filling. As for the mincemeat that is mixed with the ice cream, we don't know anyone who has made mincemeat from scratch for years.

Almost any wine can be drunk with the holiday dinner—red, white, rosé, or champagne. One wine from California which is particularly complementary to turkey is a white Pinot Noir called "Eye of the Swan."

Roast Turkey with Giblet Gravy

8 to 10 servings

If your turkey is frozen, thaw it according to the directions on the wrapping. It should be thawed slowly which, for a bird this size, means approximately 48 hours at room temperature; if the bird thaws sooner than expected, simply put it in the refrigerator until ready to cook.

Before preparing the turkey itself, make either the corn-bread stuffing or the sausage-rice stuffing.

Preheat the oven to 350 degrees.

Remove the giblets from the turkey and dry it thoroughly inside and out with paper towels. Reserve the giblets (the liver has already been taken out if you are making the sausage-rice stuffing). Salt and pepper the turkey's body and neck cavities and loosely stuff both cavities with the dressing; do not pack in the stuffing as it expands during the cooking. Either sew up the turkey cavities or skewer them shut. If you use skewers, you should lace together the ones closing the body cavity with kitchen string, as though you were tying a shoe.

To truss the turkey, use plenty of kitchen string, a piece about 6 feet in length. With the turkey positioned breast side up, start at the midpoint of the string and tie together the ends of the turkey legs, then run the string around the tail to catch it up against the legs. Run the 2 lengths of string from the legs across the breast and through the joints of the wings at the back to really secure them against the body of the bird. Turn the turkey over and knot the string against the back. Rub the bird all over with the vegetable oil, and rub salt and pepper into the skin. Sprinkle the top and sides of the turkey evenly with the paprika and garlic powder, and rub both into the skin.

1	14- to 16-*pound turkey, fresh* OR *frozen*
1	*recipe for turkey stuffing (page 213)*
	Salt and freshly ground black pepper to taste
¼	*cup vegetable oil*
½	*to 1 teaspoon paprika*
¼	*teaspoon garlic powder*
1	*medium onion, quartered*
2	*carrots, scraped and broken in half*
2	*celery stalks, broken in half*
2	*to 3 sprigs fresh parsley*
4	*to 6 peppercorns*
6	*tablespoons flour*
½	*to ¾ teaspoon gravy seasoning sauce (optional)*

In a 10 × 15 × 3-inch roasting pan, place about 1 inch of water, the turkey giblets, onion, carrots, celery, parsley, and peppercorns. Place a flat or V-shaped adjustable rack in the pan; grease the rack well with butter or oil. Place the turkey on the rack, breast side up. Roast the turkey about 15 minutes per pound for most frozen turkeys; if you're fortunate enough to obtain a fresh bird, the cooking time may be reduced to 12 minutes per pound (check with your butcher). About 2 to 2½ hours into the cooking, check the turkey to see if the top is getting too brown; if this is happening, cover the top of the bird loosely with a piece of foil.

When the turkey is done, place it on a warm serving platter and cover the whole bird loosely with foil while you make the gravy.

Remove the vegetables and turkey neck from the roasting pan and discard. Using a slotted spoon, remove the rest of the giblets to a cutting board and cut up the gizzard and heart into a fine dice. Skim off most of the fat from the liquid in the pan. Measure out 3 cups of this turkey stock, discarding any excess stock. Return the stock to the pan and season with salt and pepper.*

Place the roasting pan over low heat and scrape up the particles from the bottom of the pan. In a small mixing bowl, blend the flour with ¾ cup cold water until smooth; add a little turkey stock to this mixture and stir until smooth. Pour the flour mixture into the turkey stock and stir constantly over low heat until the stock is thickened to the desired consistency; add the optional gravy seasoning sauce and stir. Stir in the diced giblets and taste to correct seasoning. Pour the gravy into a warm gravy boat or other small serving bowl and keep warm while the turkey is being carved.

---

* Some people may find the gravy preparation easier if they measure out the stock into a medium-size saucepan.

Herbed Corn–Bread Stuffing

8 to 10 servings

Prepare the two packages of stuffing according to package directions. In a large mixing bowl, combine the two stuffings, the onion, sage, salt, and pepper. Taste to correct seasoning.

Stuff the turkey loosely with the stuffing according to the turkey recipe directions (page 211); do not overstuff. If you have any excess stuffing, put it in a small casserole dish, dot with some butter, and bake in a 350-degree oven for 20 to 30 minutes. Serve with the turkey.

1   8-ounce package herb-seasoned stuffing

1   8-ounce package corn-bread stuffing

1   large onion, finely chopped

Sage to taste

Salt and freshly ground black pepper to taste

Sausage–Wild Rice Stuffing

8 to 10 servings

Thoroughly wash the wild rice. In a medium saucepan, bring to a boil 2 cups salted water, add the rice, and cook over medium heat, covered, for 30 minutes. Drain in a sieve or colander and run cold water over the rice; make sure the rice is well drained. (The wild rice will not be completely cooked at this point; the cooking will be finished inside the turkey.) In a large mixing bowl, combine the wild rice and the cooked white rice.

In a medium skillet, melt the butter and oil over low-medium heat and sauté the turkey liver until cooked through, about 5 minutes; add the onion and sauté until tender. Season to taste with salt and pepper and let cool. Scrape the onion mixture into the bowl of rice.

In the same skillet, brown the sausage over medium heat, breaking up the meat as you

½   cup wild rice

2   cups long-grain white rice, cooked (about ¾ cup uncooked)

3   tablespoons butter

1   tablespoon vegetable oil

1   turkey liver, finely chopped

1   cup onion, finely chopped

Salt and freshly ground black pepper to taste

1   pound bulk pork sausage

½ cup dried apricots,
finely chopped

cook it. When the sausage is no longer pink, pour off all the fat and let cool. Scrape the sausage into the rice along with the apricots; stir to combine the ingredients. Taste to correct seasoning.

Stuff the turkey loosely with the stuffing according to the turkey recipe directions (page 211); do not overstuff. If you have any excess stuffing, put it in a small casserole dish, dot with some butter, and bake in a 350-degree oven for 20 to 30 minutes. Serve with the turkey.

Squash and Corn Custard

8 to 10 servings

2   acorn squash, about
     1½ to 2 pounds each

6   tablespoons butter,
     softened to room tem-
     perature

4   tablespoons maple
     syrup

     Salt and freshly
     ground black pepper
     to taste

2   10-ounce packages
     frozen corn, thawed
     OR 2 16-ounce cans
     whole-kernel corn,
     drained

4   eggs

1½   cups light cream

Preheat the oven to 375 degrees.

Halve the squash and remove all seeds and fibrous material from the centers. Spread 2 tablespoons of the butter over the cut surfaces of the squash and place a tablespoon of maple syrup in the depressions of each squash; sprinkle squash with salt and pepper. Place the squash in a shallow baking dish and bake for 50 minutes. Remove from the oven, and when cool enough to handle, scoop out the squash meat, along with the melted butter and syrup, into a large mixing bowl or the container of a food processor fitted with the steel blade. Add the remaining butter and either mash the squash by hand or purée in the food processor. Let the squash cool completely.

Dry the corn thoroughly on paper towels. In a large mixing bowl, stir the corn into the squash and season to taste with salt and pepper. *At this point, the squash mixture can be held for several hours or stored in the refrigerator, covered, for 1 day.* Let the squash come to room temperature for 30 to 45 minutes before cooking.

Preheat the oven to 350 degrees.

In a medium mixing bowl, beat the eggs well and then beat in the cream; add to the squash mixture, stirring vigorously. Pour into a greased, deep 3- to 4-quart casserole and bake for 60 minutes, or until a toothpick inserted in the center comes out clean. Serve immediately.

Carrot–Sweet Potato Purée

8 to 10 servings

Preheat the oven to 375 degrees.

Wash the potatoes and bake for 45 to 60 minutes (the baking time will depend on the size of the potatoes). When cool enough to handle, cut open the potatoes and scoop out the flesh, placing small chunks of it in the container of a food processor which is fitted with the steel blade.

While the potatoes are baking, trim off the ends of the carrots, scrape them, and cut into 1-inch chunks. In a large saucepan, bring the chicken broth to a boil, add the carrots, and cook over low-medium heat, covered, for 15 to 20 minutes, until tender. Drain and add to the food processor.

Process the potatoes, carrots, and 10 tablespoons of the butter in the food processor until you have a smooth purée (you can also process through a food mill); this will have to be done in 2 or 3 batches. Spoon the purée into a large mixing bowl and season to taste with salt and pepper. Add the wine a little bit at a time, taking care not to use more wine than the purée can absorb. Taste to correct the seasoning. Spoon the purée into a greased, deep 2½-quart casserole dish and smooth over the top. *At this point, the purée can be held for 2 to 3 hours, or stored in the refrigerator,*

6 *medium sweet potatoes (yams), about 4 pounds*

2 *pounds carrots*

2 *cups chicken broth OR chicken stock*

12 *tablespoons butter, softened to room temperature*

Salt and freshly ground black pepper to taste

¼ *cup Madeira wine OR Marsala wine*

Pecan halves OR walnut halves for garnish

covered, for 1 day. Let the purée come to room temperature for 1 hour before cooking.

Preheat the oven to 350 degrees.

In a small saucepan, melt the remaining 2 tablespoons of butter. Gently press the pecan halves into the purée in an attractive pattern and brush the entire top of the purée with the melted butter. Bake the purée, uncovered, for 30 minutes, until heated through and bubbling around the edge. Serve immediately.

Green Beans with Water Chestnuts

8 to 10 servings

2½ to 3 *pounds fresh green beans*

1 *8-ounce can sliced water chestnuts, drained*

6 to 8 *tablespoons butter*

Salt and freshly ground black pepper to taste

Snap off the stem end of the beans and break into approximately 2-inch lengths. In a large kettle, bring 4 to 6 quarts salted water to a boil, plunge in the beans, cover until the water returns to a boil, and then cook, uncovered, for 5 to 7 minutes, until barely tender. Drain in a colander and run cold water over the beans. Pat the beans dry on paper towels. *At this point, the beans can be held for several hours, or they can be refrigerated, covered, for 1 day*. Let the beans come to room temperature for 45 to 60 minutes before reheating.

Dry the water chestnuts on paper towels and cut each round slice in half.

In a large skillet, melt the butter over medium heat until bubbly. Add the beans, water chestnuts, salt, and pepper, and sauté gently over low-medium heat, tossing constantly, until the beans are completely heated through. *At this point, the beans can be held in the skillet, covered, for 15 to 20 minutes over very low heat*. When ready to serve, place in a warm serving dish and pour on the butter. Serve immediately.

Braised Brussels Sprouts

8 to 10 servings

In a large skillet, bring the chicken broth to a boil and add the Brussels sprouts; when the broth returns to the boil, lower the heat and simmer, covered, for 10 minutes, until barely tender; stir occasionally. Drain the sprouts in a colander and reserve. *At this point, the Brussels sprouts can be held for 1 to 2 hours.*

In the same skillet, melt the butter over medium heat until bubbling. Return the Brussels sprouts to the skillet along with the sesame seeds, lower the heat slightly and sauté, tossing constantly, until thoroughly coated with the butter and heated through. Season to taste with salt and pepper. *At this point, the Brussels sprouts can be held in the skillet, covered, for 15 to 20 minutes over very low heat.* When ready to serve, place in a warmed serving dish and pour on the butter.

2	cups chicken broth OR chicken stock
3	10-ounce packages frozen Brussels sprouts
6	tablespoons butter
¼	cup sesame seeds
	Salt and freshly ground black pepper to taste

Pumpkin Cream Pie

6 to 8 servings

Soften the gelatin in ¼ cup cold water. In the top of a double boiler, combine the pumpkin, brown sugar, eggs, cinnamon, nutmeg, ginger, and salt. Cook over simmering water, stirring, until thickened. Off the heat, stir in the gelatin and let the mixture get cold (this is important; if the pumpkin mixture isn't cold when the cream is added to it, the cream will curdle).

In a medium mixing bowl, whip the cream to stiff peaks and fold into the pumpkin mixture until completely blended. Pour into the pie shell and refrigerate until set, about 4

1	envelope unflavored gelatin
1½	cups fresh or canned pumpkin
½	cup light brown sugar, packed
2	eggs, well beaten
2	teaspoons cinnamon
½	teaspoon nutmeg
½	teaspoon ginger

¼ teaspoon salt

½ cup heavy cream

1 9-inch pie shell, baked

Whipped cream topping (optional)

hours. *At this point, the pie can be stored in the refrigerator for 2 to 3 days.*

When ready to serve, garnish with the optional whipped cream topping around the edge of the pie.

Frozen Mincemeat Pie

6 to 8 servings

1 9-inch graham cracker pie crust made from packaged graham cracker crumbs

1 quart rich vanilla ice cream, slightly softened

1⅓ cups mincemeat flavored with brandy and rum

Make the graham cracker pie crust according to the package directions; watch the crust carefully while it is in the oven so it doesn't burn. Let the crust cool completely, then refrigerate for 30 minutes.

In a large mixing bowl, blend the ice cream and mincemeat, taking care not to stir too long, or else the ice cream will melt more than it should. Spoon the ice cream into the pie crust and smooth over the top. Place the pie in the freezer and freeze overnight. *At this point, the pie can be stored in the freezer, covered, for 1 month.* Let the pie stand for 10 minutes before cutting into wedges and serving.

6

Fast Food
to
Go with Drinks

Fast Food to Go with Drinks

People who don't have time to cook great little dinner parties have even less time to figure out what appetizers to serve while guests are relaxing with glasses of whiskey, wine, or mineral water. What this usually means is that the hors-d'oeuvre course gets short shrift in the overall planning of the affair—with a supermarket or cheese shop ending up as the provider of the nibble food. This is not only an uninspired approach, it's unfortunate as well because so much of this is junk food. It really is easy to have delicious and nutritious tidbits on hand in freezer, refrigerator, and pantry; and furthermore, there are a number of decent appetizer foods that can be thrown together in just a few minutes.

We dislike thinking about appetizers, too, and admit to having lived many years offering guests nothing more than wedges of cheese and bowls of peanuts. But the writing of this chapter has convinced us that food to go with drinks can be interesting, varied, and memorable. In fact, it doesn't even require the planning necessary for the rest of the dinner party.

We have categorized the recipes in this chapter according to their main ingredients, such as cheese or meat. The reason for this is to enable you to pick two or three recipes from different categories, so that you can end up with a variety of appetizers for your party. In other words, one appetizer might feature vegetables, another might highlight fish, and the third could be nuts.

When selecting your food for the cocktail hour, you should take into consideration the food that you are serving for dinner. If your dinner is heavy Italian food, you would not prepare the salami-cheese rounds as an appetizer; if blue cheese is a predominant flavor at some point during the meal, you should pass over the curried blue cheese ball as something to eat before dinner.

The season of the year should be taken into account too. In the summer, you would certainly want to serve a vegetable dip so as to capitalize on produce at its freshest. Nuts seem to go with the winter months; and so do hot appetizers like the crab meat dip and Parmesan cheese squares.

Many of the appetizers we have created are accompanied by crackers (the spreads, the cheese balls, and so forth). We would like to encourage you to purchase crackers or wafers that are small in size and low in salt and oil; some generic names to look for are water biscuits, melba toast rounds, Scandanavian crisp flatbread, rice crackers, stoned wheat thins, rye crisps. Such crackers enhance the taste of hors-d'oeuvre food rather than bury it. Many supermarkets separate the run-of-the-mill crackers from the good varieties, putting the latter in with the breads, in the gourmet section, even above the frozen orange juice counter! Ask someone who works in the store, or search out the crackers on your own.

The number of appetizers to serve a dinner party of six is a matter of personal choice. We think three different kinds of food to munch on provides the desired variety in taste experience and appearance. Thus most of our appetizer recipes produce moderate quantities because we are assuming that you won't be relying on a single appetizer to take care of the entire cocktail hour. For larger parties, you can increase the amounts of the recipes or prepare additional recipes. A judicious selection of the appetizers in this chapter would constitute a smorgasbord for a terrific cocktail party.

If you haven't planned for the appetizers until the eleventh hour and can only manage to make two of our recipes, you can certainly rely on a storebought item to round out the homemade nibbles. We don't intend to knock all storebought appetizers. In fact, there are a number of notably acceptable ones with which you can stock your pantry shelf. Here is a list of purchased appetizers we have tried and liked very much:

---

eggplant appetizer (caponata)
marinated artichokes, mushrooms, and Brussels sprouts
smoked oysters, clams, and mussels
liver pâté
Boursin and Boursault cheeses
hot green pepper jelly (*this goes on crackers with cream cheese*)
sesame sticks
"trail" mix (*combination of nuts, raisins and other dried fruits, sunflower and pumpkin seeds*)
sardines in mustard or tomato sauce
cocktail shrimp in sauce
olives stuffed with almonds

black olives
pickled corn
dilled beans and dilled carrots
Mexican bean dip
sunflower seeds
red or black caviar
plain raw vegetables

We're sure there are others we have overlooked. Just keep snooping around in the gourmet section of the supermarket, in cheese and fine food shops, and even in gift catalogs.

Finally, remember that if you always have one or two appetizers tucked away in the freezer, perhaps one in the refrigerator which has excellent staying power (like the red sauce, the pickled pineapple, a cheese ball, the mustard dip), and a well-stocked pantry, you will never again have to worry about what tidbits to serve to temper guests' ravenous appetites.

Spicy Cheese Balls

Makes 40 to 45 balls

1   *cup flour*

½   *teaspoon cayenne pepper*

½   *teaspoon caraway seeds*

Salt to taste

8   *tablespoons (1 stick) butter, softened to room temperature*

1   *cup sharp Cheddar cheese, grated and softened to room temperature*

¼   *teaspoon steak sauce*

In a medium mixing bowl, combine the flour, cayenne pepper, caraway seeds, and salt.

In a food processor fitted with the steel blade, process the butter, cheese, and steak sauce until blended. Add the flour and continue to process until a ball of soft dough is formed. Place the dough in a bowl and refrigerate for 1 to 2 hours. *At this point, the dough can be stored in the refrigerator, covered with plastic wrap, for several days; or it can be frozen for 2 to 3 months. Let the dough thaw before using.*

When ready to bake, preheat the oven to 375 degrees.

Break off approximately 1 teaspoon of dough, roll into a small ball, and place on an ungreased cookie sheet. Repeat this procedure until you have used up all the dough; you will need 2 standard cookie sheets. Bake the cheese balls for 10 to 15 minutes, until golden brown. Let the balls cool before serving or storing in a covered container. *At this point, the cheese balls can be stored for several days.*

Cheese—Wrapped Olives

Makes 30

½   *cup flour*

1   *teaspoon paprika*

¼   *teaspoon dry mustard*

Salt to taste

In a small mixing bowl, stir together the flour, paprika, mustard, and salt.

In a food processor fitted with the steel blade, process the cheese and butter until blended. Add the flour and process until a ball of soft dough is formed.

Dry the olives well on paper towels. Take 1 teaspoon of the dough and flatten it on waxed paper with the heel of your hand to the approximate size of a silver dollar. Place an olive in the middle and wrap the dough around it, then shape the dough evenly around the olive until you have completely covered it and the dough is smooth. Repeat until all the olives are covered with the dough.

Place the cheese-wrapped olives on an ungreased cookie sheet and refrigerate for 1 to 2 hours. *At this point, the appetizers can be stored in the refrigerator for several hours; or they can be frozen for 2 to 3 months.* Let them thaw before baking.

When ready to bake, preheat the oven to 400 degrees.

Bake the cheese-wrapped olives for 10 to 15 minutes, until the dough is golden brown. Serve immediately.

1 *cup sharp Cheddar cheese, grated and softened to room temperature*

4 *tablespoons butter, softened to room temperature*

30 *pimiento-stuffed green olives*

Whole—Wheat Cheese Sticks

Makes 24 sticks

The whole-wheat flour imparts a nutty flavor to these popular cheese sticks. Serve in an upright container such as a beer stein, pitcher, or vase.

In a medium mixing bowl, stir together the flour, cayenne pepper, and salt.

In a food processor fitted with the steel blade, process the cheese, butter, and Worcestershire sauce until blended. Add the flour and process until a ball of soft dough is formed. Place the dough in a bowl and refrigerate for 1 to 2 hours. *At this point, the dough can be stored in the refrigerator, covered with plastic wrap, for several days; or it can be frozen for 2 to 3 months.* Let the dough thaw before using.

When ready to bake, preheat the oven to 375 degrees.

1 *cup whole-wheat flour* OR *regular flour*

½ *teaspoon cayenne pepper*

Salt to taste

1 *pound sharp Cheddar cheese, grated and softened to room temperature*

6 *tablespoons butter, softened to room temperature*

¼ teaspoon Worcester-
shire sauce

To form 1 cheese stick, break off approximately 1½ tablespoons of dough, roll into an 8-inch stick, and place on an ungreased cookie sheet. Repeat this procedure, placing the sticks 1½ inches apart, until you have used up all the dough; you will need 2 standard cookie sheets. Bake the cheese sticks for 15 to 20 minutes, until golden brown. Let them cool completely before trying to pick up. Serve the cheese sticks or store in a covered container. *At this point, the cheese sticks can be stored for 2 to 3 days.*

Curried Blue Cheese Ball

Makes 1 cheese ball

1 8-ounce package cream cheese, softened to room temperature

4 ounces blue cheese OR Roquefort cheese, crumbled and softened to room temperature

1 teaspoon Worcestershire sauce

2 teaspoons curry powder

1 teaspoon tarragon, crumbled

1 teaspoon dry mustard

⅛ teaspoon ground ginger

3 tablespoons fresh parsley, finely chopped

In a medium mixing bowl, cream together the cream cheese, blue cheese, Worcestershire sauce, curry powder, tarragon, mustard, and ginger. (Note: You can blend in a food processor, too, but this will create a soft cheese mixture which will have to be put in the refrigerator for 2 to 3 hours, until it stiffens up to hold the shape of a ball.) Shape the mixture into a ball and roll in the parsley to cover. Wrap tightly in plastic wrap and refrigerate for at least 1 hour before using. *At this point, the cheese ball can be stored in the refrigerator for 1 to 2 weeks.*

Horseradish Cheese Ball

Makes 1 cheese ball

The amount of horseradish you use in this popular cheese ball depends on how emphatic you want its flavor to be.

In a food processor fitted with the steel blade, place the 2 cheeses and process until smooth. Add the horseradish and butter and process briefly to blend. Spoon the cheese mixture into a bowl and refrigerate about 3 hours, until it is stiff.

Place the cheese mixture on a piece of waxed paper and shape into a ball, then roll in the chopped nuts to cover. Wrap tightly in plastic wrap and refrigerate for at least 1 hour before using. *At this point, the cheese ball can be stored in the refrigerator for 1 to 2 weeks.* Serve with crackers, preferably the unsalted variety.

5 *ounces sharp Cheddar cheese, grated and softened to room temperature*

3 *ounces cream cheese, softened to room temperature*

About 3 tablespoons horseradish, drained

1 *tablespoon butter, softened to room temperature*

¼ *cup walnuts, finely chopped*

Peanut Butter–Cheese Ball

Makes 1 cheese ball

You will have a hard time keeping away youngsters and adults alike from this smoothly rich concoction.

In a food processor fitted with the steel blade, place the 2 cheeses and process until smooth. Add the peanut butter and the butter, and process until completely blended. Spoon the mixture into a bowl and refrigerate about 3 hours, until it is stiff.

Place the cheese mixture on a piece of waxed paper and shape into a ball, then roll in the chopped raisins to cover. Wrap tightly in plastic wrap and refrigerate for at least 1 hour before using. *At this point, the peanut butter–*

4 *ounces sharp Cheddar cheese, grated and softened to room temperature*

3 *ounces cream cheese, softened to room temperature*

6 *tablespoons smooth peanut butter*

1 tablespoon butter, softened to room tempera-
ture

¼ cup raisins OR dates,
finely chopped

cheese ball can be stored in the refrigerator
for 1 to 2 weeks. Serve with an assortment of
crackers.

Cheese Spread with Chutney and Ham

Makes 2 cups

This is a delightful blend of sweet and salty flavors.

1 cup sharp Cheddar
cheese, grated

6 ounces cream cheese,
softened to room tem-
perature

1 4½-ounce can deviled
ham

¼ cup chutney

2 to 3 scallions (white
part only), finely
chopped

2 tablespoons dry sherry

In a food processor fitted with the steel blade,
place the cheeses, deviled ham, chutney, scallions, and sherry; process until smooth. (Note:
The spread can be prepared by hand, but you
will have to chop up the chutney and the texture will not be as smooth.) Spoon into a serving bowl or crock and chill until firm, about
2 hours. At this point, the cheese spread can
be stored in the refrigerator, covered, for several days. Serve with crackers.

Parmesan Cheese Squares

Makes 48 squares

This is a last-minute appetizer that takes no time at all to make and will be eaten in even less time.

Preheat the oven to BROIL.

Lightly toast the bread. Trim away the bread crusts and cut the bread into quarters.

In a small mixing bowl, combine the Parmesan cheese, mayonnaise, and hot pepper sauce. In another mixing bowl, beat the egg white to foamy and fold into the cheese mixture. Spread this over one side of the small squares of bread.

Place the bread squares on an ungreased cookie sheet and broil 6 inches from the heat about 2 to 3 minutes, until the tops are puffed up and golden brown; watch constantly to see that the squares don't burn. Serve immediately.

(Note: If you make the entire recipe for a party of 6 to 8 people, broil only half the bread squares for the first passing of the appetizer, then broil the rest of the squares after the first batch has been eaten.)

12 *slices very thin white bread, preferably square-shaped*

6 *tablespoons Parmesan cheese, grated*

6 *tablespoons mayonnaise*

Dash hot pepper sauce

1 *egg white*

Mustard Dip

Makes ¾ cup

½ cup mayonnaise

¼ cup sour cream

2 tablespoons Dijon mustard

1 tablespoon red wine vinegar

1 teaspoon mustard seeds (optional)

In a small mixing bowl, combine the mayonnaise, sour cream, mustard, vinegar, and the optional mustard seeds. Spoon into a small serving bowl and chill. *At this point, the dip can be stored in the refrigerator, covered, for several days.* Serve with raw vegetables such as carrots, celery, zucchini, cucumber, and snow peas, or with barely cooked green beans.

Curry Dip

Makes 1½ cups

½ cup mayonnaise

1 cup sour cream

1½ teaspoons onion, grated

1 tablespoon curry powder

1 teaspoon red wine vinegar

1 to 2 teaspoons poppy seeds (optional)

In a medium mixing bowl, combine the mayonnaise, sour cream, onion, curry powder, and vinegar. Spoon into a small serving bowl, sprinkle the optional poppy seeds over the top, and chill. *At this point, the dip can be stored in the refrigerator, covered, for several days.* Serve with raw vegetables such as carrot sticks, mushrooms, cauliflower or broccoli flowerettes, green or red pepper strips, or with cooked green beans.

Green Sauce

Makes approximately 1 cup

In a food processor fitted with the steel blade, place the parsley, onion, mustard, sugar, paprika, salt, pepper, and vinegar. Turn on the machine and slowly pour in the oil through the feeder tube; process until the parsley and onion are completely puréed and smooth. Scrape into a small serving bowl and chill. *At this point, the sauce can be stored in the refrigerator, covered, for 1 to 2 days.* Serve with raw vegetables such as carrot and celery sticks, mushrooms, cauliflower, and zucchini or yellow squash fingers.

2 *cups fresh parsley, packed*

2 *medium onions, quartered*

½ *teaspoon dry mustard*

⅛ *teaspoon sugar*

¼ *teaspoon paprika*

Salt and freshly ground black pepper to taste

¼ *cup red wine vinegar*

¾ *cup vegetable oil OR a combination of vegetable and olive oil*

Red Sauce

Makes 1 cup

This nippy sauce will bring back memories of a south-of-the-border vacation or simply the last time you dined in a Mexican restaurant.

Wash the green pepper, seed and finely chop it. In a medium mixing bowl, place the green pepper, tomatoes, and onion. Stir in the chili pepper, tomato paste, horseradish, and sugar until well blended; taste to correct seasoning and add a little more chili pepper if you like a hotter sauce. *At this point, the sauce can be stored in the refrigerator, covered, for 1 to 2 weeks.*

Shortly before serving, taste the red sauce again to correct seasoning, and if the sauce has lost some of its zip (as it is apt to do when stored for a length of time), add a dash or two

1 *small green pepper*

1 *16-ounce can tomatoes, drained and chopped*

1 *very small onion, finely chopped*

1 *teaspoon green chili pepper OR jalapeña pepper, finely chopped*

1 *tablespoon tomato paste*

1   *teaspoon horseradish*

½   *teaspoon sugar*

    Dash hot pepper sauce
    (optional)

of the hot pepper sauce. When ready to serve, spoon the sauce into a small bowl and place on a serving platter, surrounded by plain tortilla chips or corn chips.

Chick–Pea Spread (Hummus)

Makes 2 cups

½   *small onion*

2   *small cloves garlic*

1   *20-ounce can chick-peas, drained*

1   *teaspoon Dijon mustard*

1   *teaspoon soy sauce*

2   *tablespoons lemon juice*

    Dash hot pepper sauce

    Salt and freshly ground black pepper to taste

¼   *cup vegetable oil* OR *a combination of vegetable and olive oil*

2   *tablespoons fresh parsley, finely chopped*

In a food processor fitted with the steel blade (see below for electric blender directions), chop the onion and garlic until fine. Add the chick-peas, mustard, soy sauce, lemon juice, hot pepper sauce, salt, and pepper. Turn on the machine and slowly pour in the oil through the feeder tube, processing until the mixture has reached a spreadable consistency (adding more oil if necessary). Taste to correct seasoning, then scrape the chick-pea spread into a serving bowl and refrigerate until slightly stiff. *At this point, the chick-pea spread can be stored in the refrigerator, covered, for several days.* Allow the chick-pea spread to come to room temperature for 30 to 45 minutes before serving. Sprinkle with the parsley and serve with sesame crackers or warmed pocket bread.

(Note: You can make the chick-pea spread in an electric blender, but you will have to chop the onion and garlic by hand. Also, you need to add the oil to the container before turning on the machine, or you might stall it. You can also make the spread by pressing the chick-peas through a food mill, then stirring in the rest of the ingredients.)

Spinach–Stuffed Mushrooms

Makes 32 stuffed mushrooms

These appetizers are colorful, nutritious, and extremely popular.

Cook the spinach according to the package directions.

In a medium saucepan, melt 2 tablespoons of the butter over low heat; off the heat, stir in the flour until smooth. Add the creamed spinach, salt, and pepper to the saucepan and cook over low heat, stirring constantly, until the spinach is very thick. Stir in the Parmesan cheese and continue stirring until it is nearly melted. Remove from the heat and reserve.

Wash the mushrooms, dry them on paper towels, and twist out the stems; discard the stems or save for another purpose.

In a large skillet, melt the remaining 1 tablespoon of butter and the oil over low-medium heat and sauté the mushrooms, top side down, for 2 minutes, until slightly browned; turn and sauté for 1 more minute. Remove the mushrooms with a slotted spatula and let cool slightly. Fill each mushroom cavity with about 1 teaspoon of the spinach mixture. *At this point, the mushrooms can be stored in the refrigerator, covered with plastic wrap, for several hours.* Let them come to room temperature for 20 to 30 minutes before cooking.

Preheat the oven to 375 degrees.

Place the mushrooms on an ungreased cookie sheet and bake 10 minutes until heated through. Serve immediately.

(Note: If you make the entire recipe for a party of 6 to 8 people, bake only half the mushrooms for the first passing of the appetizer, then bake the rest of the mushrooms after the first batch has been eaten.)

1 *10-ounce package frozen creamed spinach*

3 *tablespoons butter*

3 *tablespoons flour*

Salt and freshly ground black pepper to taste

2 *tablespoons Parmesan cheese* OR *Romano cheese, grated*

32 *medium mushrooms*

1 *tablespoon vegetable oil*

Pickled Pineapple

14 to 16 servings

This tastes something like watermelon pickles with pineapple overtones. Goes nicely with barbecued nuts, spicy cheese balls, and ham roll-ups.

1 20-ounce can chunk pineapple in unsweetened juice

1 cup white vinegar OR cider vinegar

1 cup sugar

Dash salt

8 whole cloves

2 sticks cinnamon OR 2 teaspoons ground cinnamon

Drain the pineapple and reserve 1 cup of the juice. In a small saucepan, place the pineapple juice, vinegar, sugar, salt, cloves, and cinnamon. Bring the liquid to a boil and boil gently for 10 minutes. Add the pineapple and bring to a quick boil, then remove from the heat and allow to cool. Pour the pineapple and liquid into a refrigerator dish, cover, and refrigerate for 2 days. *At this point, the pickled pineapple can be stored in the refrigerator, covered, for several weeks.*

When ready to serve, drain the liquid well, place the pineapple in a decorative bowl, and serve with toothpicks.

Barbecued Nuts

Makes 2 cups

¼ cup butter

¼ cup steak sauce

2 teaspoons celery salt

⅛ teaspoon cayenne pepper

2 cups pecan halves, walnut halves OR whole almonds

Preheat the oven to 350 degrees.

In a medium saucepan, melt the butter over low heat. Off the heat, stir in the steak sauce, celery salt, and cayenne pepper. Add the nuts to the butter and stir to coat well.

Spread out the nuts on an ungreased cookie sheet and bake 20 minutes; stir once. Drain the nuts on paper towels until cool. *At this point, the nuts can be stored in a tightly-covered container for several days.*

Cinnamon–Sugared Nuts

Makes 2 cups

These nuts are especially nice to make up for the Christmas holidays.

Preheat the oven to 250 degrees.

In a medium saucepan, melt the butter over low heat. Off the heat, add the walnuts and stir to coat with the butter.

Take 2 plates or pie plates. In one, lightly beat the egg white until foamy. In the other plate, mix the sugar, cinnamon, and nutmeg. With a slotted spoon, remove the nuts from the butter and put into the egg white, tossing to coat them thoroughly; this can best be done with your hands. Transfer the nuts to the plate with the sugar and toss again to coat well, using your hands if necessary.

Spread out the nuts on an ungreased cookie sheet. Bake for 45 minutes, stirring occasionally. Let cool. *At this point, the nuts can be stored in a tightly-covered container for 1 week.*

2	tablespoons butter
2	cups walnut halves OR pecan halves
1	egg white
¼	cup sugar
½	teaspoon cinnamon
¼	teaspoon nutmeg

Spicy Peanuts

Makes 1½ cups

When these peanuts are cooking, the aroma in the house is heavenly.

Preheat the oven to 350 degrees.

In a medium saucepan, melt the butter over low heat; off the heat, stir in the 2 tablespoons of cumin and the ginger. Add the peanuts to the butter and stir to coat well.

Spread out the peanuts on an ungreased cookie sheet and bake 15 to 20 minutes; stir once while baking. Scrape the peanuts into a paper bag, add the remaining 1 teaspoon of cumin, and shake the bag vigorously to distribute the cumin. Let the peanuts sit in the bag until completely cool. *At this point, the peanuts can be stored in a tightly-covered container for 1 week.*

4	tablespoons butter
2	tablespoons plus 1 teaspoon ground cumin
½	teaspoon ground ginger
1	12-ounce jar dry-roasted peanuts

Ham Roll–Ups

Makes 32 to 48 roll-ups

Whipped cream cheese comes in an 8-ounce container. Thus you can make additional ham roll-ups, if you want; or you can use the leftover cream cheese for sandwich or cracker spreads. When shopping for this hors d'oeuvre, look for skinny scallions.

4   *thin slices boiled ham, each measuring 4 x 6 inches*

4   *ounces whipped cream cheese*

1   *tablespoon horseradish*

16 *scallions*

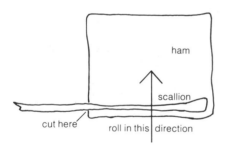

Stack the ham slices and cut into quarters; you should have 16 pieces of ham, each measuring approximately 2 × 3 inches.

In a small mixing bowl, blend the cream cheese and horseradish. Spread ½ teaspoon of the cheese mixture evenly over each piece of ham, taking care to spread out to the edges of the ham.

Cut off the root end of the scallions and remove any discolored leaves; each scallion should have a diameter of no more than ¼ inch. Place a scallion at the longer edge of one piece of ham and cut off the green end of the scallion to fit the ham (see diagram). Roll up the ham around the scallion until it binds; wipe away any cheese that oozes out. Repeat this procedure for the rest of the ham and scallions.

Place the rolls of ham on a flat surface. Using a very sharp knife, cut each roll into 2 or 3 pieces; cutting in half yields 32 roll-ups, into thirds 48. *At this point, the ham roll-ups can be stored in the refrigerator, covered, for several days.*

Serve on a platter or plate.

Omelet–Liverwurst Rolls

These visually appealing pinwheels with a subtle flavor blend of liverwurst, cream cheese, and sherry will elicit rave comments about how delicious they are, and how filling. On a platter they look like little yellow and pink jelly rolls.

To make 1 omelet: In a small mixing bowl, lightly beat 2 of the eggs with ½ tablespoon cold water; lightly beat in some salt and pepper.

In an omelet pan, melt 1 tablespoon of the butter over low-medium heat and pour in the eggs; sprinkle 1 teaspoon of the chives evenly over the top of the eggs. Cook the eggs over medium heat for 4 to 5 minutes, until they are no longer runny. Remove the pan from the heat and cover for 2 to 3 minutes. Carefully remove the omelet to a plate so that the browned side faces up. Let it cool, then refrigerate for 1 hour.

Repeat the procedure for 2 more omelets.

To make the liverwurst spread: In a medium mixing bowl, cream together the liverwurst, cream cheese, and onion. Gradually add the sherry until the mixture has reached the point where it is easily spreadable.

Remove the omelets from the refrigerator and place on a piece of waxed paper. Spread the browned side of each omelet with a third of the liverwurst spread (about 3 tablespoons per omelet), spreading out to about ½ inch from the edge of the omelet. Carefully roll up the omelet jelly-roll style and refrigerate for 1 to 2 hours. *At this point, the omelet rolls can be stored in the refrigerator, covered, for 1 or 2 days.*

Shortly before serving, slice each omelet roll into ½-inch pieces, discarding the end pieces; each omelet roll should yield 6 or 7 appetizers. Place the little omelet-liverwurst rolls, with the cut side facing up, on a serving platter.

Omelets

6 *eggs*

Salt and freshly ground black pepper to taste

3 *tablespoons butter*

1 *tablespoon fresh chives, finely chopped*

Liverwurst Spread

4 *ounces liverwurst* OR *braunschweiger, at room temperature*

3 *ounces cream cheese, softened to room temperature*

1 *tablespoon onion, grated*

1 *to* 2 *tablespoons dry sherry*

Salami—Cheese Rounds

Makes 24 rounds

Because they are filling, the salami-cheese rounds are great to serve when you know you're going to be stuck with an overly long cocktail hour. The recipe is easy to expand.

24 slices small party rye bread

4 tablespoons tomato paste

8 slices salami (Italian, hard, or Genoa), about 3½ inches in diameter

6 slices Provolone cheese, about 4½ inches in diameter

¼ to ½ teaspoon oregano, crumbled

Spread each slice of the bread with ½ teaspoon of the tomato paste. Cut each slice of salami into thirds and each slice of cheese into quarters (stacking the meat and the cheese makes this go fast). On each slice of bread, place a piece of salami and then a piece of cheese. Place the salami-cheese rounds on an ungreased cookie sheet and sprinkle a tiny bit of oregano over each round. *At this point, the appetizer can be stored in the refrigerator for 2 to 3 hours.*

When ready to cook, preheat the oven to 350 degrees.

Bake the salami-cheese rounds for 15 to 20 minutes, until the cheese is bubbling. Serve immediately.

Salmon Ball

Makes 1 ball

5 ounces sharp Cheddar cheese, grated and softened to room temperature

3 ounces cream cheese, softened to room temperature

1 7¾-ounce can red sockeye salmon, drained

1 tablespoon butter

In a food processor fitted with the steel blade, place the 2 cheeses and process until fairly smooth.

Remove any bones and skin from the salmon and discard. Add the salmon, butter, parsley, onion, lemon juice, and the optional liquid smoke to the cheeses and process until smooth. Spoon the salmon mixture into a bowl and refrigerate about 3 hours, until it is stiff.

Place the salmon mixture on a piece of waxed paper and shape into a ball, then roll in the chopped nuts to cover. Wrap tightly in plastic wrap and refrigerate for at least 1 hour before using. *At this point, the salmon ball can be stored in the refrigerator for 1 to 2 weeks.* Serve with crackers, preferably unsalted ones.

3 *tablespoons parsley, finely chopped*

1 *teaspoon onion, grated*

1 *teaspoon lemon juice*

2 *to 3 drops liquid smoke (optional)*

¼ *cup pecans* OR *walnuts, finely chopped*

Hot Crab Meat Dip

6 servings

In a medium mixing bowl, combine the cream cheese and cream. Add the crab meat, onion, garlic, horseradish, salt, pepper, and almonds. *At this point, the crab meat mixture can be stored in the refrigerator, covered, for several hours.*

When ready to cook, preheat the oven to 350 degrees.

Spoon the crab meat mixture into a greased, 1-quart baking dish (one that you can bring to the cocktail table) and bake for 30 minutes. Sprinkle with a little paprika and serve immediately with crackers. If you want, you can keep the dip warm over a food-warming flame.

1 *8-ounce package cream cheese, softened to room temperature*

3 *tablespoons heavy cream*

1 *7-ounce can crab meat, drained*

2 *tablespoons onion, finely chopped*

½ *clove garlic, finely chopped*

1½ *tablespoons horseradish*

Salt and freshly ground white pepper to taste

¼ *cup almonds, slivered or sliced*

Paprika

Sardine–Olive Spread

Makes 1 cup

Don't worry about a guest who might dislike sardines. Not only will he love this spread, he probably won't guess the main ingredient.

1 3¾-ounce tin plain sardines, drained

1 3-ounce package cream cheese, softened to room temperature

3 scallions (white part only), finely chopped

1 tablespoon dry sherry

1 teaspoon lemon juice

1 teaspoon paprika

4 pimiento-stuffed green olives, finely chopped

1 egg, hard-boiled and finely chopped

1 tablespoon fresh parsley, finely chopped

In a food processor fitted with the steel blade, place the sardines, cream cheese, scallions, sherry, lemon juice, and paprika, and process until smooth (you can also blend the ingredients by hand). Spoon the mixture into a medium mixing bowl and fold in the olives and egg. Spoon the spread into a crock or serving dish and sprinkle with the parsley. Chill the spread for 2 to 3 hours. *At this point, the sardine-olive spread can be stored in the refrigerator, covered, for several days.* Serve with crackers or melba toast rounds.

Clam Dip

Makes 1 cup

1 6½-ounce can minced clams

1 3-ounce package cream cheese, softened to room temperature

1 teaspoon lemon juice

Dash hot pepper sauce

Drain the clam juice from the clams and reserve both.

In a small mixing bowl, slowly blend most of the reserved clam juice into the cream cheese until you have reached a consistency that is on the runny side; add the juice just a little at a time, so that it gets thoroughly absorbed into the cheese before you add the next spoonful.

Add the clams, lemon juice, hot pepper sauce, salt, and pepper to the mixture and thoroughly blend. Taste to correct seasoning. Chill for 2 to 3 hours. *At this point, the clam dip can be stored in the refrigerator, covered, for 2 to 3 days.* Serve with ruffled potato chips.

Salt and freshly ground black pepper to taste

Smoked Oyster Spread

6 to 8 servings

This spread can be assembled in a jiffy, yet is so unusual.

Cut the cream cheese in half lengthwise through the middle so that you have 2 rectangular blocks of cheese.

In a small mixing bowl, mash the oysters with a fork and stir in the almonds. Spread the oyster mixture over the top of one of the blocks of cheese. Place the other block of cheese on top to form a layered effect. *At this point, the cheese can be stored in the refrigerator, covered in plastic wrap, for several days.*

Shortly before serving, spread the sour cream over the top and sides of the cheese until completely covered. Sprinkle the parsley over the top and sides. Serve with an assortment of crackers; unsalted sesame crackers and water biscuits are especially nice.

1 *8-ounce package cream cheese*

1 *3½-ounce tin smoked oysters, drained*

2 *tablespoons almonds, finely chopped*

⅓ *cup sour cream*

1 *tablespoon parsley, finely chopped*

Index

K

kugel, zucchini-carrot, 178

L

lamb in mixed grill, with pork and liver, 70
lemon bread, 186
lemon-lime chicken breasts with artichoke hearts, 24
lima bean soup, cream of, 145
limeade mousse, 38
liver in mixed grill, with pork and lamb, 70
London broil, marinated, with olive garnish, 192

M

marinade(s)
    for beef, 57, 192
    for fish and shellfish, 47, 52
    for lamb, 70
    for liver, 71
    for pork, 70
meat and zucchini moussaka, 132–34
meat appetizers, 236–38
melon and pineapple platter with green grapes, 180
melon soup, 160
mincemeat pie, frozen, 218
minestrone casserole, 160
mixed grill of lamb, pork, and liver, 70
moussaka, meat and zucchini, 132–34
mousse
    after-dinner drink, 116
    limeade, 38
mushroom(s)
    pilaf, with celery, 47
    risotto, 141
    soup, 90
    spinach-stuffed, 233
mustard dip, 230

N

new potato salad, 78
noodles. *See also* specific pasta recipes
    buttered, 65
    paprika–poppy seed, 104
nuts
    appetizers, 235
    barbecued, 234
    cinnamon-sugared, 235

O

olives
    cheese-wrapped, 224
omelet, pipérade, 176
omelet-liverwurst rolls, 237
orange crème brûlée, 110
orange juice, sherried, 183
oyster spread, smoked, 241

P

paprika–poppy seed noodles, 104
parfait, peppermint, 26
Parmesan cheese squares, 229
parsley-lettuce soup, 23
parslied rice, 122
pasta. *See also* noodles
    pasta primavera, 53
    pasta with peas and mushrooms, 109
peach-cassis ice, 43
peach upside-down cake, 72
peanut butter–cheese ball, 227
peanuts, spicy, 235
pea soup, green, 63
peppermint parfait, 26
pie, frozen mincemeat, 218
pie, pumpkin cream, 217
pilaf. *See also* rice
    apricot-cashew, 25
    mushroom-celery, 47
    tomato, 99
pineapple
    pickled, 234
    slush, 60
pocket bread (pita), toasted, 135